SAVING MANDELA'S CHILDREN

Dianne Lang © 2007

First Edition 2007 (with addendums of proof)
Second Edition 2015 (without addendums of proof)
Third Edition 2018 (without addendums of proof)

THIS IS A TRUE STORY

No names have been changed to protect those involved.

The events in this book have been recorded as honestly and as accurately as I can manage. Many led to huge frustration and anger. The occasional use of strong language is an honest reflection of that frustration and anger.

Saving Mandela's Children

This book is dedicated to all the children of South Africa who are still abused, neglected, abandoned and orphaned, who are affected and infected by HIV and AIDS and whose voices are still unheard, as well as to those women and men who work tirelessly for the good of the children.

And to my family and my biological children who have suffered because of my choices to care for Mandela's children.

Saving Mandela's Children

In the 1993 Nobel Peace Prize Ceremony in Norway, Nelson Mandela said: "Children are the most vulnerable citizens in any society and the greatest of our treasures."

In the 1996 Summary of the first year of the Nelson Mandela Children's Fund, Nelson Mandela stated:

"The children must, at last, play in the open veld, no longer tortured by the pangs of hunger or ravaged by disease or threatened with the scourge of ignorance, molestation and abuse, and no longer required to engage in deeds whose gravity exceeds their tender years.
The reward of the ending of apartheid will and must be measured by the happiness and welfare of the children.
The children who sleep in the streets, reduced to begging to make a living, are testimony to an unfinished business. There can be no keener revelation of a society's soul than the way in which it treats its children."

This book shows that if the ending of apartheid is to be measured by the happiness and welfare of the children, apartheid was a far more lenient master than the democracy we now have.   Mandela's children have not only been forgotten, their rights have been systematically violated by the very government that wrote the Constitution to protect the children.

The death of a dream

I am so tired. The tears sting my eyes as I struggle to open the padlock on the security door, and then open the locked door while balancing the files of court documents in one arm and my bag in the other. How many times do I have to bend down and look a child in the eyes and say "I love you still", and then wrench their little arms from around my legs or waist while they are being pulled away from me by an abusive parent, a family member, a stranger or a social worker? Another day in court. Another child I could not save. Another court case where the outcome was a fait accompli. The child's fate was sealed before we even had a chance.

I lock the doors behind me, put the kettle on, make a cup of coffee and flop down on the couch. The tears slowly flow down my cheeks and, before I realize it I am howling. Great big sobs are forcing their way out from deep within my chest. I am struggling to breathe. I am drowning in my grief. My mind is numb. I cannot think coherently anymore. My thoughts are move between my own pain and, then to the children that have been taken away. I remember what my mother told me.

"Dianne, you are farting against thunder".

Perhaps she is right. No matter what I do, no matter how hard I try, no matter how much I love, I can't seem to make the social workers or the Commissioner of Child Welfare understand that the interests of the children come first.

And I hear my own voice howling in the emptiness and silence and wonder if the sound is really coming from me. Have I become insane? Have I finally and truly lost it? Is this the moment that I give up and leave it all behind?

I struggle to bring my breathing under control and to stop the hideous howling that is coming out of my mouth. I grab a tissue and, wipe the snot and tears away. I look at the horrible distorted face staring back at me from the mirror. The vision staring back at me makes me start crying all over again, and now I can't stop. I lie down on the couch and bury my head in a pillow and, sob until I fall asleep. I wake up hours later, cold and disorientated. And then I remember.

I found nine year old Kelly one ice-cold winter's night in May 2002, in Lusaka, a shanty township made up of dwellings built from corrugated iron, bits of wood, plastic, cardboard or anything that can serve as cover for the severe winters and summers. The township is adjacent to Middelburg, a Karoo town in the Eastern Cape, and is the oldest township in South Africa.

Kelly was sitting with her seven year-old friend, Jane, in what would serve as a street, although it is nothing more than a strip of gravel between dwellings. They had covered themselves with a piece of cardboard to keep themselves warm. Kelly was dressed in a tracksuit top that only reached her elbows and, had on a pair of track pants that reached her knees. Jane was wearing a very short school dress. Neither girl had any underwear and, both were barefoot. Kelly had a very large scar running along her face where she had been stabbed during a gang rape.

Both girls had lice and scabies. Both had been raped. Neither girl had had anything to eat in four days. Their last meal had been on the rubbish dump, the place known to the street children as "The Restaurant". They had also never attended school.

I reported the child abuse and rape to the police and a docket was opened.

Within weeks of the arrival of the girls, they too settled in with the other children, and were clean, healthy, happy, and attending school. But, as with all children who have lived on the street and who have been subjected to such a cruel upbringing, it is not easy to adjust to living in a house with others. It is also not easy for others who are have been socialized to live with such children. Children who have lived on the street and who have been subjected to abuse do not know how to eat with a knife and fork, nor to eat from a plate. They are used to scraping food from pots or plastic bags; or off the street with their fingers. Kelly told me how she used to scrape the banana skins off the tar road after a car had ridden over them.

They have never used a tooth brush or a toilet and have no idea of how to use toilet paper. They do not know how to blow their noses. They have to be taught how to get dressed, irrespective of their age, because they have never had any other clothes other than the ones they have on, so therefore have never had to take them off to put other clothes on.

Bathing is a major problem and struggle, as they either don't want to get wet or want to keep their clothing on. They do not understand that they have their own shoes and cannot just wear anyone's shoes, so this also causes consternation with the other children when new children come in and grab any pair of shoes to wear. Children are renowned for teasing one another. The tragedy of the teasing of these children is what they tease one another about.

"The man that raped you was a grandfather but the one that raped me was young".

It soon came to our notice that Kelly, Lindelwa and Evelyn, three of our young children, had all been raped by the same man. This man (at the time of writing) is still walking around the town, despite it being reported to the police and dockets being opened for all three offences. In the case of Evelyn, three male police came to take the statement from her. She told her story up until the point of penetration and, then she refused to continue speaking. Lindelwa told her entire story to all three male detectives, which I thought was very brave for an eleven year-old girl. She also mentioned the name of her rapist as well as the address at which he stayed. I requested the police to send a female detective to take her statement. No female detective was ever sent. In the case of Kelly, no detective ever bothered to take a statement.

The police dockets went to the Public Prosecutor, but he refused to prosecute. When I requested reasons for refusal to prosecute, it was stated that there was insufficient evidence, and that the problem had been socially taken care of since the children were now in my care. I have written to the Head of Public Prosecutions requesting an investigation into the reasons why it was thought there was insufficient evidence. Surely the police investigated the cases thoroughly, since rape is a serious offence and three children identified the same man as the rapist?

The children also play-act their rapes and sodomies for months after coming into care. Often, too, the children will use sticks or toothbrush ends to stick into their vaginas and anuses to show one another what had been done to them. It takes a lot of patience and counselling to get the children past their sex games and, to the point where they realize that what has been done to them is not acceptable or normal. As time passed, Kelly and Jane became more and more settled in and socialized with the large family that we had become. They became happy and carefree children.

One late afternoon in August 2002, a little squint-eyed boy whom I had often seen with a group of street boys came to see me. He told me that he wanted to come and live with me.

"Mama D", he said, "I am tired of living on the street and since you are looking after my sister, it is my right to live with you".

It turned out that his sister was Kelly. The little boy was 10 year old Shaun, or Gigi, as he was known in the township. Shaun was on the Department of Social Development Register, so I made the necessary enquiries and was told that there was no problem with the child living with me. By the time Shaun came to live with us, there were thirty-four of us in our home. Shaun was clever, witty, smart, and loveable. He was also a talented gumboot dancer. The gumboot dance is the dance that the men on the mines in South Africa dance. And I fell in love with Shaun instantly. He always came up with the most amazing things.

One day he stroked my arms and said, "I love the fat on these arms, because these are the arms that are growing me".

Shaun lived life with abandon, in-between forcing him to go to school.

I remember how Kelly grew from the frightened, abandoned, emotionally damaged child she was to the confident and child she became, the child with courage, determination and the beautiful smile. I remember the pranks got up to as well as the compassion that Shaun showed at all times; the spirit of survival that he showed; his enthusiasm for life. I remembered the laughter, the love and the joy and security we shared by being together in this large family.

And I remembered with disbelief the telephone call I received yesterday the Social Worker, Pumza Mobo, to tell me that I was to bring Kelly and Shaun to the Magistrate's Court because their aunt was going to foster the children. I relive it in my mind.

"What aunt?", I ask.

"Their mother's cousin's sister", she said. "Have you investigated and done the report?", I asked in disbelief. "Yes".

"What are the circumstances?", I asked.

"She lives alone and is willing to care for the children", Pumza replied.

"But where has this aunt been for the past three years?", I asked.

Silence.

"Be at court at 7h45", the social worker tells me, "and don't forget to bring the children".

The time is 16h30. The offices of the Department of Social Development close at 16h30. I have no time to argue the case or do anything about what is going to happen. Pumza Mobo has timed this to her advantage perfectly.

I see myself as I walk down to the children's home from the office. I am stunned into disbelief at what is happening. I call Kelly and Shaun and tell them that we have to go to court tomorrow and that their aunt wants them to go and live with her. I ask them if they are happy about that. They are not. They say they will go for the weekend but not forever. I tell them that family is better than staying in a children's home forever, but I will try and speak to the magistrate to get him to let them stay a while longer or let them come home to me for weekends. I try and get them prepared in case things do not go according to what they want, and for that matter, according to what I want.

The Department of Social Development has a mandate that all children are to be re-unified with family as soon as possible after being removed from their home. In Kelly and Shaun's case, they were not removed from their home, but from the street. Re-unification also means that the child or children are given a period of adjustment, so that they get used to their new family circumstances and that there is as little trauma associated with the move to their new environment as possible.

We are at court at 7h45. Kelly and Shaun are holding tightly onto my hands. The social worker and Trudie, the nursery school teacher, are there. I look around for someone else. I ask the social worker where the aunt is. She points to Trudie. I gasp. I am shocked. I cannot believe what I am seeing or hearing. Something cannot be right. Every day I see Trudie. She has not mentioned that she is the aunt of the children. She has never visited the children. The children have not mentioned her, nor have they ever made any fuss of her. I am completely dumbfounded.

"What is going on here, Trudie? If you wanted the children, why did you not discuss it with me?", I question her.

"Pumza told me to take the children and I assumed you knew about it", she said, indicating the social worker.

Just then, we are called into the court room. The magistrate, who now assumes the position of Commissioner of Child Welfare, looks at all the papers, asks the "aunt" if she is willing to take the children, then asks the social worker if she is satisfied with the arrangements, and when he gets the affirmative starts making out the order.

I attempt to make myself heard by telling the Commissioner that the children have been with me for three years, that they need a period of adjustment before the final move, and that I have not been given a chance to see the report. He tells me that children need to be with their families and that is all that matters. With that, the order is signed and we are dismissed. I am shocked. Thoughts run through my head. I want to shout out loud that it is all a set up. That if the social worker was not sleeping with the Commissioner of Child Welfare, maybe the children's rights would be observed!!!! In whose interest was the order made out?

We walk out and the children cling to me. I ask the aunt to please let the children visit and then she and the social worker start pulling them away from me, shouting at the children to get into the car. I watch with disbelief as the children are bundled into the social worker's vehicle. I stand on the court house steps and watch the car drive away, the children's faces awash with tears, pressed up against the windows of the car.

I get up and wash my face. I am no longer so cold and disorientated. I have had a cup of coffee but I need to talk. I need to be with other human beings who care. I need to talk to Nonqaba. I put on a jacket and walk down the road. Three houses of children in the same street, but this evening the sound is muted. There is a sadness hanging over all the homes. Shaun and Kelly are gone.

I remember overhearing Shaun telling some of the other children one day, "Life is better when she is around", pointing over his shoulder at me.

They were part of the family. I must remember to tell the children that although these two are gone, they are not dead, not like the others. I fall into Nonqaba's arms. I can see she has been crying too. But her tears are of anger.

"That woman is not the children's aunt! And she has already got 8 children that she is fostering. She only does this to get the foster-care money", shouted Nonqaba, clearly angry and agitated.

"I am going to see that Pumza Mobo. She is a liar. I don't know what she is trying to do with this community", she ranted.

The situation regarding the two children was worse than I thought. Not only were they suddenly uprooted from a place where they were safe and happy with no preparation for the move, but now they were in a place where they were not with family as they were led to believe, but with a group of children. Kelly is now living in the same township where her rapist is still walking free. The interest of the child was clearly not a priority. The priority was foster-care grant for the foster mother, and an easy solution for the social worker whose mandate was to ensure that as many children were removed from my care as possible, regardless of where and how they are placed.

Section 28 (2) of the South African Constitution states:

A child's best interests are of paramount importance in every matter concerning the child.

What does this really mean to the child?   It may as well not exist as far as the child is concerned, because in this case the child's interests were clearly not taken into consideration and, in fact, according to the constitution, the children's rights were violated.

Nonqaba and I put the children to bed and when all was quiet, made a cup of tea and sat at the kitchen table, talking about the problems caused by the authorities. Why, when the authorities had no alternative to us, did they give us such a hard time? Why did they not want to assist us with what we were doing?   Why would they not work with us? After all, these children belonged to all of us. They were the throw away children of the community. We did not receive any grants for them.   We did not take anything from the authorities.   We were no threat to the social workers. Or were we? Were we showing them up by doing what we were doing?   Were we doing what they were being paid to do because they were not doing it? Was it professional jealousy? We had tried attracting the bees with the honey. It had not worked.   We were now standing up to them. We were studying the Child Care Act and the South African Constitution.   We were using the laws when dealing with the social workers, but even that did not always work. They would catch us off guard, like they did with Kelly and Shaun.

We had another problem. Shaun was part of the drama performance we were taking to the Grahamstown National Arts Festival. We had been practicing for weeks and the gumboot dancers' performance was excellent. Their precision and synchronization was unbelievable for children of their age, and Shaun was an integral part of the performance. The venue had been booked and paid for, the accommodation had been booked and paid for, the advertising had been done and above all, Shaun was looking forward to the ten days of performing in Grahamstown. Now we would have to look at the whole play and try and get the boys to perform without one of the team.

The welfare knew that Shaun was part of the team and that we were going to Grahamstown. No one from Middelburg had ever performed at the Grahamstown National Arts Festival before, and this was a really big event in all our lives. We were going to be performing against seven hundred other professional performances. How could that social worker do this to us, and more specifically, to Shaun? Did she not have any compassion, any vision, any thought for the future of the children?

I left Nonqaba to go to bed, hoping that a new day would bring a new perspective on everything. I did not have the energy to bath. I just lay on the bed. Despair was the only thing I felt. Total despair. Total exhaustion. Not depression. Despair. Depression is a sadness, one you can speak about, a condition that can be treated with medication. Despair is a dark pit in the mind from which there is no escape, no words to describe and no medication to relieve. No place to go. No way to turn. No way out. I think of death. I feel I cannot carry on. There seems no reason to take the children in, protect them, love them and to let them go the way Shaun and Kelly left today. I know what will happen to them. They will stop going to school. They will return to the streets. The foster care grant will be misused. It has happened hundreds of times before. What help did I really give to Kelly and Shaun? Would it not have been better to leave them on the street, because then they would have known no better? Perhaps they would have been dead, but now they were suffering indescribable heartache, the wrench from the safety of our home; the love; the security.

What had I really achieved by taking them in for three years and loving them the way I had? I think of taking an overdose. But I don't have the energy to get off the bed. I hope God will be kind enough not to let me wake up tomorrow.

A South African on a mission

The road stretches ahead of me, shimmering in the heat of the Karoo summer. A song starts playing on the compact disc that I have put into the player. I start singing along with it, "these boots were made for walking", and a smile plays on my lips as I turn to look at Patience's face; to share the delight in this song of ours.

But there is no one in the seat. Only my bag rests on the seat. She will never share my journey again. My best friend.

I try hard to blink the tears away so that I can focus on the road. It is useless. I drive over to the shoulder of the road and try to pull myself together. I refuse to think about how she died. I cannot allow these thoughts to enter my head. I know that if I let her death, the actual way she died and, the last time I saw her enter my head, I will lose my mind. I shut it off. I look around the vehicle for the bottle of water and take a swig of it. I light a cigarette and take a long, hard pull, letting the smoke stay in my lungs by holding my breath until it feels like they will burst, and then slowly blow the smoke out the side window. What brought me to where I am today?

I start my vehicle and pull away. It is the car, the road and me. I let my mind wander to when it all started. Was it that cold winter night in Middelburg or was it further back yet? Where does a journey really start? Where did the journey to the death of Patience really begin?

I was flying back home to South Africa from a trip to visit my daughter in Scotland when I had a panic attack on the plane. There was no warning and no reason for it. I sat there wondering what could have brought it on and with utter disbelief, I realized that I did not want to go home. The high crime rate, the corruption, the unemployment and, the AIDS did not fill me with patriotism, or even the desire to live in South Africa any more. The freedom from crime and the underlying stress that we, as South Africans', feel everyday, that I had enjoyed in Scotland had highlighted how we lived in South Africa. However, I rationalized that since I was the fifth generation to be born in this country, I was African and since I was African, I would have to live in Africa. And if I had to live in Africa, I would make Africa a better place to live. As an African, I would not become one of the many moaning "whites"; lamenting a by-gone age when crime was negligible and life was easier for all of us. I would have to do something about the situation.

When I look back, I cannot begin to assimilate how naïve I was, thinking that I could make a real difference.

Having been brought up in the Transkei, an area of South Africa which had been self-governing and under tribal law, I was shocked as an adult to be confronted with apartheid. My entire life as an adult had been dedicated to alleviating the suffering of others and to this end, I become involved in making a difference, in my own small way, to the ending of the injustice of apartheid. I proudly carried the illegal ANC card and literature, was a member of the Black Sash, and did everything I could to assist in the struggle.

18

Saving Mandela's Children

Like millions of other white South Africans, I too put my "yes" vote on the referendum to give the vote to all. My struggle today is still for the alleviation of the suffering of others, irrespective of what government is in power. Oppression remains oppression. Suffering remains suffering. And the suffering of children is the worst suffering imaginable. Children have no voice but mine and yours.

Doing something about a situation where I had no experience was out of the question. I could do nothing about the crime. I could do nothing about the poverty. I could do nothing about the unemployment. But since I had a semi-medical background, I figured it would not take me too long to become up-to-date on the AIDS situation, and then to do something about that. I am an all or nothing person. If I am going to do something, I will do it to the best of my ability or I will not even attempt to do it. Once I have my teeth into something, I became just like a terrier, I hang on and tear away at it, stopping at nothing until I have the success I want. Often, it is innocent naivety that gets me what I want, because I never think I cannot do something. I act before I think, and as my close friends tell me, I go where angels fear to tread. I never see it that way, though. If I see that a job needs to be done, I go and do it. I never think twice about it. I do the job and then think about it afterwards and often surprise myself by my audacity.

Within two weeks of that plane landing at Johannesburg International Airport, I ran my first HIV and AIDS workshop. I discussed my idea with Patience, my friend, and we decided that this was the way to go. I hardly slept during those two weeks. I went on to the internet and printed out every article I could find on HIV and AIDS. I read almost right through the night. I went to the library and took out all the books on HIV and AIDS. I went to the municipal AIDS clinic and got all the information available to the public. I read up on anti-retroviral treatments, the African National Congress (ANC) AIDS policy, every bit of information from the World Health Organization, from the Treatment Action Campaign (a non-governmental organization lobbying government to give anti-retrovirals to citizens) and spoke to those who were diagnosed HIV-positive. I found a venue, booked and paid for it. The workshop was advertised, leaflets and booklets printed. Knowing that it is easier to learn through song and dance, Patience and I put words to the rhythm and music of the freedom songs we used to sing prior to the elections.

After extensive advertising and with refreshments, T-shirts, motivation, enthusiasm, energy and the rhythm of the freedom songs filling our hearts, we opened the doors to our first HIV and AIDS workshop. Here we were, Patience and I, ready to make the difference to AIDS in Africa. And only one person arrived.

"Patience, what are we going to do", I asked.

"Let us do it anyway", she replied.

"Yeah, let us pretend the whole hall is filled with people", I said.

And that is what we did. That single delegate got the full Monty. We sang and danced. We lectured and performed. We taught the motto that we had decided on: "You can live with HIV!!"

The following week, we had seventeen delegates, including the delegate, Moses, from the first week. He obviously enjoyed it so much, he decided to return. Moses helped us with the singing and dancing and got the others to join in as well. It was a good workshop. By the third workshop, bush telegraph was working and Patience and I were so excited because when we arrived at the hall, there was a queue waiting at the door. The hall that we were hiring was just off the main street of the Central Business District of Port Elizabeth. As it had been an old shoe factory, it was upstairs, and there were a number of stairs that had to be climbed. Moses had become the unofficial third course leader and was assisting the very sick up the stairs. There was no sitting room for them, so we moved those who were not so ill on to the floor and put two or three chairs together for make-shift beds for those who were sick.

Before we started, I ran down the other outside stairs to the toilet and found three beautiful white feathers lying on the ground. I just knew that this would be a workshop that would be guided by the angels. While I was in the toilet, I could hear Patience's clear and brilliant voice singing the welcome song. Moses' voice joined in on the second line. I climbed the stairs back to the hall with my heart filled with love for Patience and Moses and for all the people in the hall. I felt so happy. I was doing something that was making a difference.

I stood there looking around. The hall was filled with people. The posters "You don't have to die" and "Choose to live until you die" were on every available wall space. The energy was good. There was a feeling of expectancy and excitement in the hall.

Suddenly, a commotion was heard downstairs. Someone was banging on the door. Moses ran down the steps to find out what was going on. While he was busy with that, Patience and I started with another song, which was easy enough for everyone to follow, and after the first verse those who could stand were standing, swaying, singing and clapping their hands.

What was coming up the stairs, with Moses in the lead, made me look twice. It was an unbelievable sight. A fully made bed, with matching duvet and pillow was being carried up the stairs, and in the bed was a very sick woman. She too, wanted to be at the workshop that promised a way of living with HIV, instead of dying. This was truly going to be a miraculous day. And it was. Everyone left at the end of the workshop walking on their own, unsupported, singing and happy, including the woman who came in on the bed.

People were coming back again and again to the same workshop. We kept on drawing the same crowd. We then realized that these people were the ones who did not mind disclosing their status, but we were not reaching those who were HIV-positive who were still keeping their status secret. The delegates were reporting that they were feeling better, some were going back to work and others were joining other NGOs, disclosing their status and helping other HIV- positive people. Something we were doing on the workshops was working. We were doing pre- and post testing to see whether the delegates were more positive after attending and whether they were changing their life-styles. Ninety percent of delegates found the workshops made a positive difference in their lives.

Moses did not turn up at one of the workshops. He was by now such an integral part of the team that we could not start without him.

"Where is Moses?", I asked.

There was silence.

"Has anyone seen Moses?", I asked again.

There was deathly silence.

"Where is Moses?", I again asked, slightly irritated by the hush.

"He is dead", a voice at the back of the hall said.

"What?", I asked, not believing what I had just heard.

"He is dead", the woman answered.

"But that is impossible. How could he die? He was fine when he was here last week. No one dies just like that. He may have had HIV, but he was as well as I am. He could not have just died".

I was beside myself, my mind reeling, confused. What the hell was I doing here, telling these people that they could live with HIV and then Moses, so much better and doing fine, drops down dead just like that. What on God's earth was going on? It could not be. Did I have it all wrong? Was my whole theory of this HIV and AIDS wrong? Who did I think I was to lead these people down the garden path, letting them believe they could live with HIV when, in fact, they could just drop down dead with no warning? The thoughts were running round and round in my head, settling on nothing and clinging to nowhere.

"Di... Di... Di...", I felt Patience pulling at my sleeve. "Di, he did not die of AIDS. Come and sit down. Breathe. Calm down please. You have gone white. He did not die of AIDS", she whispered.

"What did he die of?", I asked.

She shook her head.

"What did he die of?" I loudly asked the woman at the back.

"He was killed by lightning day before yesterday", she said.

Oh, the relief. The incredible, undeniable relief. I am horrified now as I write this, but I felt relief that he had been struck by lightning and had not died from AIDS. I was glad because my theory still stood, and I was glad that I had not led these people down the garden path. But I was sad that Moses was dead. After all the effort and work that he had put into living; and he really was living, to be killed by such an unlikely death such as lightning hardly seemed fair.

The workshops were taking a large chunk of my financial savings, and many of the delegates had been to so many of the workshops that they were now trained to be able to run the workshops on their own in their own communities. I needed to move further afield. I approached an NGO with my theory of self-sustainable HIV and AIDS Training, and expressed my wish to work in the worst area in South Africa. All I needed was the finances to do the work. We identified Middelburg in the Eastern Cape as having one of the highest HIV and unemployment rates in the country. Armed with a good funding proposal, the Project for Conflict Resolution and Development (PCRD), a registered charity, found it easy to find the funding for work in this area. Patience and I were on our way to making our dream a reality.

Middelburg is 340 km from Port Elizabeth, so the training in HIV and AIDS awareness necessitated a lot of travelling and staying away from home. Our modus operandi was to start with awareness workshops, identify possible trainers, do Train-the-Trainer workshops and then let the trainers do workshops, thereby spreading the message. In addition to this, my dream was to have one home-based care worker per street per township, thereby ensuring that no one would die alone and afraid. This would also necessitate doing Basic Home-Based Care Workshops, identifying leaders and then training them in advanced workshops so that they could continue the training of the others. Included in the Home-Based Care Advanced

Workshops as well as the Train-the-Trainer Workshops was Basic Hospital routine training in case there was ever need of additional personnel in a disaster.

Hospital training was great fun. We used this opportunity to clean the hospital, which was filthy. It was the bucket and mop brigade. Blood and faeces were cleaned from the walls and floors. Beds were moved and floors were scrubbed with scrubbing brushes and bleach. Cupboards were moved, linen was changed that had not been changed in months. We washed the patients and put them into clean bed clothes. We fed the patients when we found that their food was just put on the bedside tables and then collected later on. The patients were too ill to feed themselves and the nurses either did not bother to feed them or did not have the time. We went into the kitchen and scrubbed the pots and pans. The pots were encrusted in filth. We cleaned every surface until the kitchen was gleaming. Unfortunately, the tiled floors of the hospital were chipped and broken, so no matter how hard we cleaned, it never did look pristine.

A ghastly thing happened during one of our hospital training weeks. I sent some of the trainees, Professor, (his name, not his profession) Jackson, Fikile and Mbulelo into the male ward to wash the patients and make up their beds. It was about 10am. I was busy in the female ward showing some of the students how to take blood pressures. Jackson came and called me to the male ward because he thought someone was lying dead in bed. When I went through to the male ward, I found that one of the patients was lying on his bed with a pillow over his face. The curtains were not drawn around his bed, although it may have been difficult to do so as the curtains did not go all the way around the three sides. I could see immediately that the man was not only dead, but that rigor mortis had already set in. Telling the students to wait, I went in search of the sister in charge to inform her that one of the patients had died.

"Sister, one of the patients in the male ward has died", I said, when I found her.

"Yes, I know", she answered, shrugging her shoulders.

"When did he die?", I asked.

"About 11 o' clock last night", she replied emotionlessly.

I was aghast. A patient was lying dead in his bed, with no curtains around his bed, in a general ward filled with other patients, for almost 12 hours and no one had moved his body. What must it have been like for the other patients? My mind boggled.

"Would you like us to move him to the mortuary, Sister?", I asked.

There was little point in getting indignant, raising a fuss, pointing out that it was beyond understanding that so little care and concern for the patients and respect for the dead was shown. This was the way things worked and raising a fuss about it would only alienate me from the hospital staff, preventing me from doing what I wanted to do. And that was to make a difference. I went back to the ward and gathered all the students around me. This was the perfect opportunity to show them how to lay out a corpse and how to transport a corpse to the mortuary. I told them that we were going to prepare the body for transport to the mortuary, which was at the back of the hospital. The ama-Xhosa have an inherent fear of the dead, so this was a major lesson that we had to get through. The students were so afraid that they stood far away from the bed. In an attempt to shield the other patients from the drama going on around the bed, I made the students stand in a line along the side where there was no curtain. The first thing we had to do was to remove the pillow covering the face of the patient. I asked if there was any volunteer who would like to do it. Professor volunteered. He took the pillow on either side with both hands and lifted it very slowly from the patient's face.

"Oh, my God", he said, "It is my neighbour".

The silence was deafening.

"I am so sorry", I said, as I took over.

The students were shocked, as most of them knew the dead patient. Professor went and sat down at the other end of the ward while Jackson comforted him. I took over the preparation of the body. Not a word was spoken by the students during the entire procedure. The students watched the procedure and assisted me in pushing the corpse to the mortuary. Once we had shut the mortuary doors, the students all started talking at once. They were so happy with themselves that they had managed to get past their fears. They climbed onto the mortuary trolley and some took the ride back to the hospital while others pushed the trolley that was going wildly out of control. Much laughter followed them.

However, their indignation was soon voiced that no one had told the family or the community that the patient had died. Living in a small community, everyone knows everyone, and if someone dies, everyone knows about it in a very short space of time. The hospital had not yet informed the family that the patient had died. This put us in a serious predicament, because there were now twenty members of the community that knew that the patient was dead, but the family had not yet been informed. Professor again volunteered to ask the sister in charge to call the family to notify them of his death before the news reached them via the bush telegraph.

Over the years of working with the hospital, we developed a good relationship with the hospital manager, the matron and the nurses. The hospital conditions improved for the staff and the patients and eventually, the hospital became one of our biggest allies in the care of the children.

The road stretches out in front of me. It is hot. The road is straight for kilometre after kilometre. In the distance I can see a mirage. It looks like a puddle of water in the road. I blink my eyes again and try and focus. My mind has been in the past. Thinking about things that have been and things that could have been. I really ought to think of the future. I force myself to concentrate on my driving. The whirr of the motor, the warmth of the vehicle, the sunlight all contribute to dulling my brain and pulling my mind back into the past... back to my friend, the little co-driver who sat with me so many times on this trip between Port Elizabeth and Middelburg.

I remember how we stood and held onto one another, that time when we heard that Anna had died. I remember it so clearly. So many things I don't remember, but other things I remember with such clarity. We were standing beside my vehicle outside the hospital when we heard the news. My beautiful Anna was gone. She was the first one I loved who died because she did not have antiretroviral medication. It was she who showed me that love was just not enough to keep an AIDS patient alive.

The day was hot. It was very hot. The temperature had already reached 26 °C and it promised to be a scorcher. There was not a breath of wind and I could feel the sweat running down between my breasts as I stood in the hall of one of the townships. The room was filled with about thirty women, all talking at the top of their voices and all at the same time. The noise was deafening.

"Oh, God, please help me to make a difference today", I quietly prayed.

"Can I have your attention, please!", I shouted, using the voice that had earned me the nickname of Mugsy when I was a child.

As the women were completing the registration forms for the HIV/AIDS home care workshop that I was going to present, a plainly dressed woman with a red shirt asked to speak to me in private.

"My daughter is very ill. She is in the hospital and the nurses tell me she has TB. I am very worried because I think she has AIDS. She has been in the hospital since Saturday and the doctor has not been to see her in four days. Will you come with me to the hospital after the workshop?", she asked as she shifted her glasses up and down her nose in agitation.

"How old is your child?", I asked.

"She is 25. She has two small children", she replied.

I readily agreed to go with her to the hospital after the workshop. She went over to complete the registration form and I saw that her name was Elizabeth Kepelele.

She sat in the front row. For some reason, my attention was continually drawn to her, even though many people had asked me personal questions before a workshop, and I had not had the same feeling as I was having about her. As the workshop progressed, it felt more and more as though the whole workshop was being conducted on a level that only she and I were on. The rest of the delegates faded into the background. As more information was presented, the tears started rolling slowly and silently down her cheeks. While I presented information and answered questions from the other delegates, I was constantly aware of Elizabeth's pain. I would keep catching her eye, willing her to know that I too, could feel her pain. She did not even move her hand to wipe the tears away until the red shirt she wore was stained wet. I saw inside her soul. I saw the grief and anguish and hopelessness. And I know that she saw mine. I could do nothing but share her grief and give her hope by repeating over and over, "No one has to die from HIV".

Forty-five percent of people who are HIV+ die of AIDS. What happens to the other fifty-five percent? What is the difference between the HIV+ person who dies of AIDS and those who don't? Some scientists maintain that there is an unknown factor which causes HIV to become AIDS. What is this unknown factor? And how do we get it? I was certain that the unknown factor was extreme stress, poor diet, a feeling of hopelessness and a victim mentality contributing to a breakdown of the immune system. This is what I had learned in my workshops that I had held in Port Elizabeth, and from the many pre-and post-test questionnaires that Patience and I had analysed.

Eventually the workshop came to an end. It was still hot. Very hot. Not a breathe of wind to ease the unrelenting heat. Elizabeth, Mlungisi, one of my co-workers, Patience and I went to the hospital. The hospital had an air of neglect about it. The once beautiful white gates that stood so proudly in front of a well laid-out garden were a sad testimonial to a by-gone age when sick people were loved and cared for. The one gate had fallen off its hinges, the pillars were discoloured with peeling paint work, and the garden was overgrown with just a few flowers struggling to express themselves amongst the weeds. We walked into the hospital and past a group of young men loitering around the entrance. Empty bottles, cigarette butts, crisp packets and papers lay about the dusty floor.

Mlungisi, Patience and I followed Elizabeth as she walked down a long corridor that was badly in need of paint and into a private ward. The room had a small cupboard with a missing leg, an old chair that had seen better days, and a wash hand basin with a leaking tap. And there, lying in a foetal position in the bed, was Anna. She was dressed in a hospital gown, her back exposed because the gown no longer had any ribbon to tie it together at the back. Her eyes were wild with what I thought was anxiety until I stood close enough to her to feel the heat coming from her body. Her breath rasped in her chest and she continually made small coughing noises. When her mother called her name, she looked up confused and disorientated. Mlungisi left the room and only later did I find him sitting quietly in the car waiting for us. It was all too much for him.

"Oh, God, she's dying", I thought, "What the hell am I going to tell the mother? What hope does one give a mother in this situation?". "Elizabeth", I said, "Go and ask the sister what is wrong with Anna, and ask her when the doctor is coming and if she can give Anna something for her temperature. She is burning up".

When Elizabeth was out the room, I called "Anna, Anna, can you hear me?".

She looked up and her eyes focused on mine. She nodded.

"Anna, do you know what is wrong with you?" I asked.

Medical personnel may not give you information regarding a patient's HIV status unless that patient has given permission, or has already disclosed his or her status. It was for this reason that I was asking Anna if she knew what was wrong with her. I had already been told by Elizabeth that the hospital staff had refused to tell her if Anna had AIDS or not. Anna nodded.

"Yes", she whispered, "I have HIV".

"Can you tell your Mom please? She is so worried about you. If you tell her, then she will not be so worried and you will also feel better if you don't keep this a secret. When you keep this a secret, then it stops you from getting better", I told her.

She nodded again. Just then, Elizabeth entered the room in tears.

"The sister won't tell me what is wrong and she says that she does not know when the doctor will be coming. She also says there is very little medicine here so the patients can only have one Panado (paracetamol) twice a day. Anna had one this morning, so she must wait until later today", she said.

I was operating on autopilot, without a plan. There was no thought in what I was doing or why I was doing what I was doing, what I was saying or why I was saying it. There was no reasoning behind my decisions and actions. I had never been in such a position before and did not know what I should do. Everything that I was doing seemed to be directed by some internal force that I had no control over or any conscious awareness of. All I was aware of was the anguish of this mother, a dying child, and hospital staff that did not seem to care, or were so jaded and, lacked so many resources, or had seen so much suffering that there was no more compassion. I felt the helplessness of this mother in the face of the authority of the hospital personnel, the helplessness and hopelessness of having a sick child and two small grandchildren to care for without any male support in the home, no public transport, no income, no employment, no government grants, and no transport to even take her child home.

What I had was a vehicle, I was not intimidated by the hospital personnel or the system, I had information and education, and I felt powerful enough to help her. This is all that I was aware of. I was only aware of the fact that I could help Elizabeth.

"Anna has something to tell you, Elizabeth", I said, as I left the room and went in search of the Sister in charge.

"Sister, Anna has told me she has AIDS. In your estimation, how long do you think she has?", I asked when I found her in the duty room.

"Maybe a couple of days at the most", she said nonchalantly.

"Thank you, Sister", I replied, making my way back to Anna's ward.

Something had to be done soon. We just could not let Anna lie here in this place any longer. Her suffering was beyond endurance and the temperature was worse than anything I had ever experienced. No one was really nursing her or giving her the love and attention that she needed. With the way that things were being run at the hospital it was more than possible that Anna would die alone in that ward.

There was something almost angelic about Anna. She had the most beautiful face. Her eyelashes were so long that they almost touched her eyebrows. Because she was so thin, her cheekbones were prominent and, unlike most Ama-Xhosa, she had an aquiline nose. She also had an exquisite latte-coloured skin.

Elizabeth was talking to Anna when I got back to the ward. She stopped speaking and told me that Anna had told her that she had AIDS.

"Then I think that you should take her home and nurse her there, Elizabeth. You can love her and care for her better at home. If you want to, I can take you both home now or I can come back and fetch you both later. You can decide and let me know", I told her.

"Please take us home now", Elizabeth said.

"You will have to clear it with the Sister first", I advised her.

While Elizabeth cleared things with the Sister in charge, I packed Anna's few things and put them into the plastic packet that she had brought with her to the hospital. With utmost care, I helped her put her clothes on and, very carefully, Elizabeth and I helped her out of the hospital and into the vehicle.

Elizabeth's home was in Kwa-Nonzame, one of the three townships in Middelburg. She had one of the two-roomed houses that the government had provided at a minimum cost as part of their promised provision of houses after the ANC came into power. The houses are only between twenty and thirty square metres and sometimes house families of up to ten and twelve people. Fortunately, in Elizabeth's case, only Anna, her two bothers, her two children and herself (thereby making it seven people) lived in her house. Her home was a reflection of herself. It was exceptionally neat, clean and tidy. One room was the kitchen/lounge/ dining room, and the other was the bedroom with one large double bed in it.

We helped Anna out of the car and took her into the house and helped her on to the bed. It was still hot and the flies were out in force. I noticed an array of medicines on the dressing table. Elizabeth was eager to show me all the medicines that she had bought for Anna and had tried to cure her. There was the well-known African potato remedy, a remedy that was selling like hot cakes because of a rumour that it cured AIDS by boosting the immune system. The Minister of Health (Dr. Mantombazana 'Manto' Edmie Tshabalala-Msimang) had also added to the acceptance of this "cure" by giving it her stamp of approval. There were vitamin B tablets, multivitamin tablets, pain killing tablets, indigestion tablets, weight gain milk drinks, the large tuberculosis tablets in the clinic packet, and a myriad of African remedies. My heart broke as Elizabeth showed me each of the medicines that she had bought and told me how much she had paid. She cried as she told me that not one of the medicines that she was still giving Anna had helped. She had so little money with no income, and she had paid out so much money in the hopes of curing her child.

How futile the whole AIDS situation was in South Africa without medication for HIV, where the majority of the people believed that there was no cure, and that to be diagnosed with HIV meant you were suffering from a dirty, sexual disease that killed you. The ANC stand on HIV and AIDS had been a very well-orchestrated brain-washing of the entire population. Health department posters of giant condoms with slogans of "No cure for AIDS" were abundant everywhere. There were debates and advertisements on national television, on radio, and in all the newspapers proclaiming that the medication (antiretroviral) for HIV was poisonous and that the side effects were worse than the disease itself. It amazed me that no one ever thought that perhaps the side effect of the disease without the medication was death! There were continual arguments put forward as to why we, as the South African population, should not have access to the medication.

One of the reasons the Minister of Health at the time put forward was that the administration of the tablets was too complicated for the general population to adhere to, meaning that to eat before some medication and to eat after others was too difficult for us to do. This to me was an insult to our intelligence.

Another bizarre situation regarding the anti-retroviral fiasco in our country was that the medication was too expensive to give to our people. This argument was used in particular with regard to the prevention of mother-to-child transmission. An HIV+ mother passes the virus onto her baby, but if she and the baby are treated with ARV medication during labour and at birth, the baby has a great chance of being negative. The manufacturers of the medication offered to give it to the government but the Health department refused the offer. If the general population and the general practitioners had been informed, they would have known that they could have bought the medication for themselves for as little as R12.00. Each would have saved the lives of thousands upon thousands of children. I often wondered if one of the reasons the Health department refused this gift of medication and life for the babies of our country is because we would have been left with a lot more orphans. By saving the babies and not treating the mothers, the mothers would have still died. By not preventing mother-to-child transmission, we were dealing with two problems at once. The mother and the child could die, thereby leaving fewer orphans to deal with.

I knew that we were being brainwashed by the propaganda that the ANC were putting out to the population via the media because I had done so much research on HIV and AIDS. I had also ensured that I was getting regular updates on all AIDS information from around the world via the internet, and every day there were piles of paper to read on the latest research. However, it was extremely difficult to put this across and still stay within the agenda that the Health Department was using, while at the same time trying to give hope to people who were now convinced that they were going to die because they had HIV. It was imperative to try to stay within their agenda so as not to alienate myself from the Department of Health, but at the same time, I still needed to be able to help people know that they did not necessarily have to die of HIV if they could change the way they perceived things, if they could change their lifestyles and their diets and if they could get medicines. It was a very fine line I was walking, and one that frustrated and angered me no end.

I knew that HIV did not necessarily lead to AIDS but that one had to have HIV to get AIDS. This was a concept that was very difficult to put across to people. The people were so brainwashed. They were so afraid. Lenin said that if a lie is told often enough, it becomes the truth. How true. So much disinformation was being fed to them that they were now consulting witch doctors, and on their advice many were raping young children and babies. The belief was that the rape of a virgin would cure them of AIDS. It is not easy for those who live in the first world to understand that this can happen, but in a culture of fear and ignorance, this is commonplace. Many would think that this type of thing would only happen if the person had not had any education, but this is not true. I have a friend who is an air hostess on a major airline and is HIV+. As a staff member of the airline, she is entitled to anti-retroviral drugs free of charge. She refuses to take them as she says that the side effects are worse than the disease. After all, she says, the Minister of Health has said so. She is now in the last stages of AIDS. I am so sad that her belief system, despite her education, is allowing this very capable and vibrant mother of two to die.

Working in the field of HIV and AIDS brings one into contact with other activists and people of like minds. With so much disinformation abounding at government level, there was bound to be other information passing between activists and others who felt strongly about anti-retrovirals and the fact that people were dying like flies for lack of medication. In 2002, I happened to be having a coffee with an acquaintance and lamenting the predicament that our country was in with regard to drugs for AIDS. The acquaintance knew very little about the HIV and AIDS situation, as did most white South Africans at the time. It was still considered a "black" disease. However, she did share some rather perturbing news with me.

"My friend, Jane, works for Aspen Pharmaceutical Company. They are making anti-retroviral drugs and exporting them", she said.

"What?", I asked, aghast. "Repeat that!", I said.

"Yes, they make and export anti-retroviral drugs", she repeated.

"Are you sure?", I asked.

"Of course, I'm sure", she said.

I was mad. I was angry. I could hardly breathe. How dare the government deny our people the drugs, when they could make them in South Africa and export them and make money on them. They could tell us that the side effects were worse than the disease itself, but they could sell them to other countries and make money. Then the drugs could not be so expensive to give us as they had kept on telling us. I was so angry that my heart was pounding. I was sure that my blood pressure was rocketing out the top of my head. I got out of that coffee shop as soon as I could and contacted the TAC (Treatment Action Campaign) in Cape Town. The TAC is a non-governmental organization which has been working ceaselessly to get the government to give us medication for AIDS. I spoke with one of the top people there and told them what I had heard.

"Yes, we know", he said.

"Well, why have you not told everyone?", I asked.

"We have a strategy that we are working towards and it is not in our long term interest to upset the ANC at this juncture", he told me.

My God, did no one think that this was an urgent issue? While we have the drugs in Port Elizabeth, probably being made at a very low cost and being transported out of the country into other countries, our people are dying! I was shocked and distraught. If the TAC were not going to use the information and they were such a strong unit, having huge demonstrations, taking the government to the constitutional court, doing all these huge things, then who was I to do anything about it? I was just me! A one person task force wanting to take on the entire ANC on behalf of the entire South African population! The task was just too daunting. I was just too small and insignificant. Who would believe me?

By now my anger at the lack of drugs for AIDS patients pushed me out of staying within the ANC's health agenda on HIV and AIDS. Now I would tell everyone on all my workshops that we were making the drugs in Port Elizabeth. We were exporting them. The government was making money on them. They did save lives but the government would not let us have the drugs. Patience was equally angry. She laid the blame directly on the shoulders of Mbeki, our State President. She would puff up her cheeks in indignation and anger and the foulest words would erupt from her mouth. Patience called Mbeki (our president) every filthy name under the sun, and she was sure that he had no compassion because he had no children. She called the President "Mr Fuckup". It was then that Patience and I changed the words to the Freedom Songs we used to sing during the apartheid years, again. The first time we used the rhythm and music of the freedom songs was to get people to sing about health, safe sex and living with HIV. We changed the words, included the President's name, and demanded the drugs.

My biggest stand on the drug issue came when Patience and I were asked to coordinate and arrange the World AIDS Day in Middelburg that was going to be attended by the MEC (Member of the Executive Council) of the Health Department for the Eastern Province and his entourage on 1 December 2002. We arranged a very good day with much entertainment, using all the HIV trainers and Home Based Care Workers as well as High School pupils. During the days before the ANC took over, we would run and chant freedom songs with our right hands raised as fists. When all was ready and the dignitaries were seated, we came into the stadium running and chanting with our right hands held high as fists – singing:

"Thabo Mbeki, bring us the medicine, we are here, dying of AIDS. Bring us the medicine. You are letting us down. Bring us the medicine. We are dying of AIDS".

Of course, since the song was in Xhosa, it rhymed. The looks on the dignitaries faces was worth it although I was hauled over the coals because of it later in the day.

To further complicate issues, Thabo Mbeki, had taken the stand that HIV does not lead to AIDS, this despite the majority of the world's opinion. Then there were the statements made by the Minister of Health that the drugs were not tested properly, that HIV was caused by poverty, and that AIDS was cured by beetroot.

As late as 2005, the Minister of Health appeared on National Television stating that beetroot and lemon juice cured AIDS. In 2006, the Minister of Health added garlic to her concoctions of cures for AIDS and when questioned by media, still insists that the side effects of the drugs are more deadly than the disease itself. It is embarrassing when talking to citizens of other countries about our Minister of Health. I wonder what she would do if she were diagnosed with AIDS, since as a Member of Parliament she has free access to antiretroviral drugs. I met her on a sub-Saharan Aids Conference and she had the coldest, reptilian eyes I have ever seen on a human.

Another way in which HIV is passed from mother to child is through breast feeding. When I first started work in the townships, the municipal clinics were telling mothers who were HIV+ not to breast feed their babies and were providing milk powder to the mothers. This was in line with the World Health Organization's recommendation to stop the transmission of HIV from mother to child. However, with the complete and utter mismanagement and incomprehensible duplication of unnecessary paperwork to obtain the milk powder from the Health Department Stores in Bisho, the government head office for the Eastern Cape, the milk was not always available. This meant that the babies were being given breast milk at times, or were being given Sterimilk, a milk substitute, which has no nutritional value at all. This situation was obviously indefensible and had to change. I had meetings with the head of the local Department of Health to see if there was any way in which I could assist in obtaining the necessary milk supplies. I was told that there was no more money left for the supply of baby formula to mothers until the new financial year.

There was only one thing to do. I had to get the baby formula for the babies in Middelburg myself. I sent out emails to everyone I knew and asked them for donations of baby formula. The response was overwhelming from friends and friends of friends. Donations were even received from strangers in the United Kingdom. No donations were received from the manufacturers of the baby formulas although we pleaded our case via proposals, calls and faxes. Their answer was always "We have our own social responsibility programs". This is the standard reply when asking for any assistance from any large company within South Africa. We were able to supply the hospital and the clinics with baby formula for a couple of months, until the beginning of the new financial year.

Thinking that the crisis would then be over, I did not continue to request donations of the formula. Much to my dismay, nothing had been done by the Department of Health to make sure that baby formula would be available in Middelburg. The ineptitude and complacency were unbelievable. The babies were back to being fed Sterimilk or breast milk, even though the mothers were HIV+.

The Health Department's agenda then changed to a criminally irresponsible program for HIV mothers and their babies. I could not believe it when I heard what the mothers were telling me, so I went to the clinic and the hospital to find out for myself. The mothers told me that the clinic sisters were advising them to breast feed their babies. When I went to the clinics and the hospital, the sisters said that they had received instruction from the Health Department that they were to advise the HIV mothers to either breast feed or to bottle feed, but not to do both as doing both would lead to transmission of HIV. Although by 2005 a few of hospitals are giving treatment to HIV mothers to prevent mother-to-child transmission, the breast feeding policy still stands. This is an unbelievable situation in which the child is prevented from getting HIV at birth through treatment with Niviripine, but then is put at risk by advising the mother to breastfeed!

In 2005, after much pressure from the TAC and the outside community, the government started a very slow roll out of antiretroviral drugs for preventing mother-to-child transmission. In the hospital, in Middelburg, there was treatment to prevent mother-to-child transmission for the mother, but not for the baby!! It is like having the teaspoon but not the medicine. It would take almost a year for the correct medication to be received by the hospital.

Despite the fact that we were producing antiretroviral AIDS drugs and exporting them, our Minister of Health was grudgingly allowing "Pilot Studies" to be conducted by various organizations, amongst others, Médecins Sans Frontières, in some of the townships in South Africa. However, these pilot studies were only allowed to have a minimum number of subjects and had to fit into a strict category before being given the drugs. Unfortunately, Middelburg did not fall into one of these areas. I did try unsuccessfully to get Anna drugs via one of these organizations, but the red tape was so strict that it was impossible. The AIDS drugs were available privately but the cost was completely prohibitive. For us, we may as well have been asking for a trip to the moon.

There was so much disinformation around that even the local doctors did not know how to write a prescription for the AIDS drugs. The World Health Organization recommended that ARV treatment should start once an HIV patient's CD4 count fell to 500 and less. HIV becomes AIDS when the patient gets a secondary infection such as TB or meningitis. Women die of AIDS within six to eight weeks when their CD4 drops to 350. Men die when their CD4 count drops to 200. There is always the exception, these are generalizations. In South Africa, anti-retroviral (ARV) treatment was and is still given to patients who have AIDS when their CD4 count drops to 200. It does not take a rocket scientist to figure out that South Africans who are given the treatment have less chance of survival than others who are given the treatment in good time. The modus operandi in this is that it plays directly into the Health Department's strategy, and justifies their standpoint that ARV treatment is not a good treatment for HIV and AIDS.

The pilot studies have now retreated into the background, and thanks largely to the work of the Treatment Action Campaign and their leader, Zackie Achmat, the Department of Health is now rolling out ARV treatment at numerous hospitals and clinics.

The world has watched and listened to the propaganda. The world believes that we now have unlimited access to treatment. In fact, at the time of writing, the TAC has taken the Minister of Health to court and she has admitted that "as many as 42000 South Africans are on ARV" and she is concerned about "how many of those are dying from the side effects of the drugs". In a country where millions of people are HIV+, we are only providing medication to 42 000 people. The truth is that the access to treatment is so limited that the vast majority of HIV people in South Africa are still going untreated and we are still dying of AIDS. In Middelburg, where the hospital has eight to twelve deaths to AIDS per week, where you have to wait your turn on a Saturday to be buried because there are so many funerals going on due to AIDS, only 30 people are allowed to receive ARV treatment!! The heat was intolerable. The flies were descending on Anna like a blanket and I moved to swish them away. They were a

48

lazy bunch, because they lifted up only about a foot before settling down again.

"Do you have a tea towel or a net of some sort?", I asked Elizabeth.

She scurried off and came back with an embroidered net tea cover, and we placed this over Anna, lifting the cushions so as to make a tent over her. At least the flies would not bother her. "What do I do now? How do I take care of her?

What medicines do you think I should give her?", asked Elizabeth.

"Give her whatever she wants to eat, but make sure she drinks. Get liquid into her so she does not dehydrate", I responded.

I knew that Elizabeth had very little money and there was little food in the house. I pressed some bank notes into her hand as I left, praying that she would manage and that by some miracle Anna would get better, although I felt that she was too far gone.

Elizabeth attended the week-long workshop that we held for HIV trainers the following month. We would buy food in the town and pay women from the community to cook it for us so that we could have a good meal at lunch time. Often I noticed that some of the older women would not eat their lunch, but would take it home with them. On one occasion I saw someone pushing her food around on her plate with her fork, with tears streaming down her face. I asked her why she was crying.

"I can't eat this food, knowing that my grandchildren are at home starving", she sobbed.

She was one of the thousands of grandmothers who had lost her children to AIDS and was having to be a mother all over again to her grandchildren.

As soon as I had a chance that week, Patience and I went to visit Anna. We arrived at her home and found someone sitting outside in a pink dressing gown, watching the two children playing in the sun. I walked up to her and told her that I was there to see Anna. She looked up and smiled. "I am Anna", she said.

I was astonished. She was beautiful and serene. She had put on weight. She was strong enough to be outside and watching her children. She was talking. She had no temperature. She was getting well. She got up and invited us inside.

"Anna, I am so surprised and so happy to find you looking so well. You were so ill when I saw you last. I am so happy", I said as I gave her a hug.

I could not stop the tears of joy from running down my own face. I turned to Patience and saw the joy in her own eyes and her smile said everything. We passed a pleasant hour with Anna, talking about her children, her dreams and her sadness. Her husband had died of AIDS the year before. Every time we went to Middelburg to do training, we would include a visit to Anna, and she just seemed to get stronger and stronger. We were talking about getting her to join us as one of the Support Group Leaders and she was excited about it. Anna was a beautiful person, inside and out. She had a quiet strength about her. She never complained. She truly had the face of an angel, and once I put a scarf around her head and she looked like the Madonna. Elizabeth, her mother, had become my friend, but it was Anna that I started loving in a very protective way. I longed for her to be well. I prayed for her incessantly and thanked God each day for the miracle of her health.

As the months rolled by and more people passed through our workshops, we started building up a large network of people around us in the community. Mobile phones and electronic devices are not needed in the communities as news travels extremely fast. There was no need to even advertise a workshop. When we arrived in Middelburg, all we had to do was to tell one or two of the HIV trainers that a workshop was going to be held the next day and book a community hall, and the next day the hall would be full of people. I am sure the fact that there was free food helped to bring the people in. This did not matter in the least because the more people we reached with our AIDS awareness work, the better.

Our first couple of workshops consisted only of female delegates. It was beneath the males' dignity to attend. In one way, this was a good thing, as I could get used to doing the work I was doing in a female-friendly environment. I cut my teeth with them and we learned things together. I made a lot of mistakes along the way.

The biggest lesson I learned was to the detriment of a number of the women in the community, and even though I did not know any better at the time and should not feel guilty, I am responsible for some of the domestic abuse that took place. The Department of Health was giving us free male condoms. I felt that this was great, although it was disempowering for females since females did not have a choice in their own protection.

After much research and persuasion, I managed to get the AIDS Consortium (another non-governmental organization) to supply me with female condoms. With female condoms I would be able to tell the delegates that they would now be able to choose to use their own protection and not depend on their men. The accepted practice amongst the vast majority of African men is that they can have many women but their woman must stay faithful.

What I did, in retrospect, was quite irresponsible, knowing that we live in a patriarchal society. But I was all fired up with empowering these women, trying to get them to stand up for themselves and to stop them from dying of AIDS. And I assumed that the country was run by the rule of law, or at least the police would know that if a man refused to wear a condom and still forced sex on his wife, the wife could then charge her husband with rape. The best way to prevent HIV is to use a condom. This was in line with the government policy and I was happy to go along with it. But I wanted something more for these women. The female condom was the answer. The women had told me that their men would not use a condom because they said that it was like eating sweets with the paper on.

We had just had a law passed that gave woman the right to refuse sex if the man refused to use a condom. If the man had sex without a condom and without consent, it constituted rape and we could then lay a charge against the man. Of course, this is what I taught the women. I also taught them that they also had the choice of using the female condom. This way, the man would not have to have his "sweets with the paper on". One of the best ways to teach in Africa is to make use of imagery and humour. I asked them, "If you had a beautiful new garage, would you allow someone to park his dirty car in it?".

"No!", they would shout.

"And if it was a dirty BMW?"

"No", they would shout.

"And if it was a dirty double-decker bus?", I would ask again.

Again they would shout "No!".

"Then", I would say, "Valha 'i garage" (Close the garage), crossing my ring and index finger and holding my right hand in the air.

They would all then shout "Valha 'i garage", and mimic what I had done. From then on, whenever Patience and I drove around the township, the women would shout "Valha 'i garage" and hold their hands up in the salute of camaraderie. The women were all fired up and feeling strong and empowered when they left that first AIDS awareness workshop, equipped with their new knowledge and a bag full of male and female condoms. They were to return the next day as the workshop on AIDS awareness was a two-day workshop. Four of the women who came back to the workshop had been beaten up by their men-folk. When I enquired about it, I was told it was because they had refused to have sex without a condom.

"Well, did you go and report it to the police?", I asked.

Three were too afraid to go because their men had told them they would be killed if they did that. One had gone to the police to complain.

"What did they say", I asked.

"The police laughed at me", she said.

To say I was flabbergasted is putting it mildly. How could I work in this environment where the police did not even know how to do their jobs? Were they so compassion fatigued or so insensitive that they could laugh at an abused woman? And how were these women learn to protect themselves when my advice led to them being beaten up? After the workshop I went to the Superintendent of the Police and he had not even heard of the law regarding the use of condoms. I made it a point of showing him the law and asked him to kindly inform the members of his police force. Big mistake. I was making enemies without realizing it.

I had much to learn. My journey was only beginning, and had I known what lay ahead of me then, I doubt I would have continued. This was the culture in which I had decided to work, and I thought that I was going to be able to make a difference by making the police understand the necessity of knowing about policing domestic violence. I naively thought that it would mean a meeting with the Superintendent, and that since he was the "boss" of the police in the area, he would put it all straight and then things would be fine from there on. How wrong I was. Nothing works like that in Africa. I made a lot of mistakes along the way, but the biggest mistake was thinking like a Westerner, thinking that every one cared enough to make things work properly.

The next thing I felt was necessary was to include the men in the workshops. If the police were not going to be of any help, I would have to get the husbands, boyfriends, lovers into the workshops as well. With the help of the HIV trainers, we started encouraging the women to bring their partners. The workshops would now take on a different slant and we would be breaking a taboo for the first time. It would be about sex, something that the African men do not discuss with women and definitely not in an open way as in a workshop environment.

There was never any toilet paper in the toilets in the community halls so we had to provide it. Whether we took 4 rolls of toilet paper or we took 20 rolls, there were never any rolls left at the end of the day. With a little thought, the trainers and I put together an "ice breaker", a game to break the ice before the start of the workshop. Ice breakers are also used during workshops to keep people alert and to stop them from falling asleep in the heat.

We passed a couple of toilet rolls around the hall and told them to take as much as they thought they would need for the day, no more or no less. Some people took five to six pieces while others rolled and rolled the toilet paper around their hands and then stuffed it into their pockets. When everyone had their paper, we called them up one at a time and asked them to unroll their toilet paper. With their unrolled toilet paper, they were to tell us one thing about themselves for every piece of toilet paper on their roll. Those who had taken so much tried to get rid of it while they were still sitting in their seats, but those sitting next to them would not allow them to do it, because they saw the humour in people trying to tell a story about themselves that would take as long as the number of pieces of toilet paper they had taken. Never again did we use more than 6 rolls of toilet paper a day.

Another icebreaker that we used was to begin the day by asking everyone in turn to tell us about themselves honestly but to tell one lie. The rest of the delegates were then given three chances to find out what the lie was.

Mbulelo stood up and said, " My name is Mbulelo. I am 27 years old. I went to Nonyaniso School. I lived most my life in Johannesburg. I am an armed robber. I am not married. I have one son. I came to Middelburg in 1999. Which is the lie?"

"You are an armed robber", everyone said.

"It is the truth", replied.

After another two unsuccessful guesses, he told us that he never went to Nonyaniso School. With an HIV Trainer who was also an armed robber, I dreamed for days about how to get the anti-retroviral druga for Anna from Aspen Pharmaceuticals.

The men in South Africa also prefer dry sex and, for this reason, many women use various concoctions such as alum and vinegar in their vaginas to remove the natural lubrication. The lack of education and information, and the willingness to please their men, lead women to do things that are extremely harmful to their bodies and that puts them more at risk of getting HIV. All this makes the transmission of HIV more rapid because dry sex causes lesions through which the virus can enter the vagina. The vagina is also the perfect breeding ground for the virus as it is warm and moist. There is no foreplay and no enjoyment of sex for the female. Men just push a woman's legs apart, insert their penises and with a few thrusts, (or many if the man is drunk, which is often the case) it is all over.

Our first integrated workshop was quite an education for all of us. I was learning as I was teaching and I had to be one step ahead of the class. This I managed by asking questions and using the answers as a basis to continue the lessons. What I found incredibly astonishing was that the men did not know what the vagina looked like. Sex was always conducted in the dark or with the woman's skirt or dress pulled up around her waist. I asked the men to draw the vagina and not one of them could do it. They did not know anything other than that there were the outer labia and two holes. They knew nothing about the clitoris or its function. My drawing is atrocious and the drawing of a stick man takes all my creative drawing talents. Drawing a large penis and testicles on one piece of flip chart paper and a large vagina with all the bits and bobs on another was producing screeches of laughter from Patience and at times, I was laughing so much that I had to cross my legs not to pee in my pants. Eventually, after many tries and much laughter from the entire class, I had a diagram of both male and female organs and I put them up with Blue Tack. After an unexpected quiet from everyone, the men began to laugh. They were in fits of laughter, not about the vagina, but about the penis.

"Is that the size of a white man's penis?", they wanted to know. "Black men have much larger penises than that".

The workshop was turning out to be a lot of fun and the initial worry that I had about this being such a taboo subject was gone. We discussed the various parts of the organs, and the clitoris was the part that everyone was most interested in. The men were amazed that there was a part on the female that would give females the same pleasure that they themselves got from sex. The importance of foreplay and lubrication was discussed and why dry sex was not only uncomfortable and unpleasant for the woman, but why it added an extra risk for transmission of the HIV virus. The men were eager to go home and try to find this clitoris thing and to play with it. I had to explain to them that they had to be gentle, otherwise it would be painful and quite unpleasant for the female. I also explained that if they were to initiate foreplay and the woman enjoyed sex, they would be the lucky ones because they would get sex a lot more often.

We discussed the merits of both male and female condoms and the men were all very interested in returning home to try out the female condoms.

One constant question that arose from the workshops was why it was necessary to be tested for HIV. I could see the point and still do. The Health Department were having VCT (voluntary counselling and testing) sites at clinics, urging people to get tested. I never did understand the need to be tested when we were not receiving the medication. What was the point? Knowing whether you are HIV+ or not, makes absolutely no difference if you are not going to get the medication. People were reluctant to be tested because they were afraid of the diagnosis. If they did not know they were HIV+, they could live in denial. If they knew they were positive, then they would die. To know that you are HIV+ and not to be able to have the medication is pointless. The best way to live, as I assured everyone, is to live as though we are all positive. This would mean that we would change our lifestyles, ensure a good diet (within our financial means), and use condoms. The combined workshops were a tremendous success, and the women reported back that they were having good sex, with forty percent of them using condoms for the first time.

There was and still is a huge stigma attached to being HIV+, and everyone who is HIV+ says they have tuberculosis. Disclosure of status is rarely done and most keep it a secret. Maintaining such a secret is extremely stressful, and contributes to a feeling of alienation, isolation and a lowering of the immune system. This was one of the other reasons why many people refused to go to a VCT site. Although it is against the law to reveal the status of a patient, the clinic staff is not always professional enough to keep information confidential, and often the news leaks from the clinics.

I was once standing in a queue in the bank when I overheard a hospital nursing sister tell another: "Dianne Lang came in to the hospital with a migraine. She is HIV positive, you know".

I had never been tested in Middelburg, so this information was just an assumption on the part of the hospital staff. Nevertheless, in a small community, hospital staff, police, teachers and social workers hold positions of power and their word is sacrosanct. Patience and I went on a Health Department course, and registered as a VCT site. This enabled us to set up a site and to get testing equipment. We were then able to offer testing to some of the delegates. Of fifteen Trainers tested, eight tested positive. Of these trainers, four are still alive six years later, despite not being on ARV treatment. Unfortunately, after only three months, the testing equipment became impossible to obtain due to the same problems of red tape and "there is no money" in the Department of Health.

On one of our trips back to Middelburg we heard that Anna had taken ill and was in the Hospice. We went there as soon as we could, and I was shocked at how she had deteriorated. She was thin and very ill. I sat with her and chatted for a long time. She knew that she was dying. I was so sad, but at the same time, I was also angry. I was angry that we did not have the anti-retroviral drugs. The Hospice wanted to know whether there was money to bury

Anna or whether there was a funeral policy for her. When I wanted to know why, they said that they did not want her to die at the Hospice unless they were sure that there was money to bury her. We would have to take her home to die if there was no funeral policy. It was beyond me that we could be talking about burying Anna while she was still alive, as though she were just a thing that needed to stop breathing so that she could be got rid of. We were terribly upset by it. Few people in the townships had mobile phones so I drove to Elizabeth's home and asked her about it. Fortunately, she did have a family funeral policy to cover the costs of the burial, which meant that Anna could stay in the Hospice. I took Elizabeth and the children to see Anna, with the offensive policy in my hands so that I could show the Sister in charge. It was through this experience that I found out that most families have funeral policies so that they can bury their dead. The funeral policies are expensive and take a chunk out of the monthly income, but with the rate of AIDS deaths, the policy is an essential monthly expense.

I went to see Anna the next day as well. She had deteriorated so much that she was no longer speaking. She was drifting in and out of sleep. I just sat there, holding her hand, feeling completely helpless, hopeless and angry. It was the following day, while standing at my vehicle outside the hospital, waiting for the last straggling students to walk up the path, that we were told that Anna had just died. I sobbed because of the futility of it all. I cried because I had lost her. I cried because I loved her. I could not stop crying. Patience was crying too. The two of us held onto one another and our pain moved the students as well, because they started to cry as well. The emotions were shared.

"Love is just not enough", I cried. "Oh, God, we need the medicine because love is not enough", I sobbed.

Anna was gone and with her went my faith that my love would be strong enough to keep those I loved well. Sadly, many of those who trained with Patience and I also died of AIDS. I should have known that those who showed an interest in the HIV Trainer Workshops would have been those who kept the secret of their HIV status. I wish they had trusted me enough to share their secret. Perhaps I would have used my "armed robber" to get that treatment for them.

At the end of that year, the funding for the work I was doing had come to an end, but the passion and motivation to make a difference in that area had grabbed my heart and soul and I could not let go. I had to continue the work there, with or without funding.

These boots will keep on walking

We kept going back, Patience and I. Our mission, our passion and our purpose for being was in that little town of Middelburg. It was there in those people who had come to rely on us, and the community in which we loved to work. We could see we were making a difference, and we felt the response and acceptance from everyone. It did not matter what time of the day or night we would arrive in one of the townships. As we drove through we would recognize our people and they us. We would be shouting across the streets to one another, giving each other the "Vala 'i garage" salute. If we did not quite know which house one of the trainers lived in, we could just drive to the street, open the vehicle window and shout his name, and the name would be shouted from house to house until that trainer would appear out of his door and come ambling over to us.

We had by this stage established a Support Group for HIV+ people although we never called it that. It was just a group of people getting together for community work. We had also established contact with two youngsters who wanted to put a drama group together. With a little bit of funding and a lot of hard work, a drama group called the Township Prophets was soon a real contender for entertainment in the townships. Fikile and Simpiwe were the inspiration and the best actors among the performers. They co-ordinated and taught the youngsters in the community to dance and perform. They were brilliant. Using their talents, we could now teach AIDS awareness, domestic violence and child abuse through drama. Eventually, they became so well known in the area that they were being asked to entertain dignitaries from the government departments for various special occasions. We were teaching AIDS awareness in the schools, the community halls and in the streets.

One of the girls in the support group was a 23 year-old by the name of Emma. She had been pregnant when she joined the group. She gave birth to a little called she called Roseline. Emma got ill and very thin immediately after giving birth. She also had TB and had not had the treatment for the prevention of mother-to-child transmission. Emma was bottle feeding Roselene with the donated milk formula. Emma died a month after giving birth to Roselene, and her mother took over the care of the baby. Roselene's father had been working in Cape Town but came back to live in Middelburg and moved in with Emma's mother and the baby. He had a serious drinking problem, as did the baby's grandmother (Emma's mother). This was not a unique situation, as alcohol abuse is the norm in at least two of the townships, Lusaka and Midros. It is unusual for a family not to abuse alcohol.

By this stage, we had managed to buy a little house with fifteen thousand rand donated by Vodacom. It was in a very bad state of disrepair, but the trainers and Home Base Care workers put in many hours of hard work and with some tins of paint stripper, paint and brushes, we soon turned it into a lovely little office and home. It became our first "home" in Middelburg, our sanctuary in the storm of AIDS. Patience and I could now spend days in Middelburg during the week instead of driving backwards and forwards to Port Elizabeth, thereby saving money on petrol. We furnished it with second-hand furniture and decorated it on the smell of an oil rag and the wings of a prayer. We bought a medium-size tin of red enamel paint and painted a big red ribbon on the side of the house. We had not had much to do with the "white" people in the town, so I was pleasantly surprised when the next door neighbour appeared at the door one morning.

"I have come to tell you that I would like to donate some paint to you", he said in Afrikaans.

"Thank you so much", I said, "That would come in so handy", also in Afrikaans.

"Ja", he said, "It is to be used to paint out that red sign. We don't want AIDS people in this street".

In the best Afrikaans I could muster from my stunned response I said, "Thank you for your offer, but we do not need paint that badly".

I would continue to greet my gentlemanly neighbour every time I saw him, in his own language and with the greatest respect. It was three or four months after I started caring for the children that he came across to me with ten kilograms of porridge.

"This is for your children. I will buy it for you whenever I can afford it", he said.

And this same gentleman has bought the children porridge every now and again for years. Miracles do happen and people do change.

Roselene's grandmother came to our home/office, which we had now named the Care House, every week to collect milk formula and baby clothes. We had sent out e-mails to all our friends, and were getting a lot of donations of baby clothes and clothing for the HIV and AIDS patients, as well as medical supplies and small amounts of money to keep us going. However, the majority of the money was coming from my own savings.

When Roselene was nearly four months old we heard that she had died suddenly. I don't know why I continued to be flabbergasted, disbelieving and stunned by the things that continued to happen. I could not understand because Roselene had looked quite well when the grandmother had collected the baby formulae the week before. Patience and I went to the grandmother's house but no one was home. The neighbours said that the grandmother was visiting her boyfriend and that the father was at the shebeen (an illegal alcohol bar/shop). We were also told that the police had taken the baby away that morning but that the baby was already dead. The baby was four days short of four months. The neighbour said that it looked as though the baby had been bleeding from her ears, nose and mouth. We knew immediately that something was amiss. This was no ordinary death.

From the township, we drove to the hospital where we were told that she was dead on arrival, and that the body had been transferred to the funeral home. It had been a weekend of child abuse for the hospital staff. Another child had arrived dead on arrival from a beating, and another who had arrived badly beaten by the father of the child. We went to the funeral home and asked to see the body of Roselene. What I saw will stay with me for the rest of my life. Her little body was naked. Her vagina was swollen, raw and red. Her eyes were bruised, swollen and blue. There was blood in her eyes, ears, nose and mouth. Bruises covered her body. I asked Patience fetch my camera from the vehicle. I took photos of Roselene. I don't know why I did that at the time. But later, I was glad that I had done it because Patience and I would soon realize that someone was hiding the fact that Roselene had been raped and beaten to death.

Much later I regretted taking those photos. I regretted ever making a stand for Roselene because through Roselene I lost the best friend I ever had. Those photos changed my life forever and the world would never, ever be the same again for me. I asked the manager of the funeral home if I could have a copy of the death certificate. "There is no death certificate, because there is no birth certificate", he said. "There is a burial order that has been made out by the District Surgeon and stamped by the Police", he continued, as he made and handed me a copy.

This was my introduction to the complexity of birth and death certificates in South Africa. After the ANC government came into power, Middelburg's municipality was decentralized and moved to Cradock, one hundred kilometres away, together with the mayor and his elected members of the Council. All decisions regarding municipal and local government issues now took place in Cradock. In order to obtain a birth certificate, a trip to Cradock was necessary. With no public transport, taxis could ask astronomical prices for the trip. Unemployment is extremely high, and with most people struggling to feed themselves, going to Cradock to get a birth certificate was not a priority. Thus, most children were without birth certificates. This being the case, a death certificate was unnecessary and a burial order was issued.

I could not help wondering where the AIDS statistics came from when death certificates were not issued. This information would later prove to be of great benefit to the Department of Social Development when I later registered a children's home, because without birth certificates, the children did not exist and therefore did not qualify for government grants. Obtaining birth certificates for the children proved extremely difficult and in some cases impossible. A death certificate from the mother had to be obtained, a clinic card showing where the child was born had to be obtained, and with that information, a birth certificate could then be applied for. Once all the necessary documentation was submitted, the certificate could sometimes take up to eight months to obtain. More often than not, an orphan could not obtain a birth certificate at all. If a child had been living on the streets and did not know the name of the mother, getting a death certificate was impossible. To compound the problem, some mother's did not have a death certificate because they had never had their birth's registered. There was no way around registering a foundling. Without a birth certificate, a child could not be admitted to school. The Department of Home Affairs did eventually send a delegation once a month to the town hall to accept all documentation for registration. However, they were often late or sometimes did not arrive on the day they were supposed to arrive. Still...

The burial order stated that Roselene had died of AIDS! AIDS deaths do not leave a baby with bruises, bleeding from the eyes, ears and nose and bruised and violated vaginas. Roselene had been raped and beaten! Patience suggested that we go back to the grandmother and ask her what had happened. Something was very, very wrong. Feeling somewhat fearful of what we were getting into, but at the same time knowing that no one would care whether she had been abused and beaten to death, we went to the grandmother's house. This time she was at home, as merry as alcohol can make one. It certainly did not appear as if there had been a death in the family. She was totally unaffected by the whole event, showing no distressful emotions whatsoever.

"Hello, Mrs Gallant", I said. "I am sorry to hear about Roselene".

"No problem. No problem. Come inside, come inside", she laughed, gesturing us to come inside.

We sat down in her small lounge. She reeked of alcohol and her eyes were red and puffy.

"Can you tell us what happened to Roselene?", Patience asked.

"Well, I went out last night. Her father was at home and was supposed to be looking after her. I can't remember when I got home, but Roselene would not stop crying. Her father was not here. She was bleeding from her ears and nose. I made her a bottle to try and stop her from crying. I eventually fell asleep. She was lying on the bed with me.

When I woke up this morning she was very still. I looked at her and saw that she was not breathing. Her father was still not at home. I went next door and they phoned the police for me. The police took her away", she said. "Her father is not a good man", she carried on. "But you had better go in case he comes back".

"Thank you, Mrs Gallant, let us know if we can do anything", I said when we left.

"What do we do now?", I asked Patience as we were driving away. "My God, this certainly is not a death from AIDS. This is a possible rape and murder", I said.

"Let's go to the police", she replied. "OK, but let us go to the Station Commissioner. He will know what to do. There is already something wrong if the burial certificate is stamped by the police as an AIDS death, because that will mean that whoever did this to Roselene will get away with murder", I said.

We phoned the police station and made an appointment with the Station Commissioner. That afternoon, we took our story to him and he said that he would look into it, but by the manner in which he said it, I was sure that he was going to do nothing about it. It was also very strange that he first said that he knew only of a child who had been abused by his father, and who had been discharged by the hospital.

"But Commissioner, there is another child that was picked up by the police and taken to the hospital that was dead on arrival, and that child looked abused", I said.

"No other child was picked up by the police". He was adamant.

"Commissioner, we saw that child, we were at the hospital, Inspector Mpongo picked the child up and took the child to the hospital and the police have put the stamp on the burial order", I said.

"I said I will look into it, Mrs Lang", he said, getting angry with me.

"Patience, they are covering something up", I said, as we left.

"I know. You can see that for sure. They think we are stupid", she replied. "Best thing we can do is to phone the commissioner every week to find out what he has done about it. Then he will know that we know that something strange is going on", she continued. "It's also because we are women. He is one of those kinds of men that can't stand to deal with women. You could feel the way he was dismissing us, as though we were just getting on his nerves".

I thought it was a good idea to give him a call every week. This was one of our mistakes, thinking that by giving the Commissioner a call, we would be making sure that something would be done about the death of Roselene. In the meantime, Roselene was buried and no arrests were made. The commissioner continued to deny that any child had been picked up on that day, 25th August, although we had the death certificate in our possession, duly signed and stamped by his police station. We were totally ignorant of the fact that the system worked on who owed who a favour, and who was related to whom, and who paid who off with how much. Corruption and fraud were not part of our framework of thought, so we could not understand what was going on. We never once thought that it was possible that perhaps the police were covering up for someone. The only explanation we could come up with was that the Station Commissioner was lazy and ignorant and did not know how to do his job. Not once did we figure or think that he was actually a clever individual who was corrupt and was covering his tracks. We were up against a very corrupt system and were too innocent to realize it. We were just confused by what was going on, and thought that no one cared that Roselene had been murdered, when in fact, people did care that she had been murdered... her life was just not valuable enough for justice to be done. At the time this idea was beyond our thought capabilities. We were still in the dream world of thinking that people were good and could be trusted and that if something like this was happening, it was just because someone did not know how to do his job properly.

When nothing was being done about Roselene, and we were continually being fobbed off by the Station Commissioner, Kakuyi, and after we heard a rumour that Roselene's father was related to one of the police officer's, I decided that I would report the incident to the ICD. The ICD is the Independent Complaints Directorate which investigates complaints against the South African Police Services. I contacted them and spoke with a man called Kevin, who was most sympathetic to what I had to say. He made an appointment to see me, and within a week, we had our meeting. I showed him all the photographs and the burial certificate and told him how we had been fobbed off, and how the Station Commissioner had denied that such a child had been picked up by the police. Kevin told me that they would certainly investigate the incident because with the evidence it was obvious that there was a cover up. He took copies of all the photographs and the burial certificate. Kevin inspired confidence in me and I knew that he would do something about it.

Later that same day, I received a call on my mobile from Station Commissioner Kakuyi to come into his office immediately. By the sound of his voice, I knew that he was angry. As I had done nothing wrong, I knew that it must have something to do with the Roselene affair and that Kevin had started his investigation already. I was afraid. The Station Commander was not a small man. He was huge and looked not unlike Idi Amin with his uniform stretched over his extended stomach. When I walked into his office, he was standing behind his desk, the sweat pouring down his face. He was furious.

"Mrs Lang, who do you think you are? How dare you involve the ICD in this matter? I have told you many times that the child in question died of natural causes. You are making a huge thing out of nothing. You are causing trouble in this town. You had better watch out! Things will not be easy for you. Stop interfering in police business. You know nothing about anything. I am warning you to stop interfering!", he shouted.

I was shaking like a leaf. My heart was pounding and I could feel the blood rushing in my ears. I was afraid. I was terrified but I was damned if I was going to let this bully know just how afraid I was of him. He was the splitting image of Idi Amin at that moment.

"Superintendent, you never once told me the child died of natural causes and in fact, you have continuously denied any knowledge of the child", I stated.

"That is a lie", he screamed at me.

"Do not raise your voice to me, Superintendent", I said. "You are a Public Servant. You are paid by the tax payer and as such, you have a duty to respect me", I said. "I will not stand here and be spoken to like this", I continued. "If you have something to hide, then that is your problem. If not, then there should be no problem with the ICD investigating this case. Now if you will excuse me, good day, Superintendent", I said, as I walked out his office on very shaky legs.

I don't remember how I got from his office, along the passage, past the holding cells, the front office and to my vehicle. But as I climbed into it, I burst into tears of anger. Patience had been sitting in the vehicle, and she too started crying. Patience would cry if I cried, never bothering to find out the reason for my crying. If I was angry, she was angry. If I was sad, she was sad. She felt my every emotion. I was so angry and so afraid that I wondered whether it was all worth it. I immediately telephoned Kevin on his mobile and between sobs told him what had happened. He pacified me and told me to hang in there, that I had done the right thing and that we would get to the bottom of this.

The ICD needed a statement from Patience and I to open a docket to investigate the police corruption in this case. Kevin kept in contact with me but, as his work load was heavy, the investigation into the Roselene case had to wait its turn.

It was soon after the horrible meeting with Superintendent "Idi Amin" that we started getting strange phone calls. These calls would come at all times of the day and night. "Drop the case or else" would be the only words and the phone would be put down.

"You going to die".

"Do you want to look like Roselene?".

"We know where you live".

"Be careful of where you go".   Each time a different voice – a different accent.

We changed our telephone numbers, but within a week or so, the telephone calls would begin again. It got so that we were afraid to answer the telephones. The telephone messages were becoming more sinister with actual death threats, "We going to kill you unless you drop the case", being the one used most frequently. They would phone my mobile first, and then Patience's mobile and the next time it would be the other way around.

Kevin let us know that a request for an exhumation order had been put in to the Chief Magistrate in Grahamstown. The phone calls escalated. We knew that the men were that were threatening us were meaning business when the wheel nuts were loosened on our vehicle. It was obvious where the threats were coming from. Being still so naïve, we did not really take it as seriously as we should have, although we did think that it was serious enough. When someone tells you they are going to kill you, it does not really sink into your conscious mind. It kind of hangs there, but does not really penetrate. Being in a situation like that does not necessarily make one do anything about it. It is almost as if it is happening to someone else. We spoke about it often, we would get scared but then we would think, "No, things like this don't happen – it's only in the movies", and leave it at that.

After the wheel nut incident, we sat down and had our first honest chat about whether to continue perusing the situation. Soon after the wheel nut incident, we had tear gas thrown into the house. We called the police but no one ever came. The incessant phone calls never stopped. It is an unreal feeling to be threatened by the very people you are conditioned to expect to protect you. I thought that it was not worth losing our lives over and told Patience that if those wheels had come off while speeding, we would both be dead. We could not take the chance of it happening again.

"Dianne", she said, "You have always told me that if you are doing God's work, He will protect you. This is God's work we are doing. He will protect us. Why are you changing your mind now?"

"Are you sure you want to carry on with this, Patience?", I asked.

"Yes", she said emphatically, "we have to fuck up that bastard Idi Amin".

It was the Christmas holidays so we were not going back to Middelburg again until the New Year. We would be safe until then in any event, so I let it be. We had a fabulous time those holidays, spending time in creative activities, making cards, garden plaques, and spending time in the sun and walking on the beach. We laughed and joked, sang and told stories until late at night. It was a wonderful couple of weeks, apart from the horrid phone calls. Patience was four foot nothing and I am five feet ten and a half inches. Definitely a half jack and a litre. But as small as she was, she had the spirit of a giant and the heart of an angel. Patience was going home from 24 until the 27th December to spend time with her mother. On the afternoon of the 24th, I drove her into town to put her on the taxi. We sat waiting in the car until the taxi arrived. I looked down at her little size three feet and saw that the paint on her toenails was coming off.

"Oh, Patience, you will have to paint your toenails before your boyfriend comes to visit", I said jokingly.

"I know", she said, "or I won't even get him into bed".

We laughed. Just then the taxi arrived and we both jumped out the vehicle. We kissed and hugged.

"Goodbye Patience", I said. "Have a good time. Remember I love you".

"I love you more", she said as she waved and climbed into the taxi.

That was the last time I saw my friend alive.

Dear Patience
I am sitting in a psychiatric clinic, two years after you died. Dr Fanie Meyer, the psychiatrist, wants me to write a letter to you. He thinks it is time for me to let you go. He says that I have to face up to your death, that if I don't, I will forever be stuck in this grief.

So much has happened since you died. For the first three months after you died, I could not function on any level. I could not go back to Middelburg. I could not carry on with the work we were doing. I even called Kevin and told him to forget about the case of Roseline. What did any of it matter anymore? Nothing seemed to matter without you. Eventually I did go back to Middelburg and started doing more training and then one night three children landed on the doorstep. I had to start pulling myself together then. I worked incessantly. I could not let myself think. I used work so that I did not have to think. I worked nonstop with no days off and often until the early hours of the morning. I burned out. I could not cope with anything anymore, could not stop crying and then I lost the plot completely. I tried my best to carry on, but the glue came unstuck.

I still could not think about the time you died. I could not think about the last time I saw you. I could not talk about you to anyone. I could not allow my thoughts to go back to that night, the night you died. My life was frozen around that time. I tried to carry on, Patience, but just one thing too much has happened and now I need help.

Dr Meyer has been like a raft that has been sent to me in a burning inferno. These last two years have been some of the worst years of my life and in some ways, some small ways, I have had the most joy, felt loved for the first time in my life. It is the children that have brought that joy and love into my life. In some ways, they have replaced you, and in other ways, there will never ever be a replacement for you. Not ever.

I miss you so much. So many times in the first year, I would be driving along the road to Middelburg or Port Elizabeth and one of our songs would start playing on the CD and I would start singing along, turn to smile at you in the passenger seat, and you would not be there. It would just be my bag lying there and I would realize that you were gone.

For those first days after you died, I remember little other than the intense pain I felt at losing you. I could not breathe. I could not think. I was in a nightmare I could not wake up from. I drove to Miem (what Patience called my mother) *and when I saw her I just started screaming. I could hear myself but could not stop myself. I was howling like a wounded animal. I cried all day, all week. I cried every time I was alone. I cried every time my mind was not focused on something. I cried every time I did something that we used to do together. Then the weeks after that I missed you with a terrible ache – and every time I talk about you, I still cry. I miss you with a awful haunting ache. An ache so deep inside of me that it cannot be filled or taken away. I have not been able to think about those days after you died or even the night you died. Every time a thought about it comes up, I push it away because I can't face it. I can't tell anyone because I can't allow myself to think about it.*

Denny (my daughter) *sent me a card soon after you died and in the card was a little pair of angel wings. I took those wings and put them in the 4x4 van and those wings became you. I knew that if I looked at those wings, you would be there with me.*

I remember us talking about the death threats. I remember what you said. You said "Di, this is God's work and God will protect us". But He didn't, did he? He allowed them to take you away from me. The most wonderful and special friend I ever had. The way you hurt a person the most, is to take away the one you love the most. Oh, God, Patience, I miss you so much. I don't know how I have carried on without you. For twelve years, you and I saw each other every day and not a cross word was ever used. You were my soul mate, my confidante, my comfort, my other half. We shared everything. A better friend I never had.

I also remember the last time I saw you alive. Remember how we laughed about your toenails, Patience, and how you said you would do something about painting them so you could get your boyfriend into bed. I remember how whoever said "I love you" first, the other got to say "I love you more" afterwards.

That night I got a call from your boyfriend to tell me you were in Livingston Hospital. Niki (my son) *was sleeping over that night. I woke him up and we drove immediately to Livingston Hospital. I ran into the casualty department. Your whole family were sitting around but I could not see you. They were not crying or showing signs of trauma, so I was not too worried. I asked the nursing sister where you were and she calmly walked down the passage and asked me to follow. She led me down this long corridor and turned left into a small room. And there you were. Lying on your back on the bed in the middle of a room and not moving.*

I ran to your side, calling your name and touched you, and you were cold And, there was one tear on your cheek. I shouted and shouted for you to wake up, but you did not move. And I put my arms around you, and tried to lift you off the bed to take you home.   Someone was pulling me away from you and I started screaming and screaming and I could not believe what was happening. And they pulled me out of the room, and down the passage but I got away, and ran back to you. I threw my arms around you again, and tried desperately to wake you up. I screamed for you to wake up.

And then I saw your toenails – you did not have any shoes on – you had painted your toenails. Oh, God, Patience, why, why, why did they take you from me? Where was God? Someone led me out the room, and down the passage, and I broke away, and ran back to you again. I could not leave you. I just could not leave you. You had to be OK. Niki kept on telling me that you were gone, and I would scream back at him that you were not gone. He eventually grabbed me by both arms and held me tight. He looked at me and told me you were dead. I screamed and screamed. I kept on telling him that I could see you breathing.

Rushing back into your room, I held onto you, pulling you up against my chest, wiping the tear from your cheek, feeling my world crashing down around me, wanting to wake up from this nightmare that I was in, shaking you and screaming at you to breathe. It was the worst nightmare of my life. One that I know I must wake up from. I could not leave you and I still can't. You are so much part of my life.

The days and weeks before we could bury you were a blur. I try now as hard as I can, but the time after your death seems like a disjointed nightmare. I remember phoning one mortuary after another, asking for a post mortem to be done on you, and the mortuary telling me that your body was at another police mortuary. Then I would phone that mortuary, and would be told that your body was not there, but at the previous mortuary. And I would phone again and again, and each time I would be told a different story as to where your body was. Every mortuary would deny that your body was there, or I would be told that a post mortem was being done at the state mortuary. But when I phoned the state mortuary, they would not even have a record of you. Your body kept disappearing out of various police mortuaries. I wanted to know why you had died so suddenly. There was nothing wrong with you. Something very strange had happened and I was sure that the death threats had something to do with your death.

I managed to see your boyfriend. I remember that clearly because he was very upset, and was in a terrible state of shock. He too felt that there was more to your death than what met the eye. He also could not understand why we could not get your body for burial and why we could not find your body in the various police mortuaries. He went from mortuary to mortuary and no one knew where you were.

And your family started fighting about your belongings. Your sister made me give her all your savings we had been saving to buy you a house. And then five weeks later, when your body was found and the funeral was arranged, your boyfriend phoned me to warn me to stay at home because he was worried that I would be the next person to die. When I asked him why he thought this, he would not say. He just told me that he had heard things. I was too distraught to follow up what he said or to do anything about it. But then, thinking about it now, who would I have gone to anyway?

So I held my own funeral for you. I moved all the plants from the back of the house and made a special garden for you. I bricked-paved the area, put some beautiful plants in pots, put a little bench in the area and made a sign in your memory. From that little bench I could see the sea and watch the waves roll onto the sand. I used to go up there at sunset and wish with all my heart that you were there.

As we had planned to spend the week days in Middelburg and week-ends in Blue Horizon Bay, I eventually did that and moved into that little house. That is when the first children arrived. Money became more and more difficult to get hold of because there were more and more abused children arriving at the door.

Some came on their own and some were brought by the police. And I ran out of money. I had no choice. I had to sell Blue Horizon Bay and with it went your special little place. But I made another place for you in Middelburg. No matter where I go, Patience, I will always make a special place for you.

Nombasa is fine. You would be so proud of your little girl who is now a young lady. She started menstruating and I made a big fuss of her, gave her the "Now you are a young lady ...." speech. She has passed Grade 11 and is the best actress in the drama group. She is confident, responsible and has a personality just like yours. I will look after your daughter, Patience, and give her the best I can. I promise you.

I miss you so much, Patience. I loved you so much and love you still. I know that you will forever be in my heart, but I have to let you go now. I can't move on because I am stuck with the memories of our times together. All I do in our work is a reminder of you and I wonder "What would Patience think of that?" Or I want to tell you about something that happened, or hear you tell me I drive like a man. What a back-handed compliment! But that was you.

Wherever you are now, my dearest friend, I pray that you are happy. Some people say that if we mourn too much for someone who has died, we stop them from moving on. I don't know the answers to life and death. I don't really know where you are. I know that you are not that body that I saw at the hospital. I know you are out there somewhere, watching me. I also know how much you hated to see me cry, so maybe it is time for me to stop crying for you.

Remember the time we did that HIV workshop and we found all the feathers as we were going into the hall? And remember we said that the angels were with us, and that the workshop would be brilliant, and it was? Well, for the past couple of weeks, I have found a feather in the oddest of places. Is it you? Are you telling me that everything will be fine, like the workshop? I think it is you, and I also think that you are telling me to let go and move on.

Saying goodbye to you properly makes me feel like I am deserting you. I feel that if I let go of this grief I will be letting you down. For you, Patience, and in your memory, I am letting go and I am going to be well and happy. I owe you that.

Thank you for having being in my life. Thank you for being my friend. Thank you for showing me what true friendship is. You will forever be in my heart. You are still my angel.

I will love you always.
Dianne

I left the clinic in Bloemfontein, feeling vulnerable, but more in control. The first thing I did when I got to the car park before leaving the clinic grounds was to remove the angel wings from the vehicle. I had to let Patience go properly so that I could move on with my life. Going to the clinic in itself would not have helped me. The person who has helped me overcome the death of Patience and many other traumatic things that have happened during this journey has been Dr Meyer, a psychiatrist with an abundant capacity for the understanding of human nature and the ability to instil faith in oneself. Being a counselling psychologist myself, I could not go to another psychologist where I would have wasted my time playing mind games. I needed to go to someone who would challenge me, who would push me to become more than I thought I could be, and eventually become comfortable with myself and my mission. I was fortunate to meet up with the most wonderful friend and psychiatrist.

Over the years, Dr Meyer has become far more than my psychiatrist, my doctor. He has a deep understanding of my psyche, and with only one or two sentences, he knows what is needed to be said to put me back on track again. Without his indomitable resolve and faith in me and my ability, I could not have achieved what I have. I would never have got over the death of Patience without the help of Dr Fanie Meyer.

A letter written to me by my mother on 19th February 2003 after the death of Patience shows how the death affected not only me, but my family as well.

My dearest Disey
I just feel I must let you know how happy I am to hear you are getting there a little more each day. You have come a long way in a short time and still have a long way to go to be on top of everything. You will have good days and bad ones, but you're going about the bad ones by

praying your way through. I am proud of you. (I miss her too).

You will always miss your little fat friend, she was your angel in many ways, saving you, and maybe her going away has opened your eyes to many evil/bad things which she protected you from, as I see it, maybe I'm wrong.

*Looking back, Rosie (*my mom's counterpart to my Patience) *was like my crutch in those bad days, but maybe to a lesser degree than yours. I do feel for you, Di. Time is a great healer and teacher too. My only grip on life and my reason I am here today is my link to God. We have to live today, the past is past, we can do nothing about it, it came and went, likewise we can do nothing about the future, it is not yet here, but today is ours to use in whatever way we choose. Today is the womb through which the future will emerge.*

Be careful, don't trust anyone, take care of you for once in your lifetime. You are very precious and I love you dearly. Looking forward to seeing you soon. We will get to the top of the Hill soon. God Bless you.
Love, Mom

I asked for the post-mortem report many times after the death of Patience, and eventually, with a bit of ingenuity, and after more than a year, I managed to get someone to read the report to me over the telephone. The result of her death, according to the report, was due to a "burst heart". This official diagnosis of death boggles the mind. The eyewitness accounts of the two hours leading up to the death of Patience are very clear. She was walking with her boyfriend and her daughter, Nombasa, along the street towards her mother's home when an acquaintance gave each of them a piece of chicken. Each piece was given to them individually. By the time they reached home, which was within 10 minutes, Patience was sweating and complaining of stomach ache. She sat down as soon as she entered the house, and complained of a burning sensation in her stomach and said that she was getting very hot. She stood up and went outside where she collapsed. An ambulance was called. Within two hours of eating the chicken she was pronounced dead on arrival at the hospital.

I phoned Kevin at the Independent Complaints Directorate and told him what had happened to Patience. We had been in contact with him and he was aware of the death threats we had been getting. I told him that I was not prepared to continue going down the road with the case of Roseline. It was a pointless exercise without Patience and I no longer had the stamina, the motivation or the interest in pursuing this injustice. I could not deal with the death of Patience and therefore had no energy or strength to deal with Roseline. The death threats stopped with my telephone call to Kevin.

It is better to let it all go and remember Patience as she was, my very best friend...with the two of us singing at the top of our voices while travelling the road between Port Elizabeth and Middelburg, "these boots were made for walking and they're gonna walk all over you..."

Friday 13th

I open my eyes slowly. I lie still and listen to my breathing. Outside I hear the neighbour's ducks. Then I hear a child's laughter. I am alive. I glance over at the bedside clock. It is 5.30am. I lean over and turn the radio on. It is Dido singing "Life for rent". Yeah, maybe my life is for rent. Maybe it is not mine. It belongs to the children. I lie still for a couple more moments. I realize I have two choices. I can turn over, cover myself with the duvet and play dead, or I can say "Fuck them" and get up and fight. Before the thought has taken form, I fling the duvet back and race around, putting the kettle on, jumping into the shower, all the while scheming and planning my next line of attack, my next strategy on how to protect my children.

From studying the Child Care Act, I know and have documented proof that the Department of Social Development (social services) the Department of Safety and Security (police) and the Justice Department have all contravened the Act. I also know and have documented proof that Section 28 of the South African Constitution, which is amongst one of the best in the world, has been contravened by the very systems that have been put in place to ensure that the children's rights are not violated. Section 28 stipulates that every child has the right to a name and a nationality from birth, to family care or parental care, or to appropriate alternative care when removed from the family environment. The child is also entitled to basic nutrition, shelter, basic health and social care services. The child has the right to be protected from abuse and neglect, to exploitative labour practices and not to be placed at risk of well-being, education, physical or mental health or spiritual, moral or social development. The child must be treated in a manner, and kept in conditions, that take account of the child's age and to have a legal practitioner assigned to the child by the state, and at state expense, in civil proceedings affecting the child, if substantial injustice would otherwise result. From this it is apparent that a child's best interest are of paramount importance in every matter concerning the child. In this section *child* means a person under the age of 18 years.

I had written on numerous occasions to the Chief Social Worker, Mr Johan Pienaar; the Area Supervisor, Mrs Iza Ferreira; Area Manager, Mr Makasi; Director, Mr Maxhecwana, Member of the Executive Council and the Minister of Social Development on the violations of children's rights. Apart from a letter from the Minister telling me that the matter would be looked into, no reply was ever received from any of these people in authority. Each time I wrote, I would receive the same letter, "We are looking into the matter", but nothing would happen.

While I was in the shower, I decided that it was now time to request an independent investigation into the service delivery by the Department of Social Development, the Justice Department and the Department of Safety and Security in our area. As soon as I was dressed, I sat I sit down at the computer and started my fight. Letters come pouring out of the computer and were faxed to the Ministers of the various departments, with a copy to each of the officials in those departments in the local area. I was not wasting my time with anyone other than those at the very top. I even asked the President to motivate an investigation. Needless to say, he did not bother to reply.

He was probably too busy buying airplanes and submarines that we can't fly or sail. The faxes were followed up with telephone calls. I was relentless in my pursuit of my goal. I hounded them. I believed that if there was an independent investigation, the holes in the service delivery would become obvious and something would then be done, particularly since I was willing to share the proof and documents with the various investigators.

The Minister of Safety and Security answered my letter within days and sent a representative to see me. We discussed the many problems we were having with the police service, particularly that the police did not know how to police children's rights. Because children had been abused for so long, police no longer saw it as a problem. They had become habituated to the problem. Therefore, every time I went to the police with a case of child abuse, neglect or the rape or sodomy of a child, it became a nuisance case and was not investigated. Police also did not know the legal implications of removing a child from an abusive situation and placing a child in a place of safety. Although we had a good talk and lots of promises were made to train the police in our area, no training was done by the police in the three years since the promise.

The Minister of Justice answered my letter a couple of weeks later and I met with the head of magistrates, Mrs Robertson. She was horrified by the stories that I told her. One of my staff members also spoke to her of the children who had been removed from our care, and in what conditions they were now living in the township. She advised that I should not go to court without a lawyer to represent the children. This obviously was a tall order for us as we are not subsidized and all our funding comes from private donations. Mrs Robertson told me that she had already informed the court that no children's court hearings could take place without us being notified first. She assured me that no tricks could be pulled on us by the welfare. We would have ample time to get a lawyer to represent the children. How wrong both she and I were. It made no difference. It was business as usual when she left town.

I never heard from the Department of Social Development, despite continually sending letters, faxes and making telephone calls requesting an independent investigation into service delivery. I also included documentation proving that the children's rights were being violated. Weeks dragged on and soon it was months. Social Development continued to make life difficult for us by not co-operating with us. We had bought two more houses and had applied to accommodate more children. We had completed the numerous forms and submitted them for approval. We heard nothing. We wrote to find out how far the application had got. We heard nothing. We phoned to find out. We were told to wait. Four months later, we phoned again and were told we could have more children.

When I asked how many more children I could accommodate, I was told by the Area Supervisor, Mrs Ferreira, "More, but I don't know how many more yet".

It eventually took from April 2004 to November 2006 to get an updated Children's Home certificate from the Department of Social Development and only after an application to the Supreme High Court was served on the department by the Legal Resource Centre (LRC), a legal charity. The LRC was to become an integral part of our strategy in dealing with the department from 2006.

When children in need came into our care, we would notify the social worker and the clerk of the court but no paper work would be done. By law, a Form 4 needs to be signed, placing the child in our care for a period of 48 hours. Within that period of time, a preliminary investigation has to be done by the social worker and the child, and the parent or guardian or the child, and the person into whose safety the child has been put needs to be brought before the Commissioner of Child Welfare. The child is then put into the place of safety for a period not longer than eight weeks, during which time the social worker is to do an in-depth investigation and the child is to be placed on a permanent basis in a children's home or in foster care. If this is not done, it is then the responsibility of the person who is caring for the child to notify the court within 7 days that no paperwork has been delivered. I notify the court and the social worker. Nothing happens. Every seven days I notify the court and the social worker. Nothing happens. We notify them by telephone, in person, in writing, hand-delivered letters that are signed for, and by fax. Nothing happens.

This can go on for months. If a child dies in our care without the necessary paperwork, we can be held responsible. Since some of my children are HIV+ and a few have AIDS, we would be in serious trouble. Is this what they want to happen? Or are they just completely incompetent, or do they just not care? Many children were in our care for up to three years without the social workers doing the necessary paperwork and without the children being placed in the Children's Home through the Children's Court, despite the fact that we continually notified them every seven days.

I did some legal research and on Wednesday, July 21, 2004, I wrote and hand-delivered a letter to Mr Mata, the Magistrate in Middelburg, requesting to be made an Authorised Officer of the court. By doing this, I would be able to sign the Form 4s myself, thereby making the placement of the child in my care legal and cutting the social worker and the police officer out of the equation. A Form 4 has to be signed by either a social worker, a police officer, or an authorized officer of the court. I also sent a copy to the other government departments that I was having problems with.

Dear Sir
REQUEST TO BE MADE AN AUTHORISED OFFICER AND PROCESSING OF FORM 4s

I hereby make application to be made an authorized officer in terms of Section 12.1 of the Child Care Act 74 of 1983 and on the basis of a precedent in 1996 in which a matron at a local hospital in Cape Town was granted the above status.

The reason for this request is that due to the overload of work of the Social Workers, they are unable to provide the service delivery expected of them i.e. Processing Form 4s within 48 hours. The Social Workers in Middelburg are also restricted by the Social Development Department's internal rules and regulations. Social Workers in Middelburg have to submit all Form 4s to their superior in Cradock to authorize before the case is presented to the CRADOCK magistrate. This is not acceptable because the Cradock Magistrate does not have jurisdiction over the MIDDELBURG CAPE children. Only you, as the Children's Court Magistrate, have jurisdiction over our children in this area.

What has now happened, due to incorrect information being given to the Department of Justice and the SAPS, is that children who have been placed in my care are now illegally in my care (even though criminal dockets have been opened) because the Form 4 has never been processed. This is despite continuously requesting the Department of Social Development to do so.

Because of the above, we are not acting in the best interest of the child. I include letters written to the Department of Social Development, which will highlight the plight of the child. What is continuously happening is that a child is placed in our care, a criminal docket is opened, we take care of the child for weeks, months and sometimes longer than a year, and when the alleged abuser wants the child back, Social Development removes or can remove the child from our care without any recourse. This includes children who have been raped.

As an authorized Officer, I will ensure that the correct procedure is followed so that Section 28 of the Constitution is a reality in our area. The Grahamstown High Court has advised me that all Form 4s are to be rewritten, signed and submitted to you for processing. These will be submitted as soon as possible.

I respectfully request your most kind consideration in this matter.
Yours truly,
DIANNE LANG
Managing Director
Cc Area Commissioner SAPS/Investigating Officers SAPS/Department of Social Development/Grahamstown High Court

I was over the moon when Mr Mata made me an Authorized Officer of the court. I never really believed that I would get it. This meant that I no longer had to wait for a social worker to do the paper work. I could do the paper work myself and hand it in to the clerk of the court. The clerk of the court then could instruct the social worker to do the investigation and the report within the seven-day period. However, there was a clause that if a social worker or a police officer was not available, only then could I sign the form. This did not pose a problem, because social workers never seemed to be available after hours and during hours they were always too busy. The police had been instructed by the station commander not to sign Form 4s, despite it being part of a policeman's job. This piece of paper now meant that I could help the children. What a joy, what an achievement! At long last, someone was listening.

On Thursday afternoon, 12th August 2004, the Magistrate, Mr Mata, phoned me and told me that I was wanted at a meeting at his office the next morning at 11h30. I asked him what the meeting was about. He said that the meeting was between the police and the social workers. I told him that I was afraid to attend because I knew that they would be there with a hidden agenda.

"Come, Mrs Lang, if you want to let me assist you", he said.

I agreed.

When I walked into the Magistrate's office the next morning, Friday, 13th, I walked into a very hostile environment and reception. Everyone was already seated and it was obvious that they had already had discussions regarding whatever it was that they were there to discuss with me. Those present were the magistrate, Mr Mata, the Police Station Commander, Superintendent Kakuiyu, the Police Legal Advisor, Superintendent Van Loggenberg, the Police Secretary, Inspector Ronel Jenner, Social Workers, Mrs Smith and Mrs Niemand, Area Supervisor of Social Workers, Mrs Ferreira, my secretary, Nadine Titties and myself.

The Magistrate stated that since Superintendent Kakuiyu had called the meeting, Superintendent Kakuiyu would chair the meeting.

(The following is based on a recorded transcript of the meeting that was transcribed by Nadine Titties, checked and signed by the South African Police Services Commissioner of Oaths at Middelburg, and sent to everyone present at the meeting by registered post. The words used by the various people at the meeting are exact extracts from the recorded transcript and have not been changed to improve grammar or meaning.)

Superintendent Kakuiyu said, "This is an open the meeting as a open floor meeting. No one objects. Everything said and done must be and is in the interest of the children. The State President said that everything we must do must be in the interest of our children. Do you agree?"

The social workers nodded their heads. No one said anything.

Superintendent Kakuiyu continued, "The previous meeting of the Community Police Forum (of which I am the Deputy Chairperson) and Mrs. Lang went well. The same problems were discussed from Mrs Lang side and every one agreed on the aspects discussed. Every one left the meeting with comfortness. The first problem is the authorization of the Form 4, which must be discussed. Mrs Lang and Mrs Ferreira, who is the head of Social Development, must see how we can understand each other and I see Mrs Lang has got a lot of files and things and I think that it is about Form 4s too, so Ladies and Gentlemen, the floor is open".

"Before I allow everybody to speak, I just want to - and I concur with what you said, Superintendent Kakuiyu, that today we must try to discuss this issue and resolve it once and for all. Bear in mind that we are all here to serve the community of Middelburg, the interests of the children, which is more important than any other thing. I will give you an opportunity; in fact this is an opportunity for everybody to talk as Superintendent Kakuiyu has said. Mrs. Lang complaining about the fact that the Form 4s that is sent to Cradock, she does not get a reply on that. I don't know what is the problem. And yesterday Superintendent Kakuiyu came to see me about the Form 4s and to find out how it was possible that I had appointed Mrs Lang to sign the Form 4s. The house can talk", Mr Mata said.

Mrs Ferreira stated, "I want to respond briefly on the Form 4 that was sent to Cradock. Some of them were completely incomplete, some were not signed - so there was no proper assessment done. From there I want to go further. The act and the minimum standards for children with the Form 4 in these facilities and all these things. When we deal with the Form 4 we must firstly assess the situation, the circumstances, then services should be rendered to the family. Form 4 is only issued when a child's life is at risk - if the child is removed, you must remember we said that we don't have a problem if the Form 4 is submitted here but it must go via our office. We've got a child care office and from there it is canalized to the Social Workers who are responsible for that town. If a child is removed he must be brought to a Social Worker and they must report to the Children Court to clarity with a recommendation to determine whether that child is removed or not. If the Form 4 is issued, the parent must sign and if not the parent must be notified as soon as possible afterwards that the child is removed and why. There is a form 4 which should be attached to the Form 4 - Form 4A. Should the child be not in the need of care, services must be rendered to the child as well as the parents or the child must be returned to the parents as soon as possible. They must also have access to the children, wherever they are".

"I don't have a problem with any of those things. Every single one of these children is with Social Development", I said.

"Oh, No!", said Mrs Ferreira loudly, shaking her head.

"Every single child has been registered with social services. The child is also given access, except where the child is an orphan, and the parents are encouraged to visit the children once a week. Those whose parents are in jail have to write to their parents twice a month. Every time something happens with the children I notify the Social Worker", I emphasized. Now I was getting hot under the collar. I do not lie and do not like to be made out to be a liar. I had all the files lying at my feet and I could show her each child's file and which child was allocated to which social worker. This I had done with her staff.

"At the moment I don't know who you are referring to. All the children are NOT with us. We are not aware of all the children. They are definitely not processed with a Form 4. Furthermore we have got five Social Workers in town. It is impossible and perhaps also unreasonable to expect the two social workers at the Department to take responsibility for all these cases. The last I heard there was fifty three children in the CARE HOUSE. We cannot handle fifty three cases, we cannot handle fifty three cases at once. We have other work also", Mrs Ferreira said in a hostile tone.

I tried to calm down and spoke quietly as I said, "I believe and I understand that Johan Pienaar and Pumza Mobo cannot do all the work and they said that they are going to send the cases to other Social Workers".

"There is also a problem here, Mr Chair .....", Mrs Ferreira tried to get in.

Superintendent Kakuiyu cut her off by saying, "Let's start. Let's start again. We have a problem. We came here to discuss the problem. Mrs. Lang, you concur with that? Mrs Lang, you have fifty five children in your care with the other two you've got now of which I do not know how many Form 4s you have received".

"I have received eight Forms", I said.

Mrs Ferreira repeated, "There are eight Forms 4s that are legalized".

"There are eight Forms that are legal? Let's say there are fifty five children now. Eight minus fifty five gives you forty eight, is this right? In other words forty eight children are not accounted for? Now, lets start with this, lets look at this", stated Superintendent Kakuiyu.

Mrs Smith started saying something but no one heard what she was saying. Superintendent Kakuiyu asked her to repeat it. Again no one heard her and eventually she said that she could hear what he was saying. All of a sudden, everyone was talking at the same time. And everyone was talking about the number of children in my care and why I had been given the right to sign a Form 4. This incessant talking continued for about three minutes until I had had more than my fair share of being the object of other's vileness.

I stood up and in a loud voice said, "I have a suggestion. We are here at your, Superintendent Kakuiyu, invitation at this meeting. There must have been something to necessitate this meeting at such short notice. We have been beating about the bush with this. I am quite aware of the Child Care Act. I am not a Social Worker but I have studied the Act and I know what I am supposed to do. So can we please reverse and see what was the problem? Yesterday something must have happened".

Superintendent Kakuiyu said, "Ja, ek dink.... Ja". (Yes, I think ..... Yes)

I continued, "Yesterday something must have happened and I want to know why I am at this meeting?"

Superintendent Kakuiyu replied, "O.K. I think it was wrongly - information – rumours. Rumours has that you are appointed by the Higher Court as a Social Worker. There is Form 4 which is completed by the police and we had a meeting where the status quo should be handled until we have another meeting. What actually happened thereafter is that Insp. R. Jenner wanted the mother to feed the baby or the other option was to fetch the baby, put her in the cell with the mother because this is being allowed. Since we had this problem with Form 4...Form 4...I understand that way the Social Worker that there are rumours going around and that after the last meeting at the police station there was a suggestion that we should meet and that we should meet with the Social Workers and let us see how we can find ways to accommodate each other with the Form 4s and the way forward. With my opening statement I said that we should not blame each other and we are gathered here not to blame anybody and number two that is the advantage of our people and I quote the statement of our State Presidents vision and mission is to see an African Renaissance and the Magistrate concurs with me that the community out there and the youth and the children out there in Middleburg are at large, (At this point Superintendent Van Loggenberg entered the room) so that is what we were talking about before you came in, Mr van Loggenberg, and I come to the number of children that there are at the CARE House and how many are actual, according to Mrs Ferreira, legal, and I understand that there are fifty three which are not – and there are eight with Form 4s. My next question was how can we, or what can we do, as this committee, about this forty eight children - we should try and solve this problem about the forty eight children and you have forty eight children and I know you are suffering with the forty eight children that are not catered for legal and you must get done and get sponsors for everyone and there are people who are helping you".

At this point I was totally confused as to what he was saying, so I dealt with the last issue of him thinking that I have people helping me with sponsoring all the children. I inform him, "Mr Chair, I am not getting any help for any of the children, even those who are legally in my care".

He then jumped to something else and said, "There is another point. Mrs Ferreira...".

Not wanting to let him off the hook, I give it back to him "Sorry, can we deal with these forty eight which are in my care? How are we going to do it?"

I wonder if the man has any brains at all when he replies, " No, no, no, you said that there were legally eight".

"Yes, but you said that here were forty eight that were not catered for and that I should find donors for everybody. I cannot find donors for everybody. Right?", I retort.What can the idiot say but "OK, right".

"So I have a problem", I say.

"Ja" (Yes), he replies.

"Can I respond to that?" says Mrs Ferreira. "We submitted claims for the safety fees early in the financial year. We haven't heard anything further. We made inquiries; still nothing. I hope they will pay it, but it will only be for sixty days. It is only for 60 days. So it wouldn't be of much help in anycase".

"Is it only for sixty days?" asks our chairperson.

"Per child, yes. It is only for sixty days and that is the policy", says Mrs Ferreira. She seems used todealing with people of Superintendent Kakuiyu's calibre as she keeps repeating herself.

I tell them that I have had some of the children for longer than 18 months.

Mr Mata asks me, "Now, for the children you have in your care Mrs. Lang, have you signed any Form 4's... did you forward that to Social Development?"

"Yes", I answer.

"And what does Social Development do about that?", he asks.

"Nothing", I answer.

"Any investigation?"

"No"

"In respect of those children?"

"No"

Mrs Ferreira interrupted, "Sorry, when I started off, I said I received some of them. Some of them were incomplete, some of them not even signed. It did not give me anything really to determine if that child is really in need of care. It was referred to a social worker. I just want to read something from this that I have here ... it said that children under the age of six should be placed in community based programs and not residential care facilities unless circumstances are exceptional and it is proved to be in the best interests of the child".

Mr Mata asked her, "Did you bring that to the attention of Mrs. Lang, and the fact that she hasn't complied with that?"

"We have done that before", she said.

Again, I started getting agitated because a half truth is often worse than a lie. First of all, there are no Community Based Programs in Middelburg for children, whether they are under six or not, and our children's home is the only alternative to the street and to abuse. Secondly, neither she nor any other social worker had ever made any contact with us whatsoever regarding any Form 4 submitted to them.

"Mr. Mata", I said, "I sent everything to Social Development. The fact that they did not investigate it, that they did not send it around to the various social workers, the fact that they did not do their part...I was unaware that as a Place of Safety, I was to go around and write reports".

"You are not expected or allow to ...", Mrs Ferreira started saying before I cut her off .

"But then, Mrs. Ferreira, is it my fault that those children are there illegally, because I kept going back again and again to the Social Workers, to Mr Pienaar and Miss Mobo - about these children?".

And then Mrs Ferreira lost it. Completely! She did try to keep it back in the first sentence but her venom poured out. "OK, I don't want to say much here. But, please let us clarify this once and for all. In the beginning when I became aware of the CARE House, myself and Mr. Pienaar visited Mrs. Lang and when I informed her that she cannot keep children in there as it was. The next thing that happened is that there was an article in the paper implicating that I was threatening her. Whatever I said to her, she don't believe. And I am saying it to your face now. You don't believe me, you don't trust me. You do whatever you want. You don't want to cooperate with me. You don't want to co-operate with this lady for instance. You said to my face, that you don't want to work with her. We cannot work with you, Mrs. Lang, if you don't want to work with us. As it is, there is talk about the departments, the Department of Social Development of Justice, Social Security, sorry, the Police, Correctional Services, Educating. On National level there was a commitment from all these Departments that we will work as a team. And for that matter, the NGOs on Provincial and National level are partners we have to assist this matter. We cannot work as individuals. And we have to comply with the rules. Whether we like it or not. We have to".

Even though my heart was beating in my ears and I wanted to throttle the woman, I forced myself to ask with the calmest voice, "Am I not complying with this at all? Is that what you are saying?"

"Not always, she said, her voice still a couple of octaves high. "You are making your own rules at this point in time and you are intimidating my people. And I will not allow that. Because I have to comply with the law. And I will not be brought on to the red carpet because you do not want to work with us. I said it before, and I am going to repeat again now, there must be a Social Worker linked to a child. You are not a Social Worker."

Again, with the utmost calm, I said, "That is correct, Mrs. Ferreira, and I have linked every one of the children with a Social Worker".

"No, you have not".

"Yes, I have", I calmly stated again.

"Ok, let Mrs Ferreira finish and I will give you a chance", Superintendent Kakuiyu said to me. "I think let's clear the air here".

"Yes please", said Mrs Ferreira, all puffed up.

"I think what we should do is to tell Mrs. Lang", said Superintendent Kakuiyu. "Please Mrs. Lang, doesn't see it as an attack. I think we are going on how to do it now : we are going to clear the air. We are going to clear the air. You bring up your feelings. I am just sorry I don't have a flip chart here. I should have had a flip chart here so that each and every one can bring up their problems, put it on the flip chart, put it there and then say, OK, here are our problems and what is the way forward."

Oh, God, I think. Can this really be happening? We must state our problems but I must keep quiet? What is this? Am I guilty of something here but no one is telling me what I am guilty of? Is this a witch hunt? Did they all conspire to get me to confess to making money out of children? Or did they think I had some other sinister reasons for loving these children and needing to protect them?

"Thank you very much", said Mrs Ferreira. "I would love, I would love that because we can all work hand in hand because Mrs. Lang and the CARE House can also be a tremendous source in this Community for us all. But now we are sitting with a problem that when we initially assessed the CARE House, she only qualified for twenty-six children. I sent my people again, to do another assessment, because Mrs. Lang, am I right? You opened new houses and you are doing renovations and things like that".

She had calmed down by now. Maybe she was feeling bad about her behaviour earlier.

"Yes", I answer.

"OK", she says. "And there is still another house to be completed. And we are, according to the Child Care Act, there are policies that are – we are supposed to do an assessment every year, annually – which we have done now. And according to what I have got back, she does qualify for more children now. Because of the new places you have opened up. Understand? You have not received feedback yet, but I am telling you now. What I am actually saying is please let's work as a team. Now let us get back to the Social Workers. You can support me here please. There is only one social worker here today. We cannot, as I said, the Social workers are already overloaded and it is not only child care work that they are doing, it is probation work, they have projects, it's the food program, there are lots of things. What I am saying is, every time there is a Form 4, they cannot jump immediately. Perhaps they are not even in town. But there is, always, a social worker on call. 24 hours a day. There is a list, and I ask a question to you, Mr Mata, and you Miss Lang, what was the motivation for the application to authorize Form 4's?"

Mr Mata asks, " To the appointment to sign the Form 4's?"

"Yes"

"Interesting", says Mr Mata, "Because of the problem that she had told me that most of the time the Social Workers are not available to sign the Form 4s".

"Which Social Workers?"

"Social Development"

"I will say this again", said Mrs Ferreira. "There are five Social Workers in this town - two with BADISA [semi-governmentally funded non-profit organization], one with ACVV [semi-governmentally funded non-profit organization] and two with the Department. And there is always one twenty-four hours a day on standby. I spoke to my Director this morning and I told him what happened and his first question was "Did you, Mr Mata, consult with any of us before you drafted that?" What I want to know is did you consult with any of us about the Form 4?"

"I don't have to consult with anyone. I am entitled to do it in terms of the Act", said Mr Mata.

Oh, I could have jumped up and kissed him for that. I mean, here is a social worker asking a magistrate what right he has to make a decision without first consulting with her!

"Are you saying you are entitled to do that according to the Act?" she asks in amazement.

"Yes. Did you read what it states?"

Mrs Ferreira says, "I have the Act with me. I know what it states".

"I am talking about the appointment certificate".

"Yes, here is the appointment certificate. May I react on this one?" says Superintendent Kakuiyu.

Mrs Ferreira mumbles her agreement. Superintendent Kakuiyu starts to read the appointment certificate giving me the right to sign a Form 4 in terms of Section 12 of the Child Care Act 74 of 1984 when the need arises. The need would arise if a social worker or a police officer was not available. The appointment certificate is signed by Mr T Mata, Magistrate and Commissioner of the Children Court dated 2 August 2004.

Mrs Ferreira interrupts again, "I've got a question there...section 11 and 12 is when you place a child in place of safety. Shouldn't it have been done in terms of section 42?".

"Do you have a problem with the section that I cited? Do you have a problem with the appointment?", asks Mr Mata.

"I have a problem with the appointment, yes".

"What is your problem?"

"Because in that letter it says if there's not a Social Worker available. I just now said there's always one available. That's why I asked why did you not consult with us?"

"Why I did not consult with whom?"

"With the Department".

"I don't have to consult with anyone. I have the powers to appoint the person I want to appoint. Do you have a problem with that?", asked Mr Mata.

By now, Mr Mata is my hero. He may not be standing up for me, but he is standing up for himself against the Department of Social Development, and particularly against Mrs Ferreira. I am proud of him. But Mrs Ferreira is not finished yet.

She continues: "I have a problem with that. I want to say something else. She's ordered a component within those forms. It says here that children...sorry".

I have no idea what she is talking about.
"If you have an objection that she is not complying, then raise that objection, Madam", said Mr Mata.

"Let's just sort this out", she tried to say over what Mr Mata was saying. Superintendent Kakuiyu exercised his right as chairperson by bellowing, "Silence please. Let's just give Mr. Mata a chance." Mr Mata continued, "I want to finish. Even that appointment certificate before I appointed Mrs Lang I informed the Local Social Development that I am contemplating appointing Mrs.

Lang to sign the Form 4. They didn't have a problem with that."

"They are only service offices. They are not the District office or the Province. Can I just continue here?", answered Mrs Ferreira.

"Yes. They are supposed to liaise with you if they've got a problem with that. If they do not liaise with you then that is your problem", retaliated Mr Mata.

"It was already done when they phoned me", said Mrs Ferreira. "They say here that it is also believed that police have grounds that they can bring children to safety before the relevant children's Court as prescribed. And they go on and say there should be certain documents attach to that such as a Medical certificate or a report from the doctor and there must be an Affidavit made by a Police Captain and he will report it. I want to say it again that if it is submitted to you it must go through our offices for registration", she continued.

The submission of documents through Mrs Ferreira's office is not part of the Child Care Act but an internal rule within the department that hampers and often causes delays and thereby violations of children's rights. The "canalising" as the department in the area calls the submission of all documents through Mrs Ferreira's office also ensures that no social worker is able to work alone and to his or her maximum capacity. This procedure effectively ensures that social workers cannot work independently and therefore become ineffective and non-productive. The procedure also ensures that no police officer is able to carry out his or her work effectively, further violating the rights of children and making it an impossible task to fulfil the requirements of the Child Care Act to place a child legally within the specified 48 hour period.

"Thank you. I just want to stop here. Is there anyone who wants to give input according this now before I proceed? Mrs. Lang do you want to say something about what was said here?" said Superintendent Kakuiyu.

I was glad that I was at last going to be given a chance to have my say. I by now knew why I had been called to the meeting, but no one had the courage to come out and say it. They did not want to deal with the problem head on because they did not know all the facts. Perhaps they were a little reluctant to meet me head on because of previous experiences with me. However, I was not going to walk out of that court house with my tail between my legs, having sat through a deluge of verbiage from Mrs Ferreira and Superintendent Kakuiyu. Now it was my turn.

"I would like to say something about yesterday. I think that the Form 4 that was signed by me yesterday necessitated this meeting. I actually think that there is a problem and let's not go beating about the bushes. This meeting was called very quickly yesterday afternoon so it must be something to do with the signing of the Form 4 by me. Note that the authorization specifically states in the event of an emergency, when the police are not available or when a social worker is not available. Now, I would like to, if you don't mind, Mr Chair, explain what happened and why I had to sign that Form 4 yesterday".

"The truth?" asked Superintendent Kakuiyu.

" The truth. But perhaps that would be a big problem. The form that was signed was for Kayla Hoffman and Shaun Hoffman. The Form A4 and a Form 4. This situation arose like this: The complainant, Charlene Miles phoned the police station saying a child was being abused and that she witnessed this herself ".

Superintendent Kakuiyu interjected, "Mrs. Lang. I just...I think we should not discuss this in front of the Magistrate for he is the one ruling in this case".

"Mr Chair. I need to explain why I..."

Superintendent Kakuiyu spoke over my words to Superintendent Van Loggenberg, Legal Advisor for the Police, "I don't know if you concur with me and if he hears it now he won't be that objective as a Magistrate?".

Superintendent Van Loggenberg answered, "I think the Magistrate have the power to excuse himself whenever he thinks he needs to and he himself can be the judge of that". "OK, OK", said the chairperson. "I think it would be fair to Mrs. Lang to listen what necessity made this possible and what the reason was for signing the Form 4", stated Superintendent Van Loggenburg. And I could continue.

"The complainant phoned the police station and talked to Sergeant Payoyo. She said she was residing at 71 Gemsboklaan in Midros. Her name was Charlene Miles. She had witnessed a child being kicked in the stomach and that the child had been constantly abused. She stated that she had seen this with her own eyes. She ask the police to please attend that and the police told her (Payoyo) to phoned Dianne Lang as she is dealing with child abuse. I was not in town that day. The following day she phoned the police station and was told again to phone Dianne Lang. She phoned me and I phoned the police station. I then told them about the problem".

" To whom did you speak to at the police station?", asked Superintendent Kakuiyu.

"To Makhle."

"Makhle. Is that the same day?", asked Superintendent Kakuiyu.

"This day I was not there. I was not in town", I answered.

Now Superintendent Kakuiyu seemed to be getting hot under the collar. "What are you saying? I understand. I think it would be appropriate if we break for five minutes".

I was having none of this. I had only just begun and my story had not been told yet. I continued.

"I phoned Sergeant Pongolo and asked him to come and fetch the children".

"Just questions I want to raise that is concerning me", said Superintendent Kakuiyu.

"Please may I ask Mrs. Lang something?", asked Mrs Ferreira. "Just before I came in here I had a phone call from Pumsa Mobo. The mother of this Hoffman children are at the office now. She's apparently breastfeeding. She said she went yesterday and asked to feed the baby and she was refused."

So, I was right. The reason I had been brought here so suddenly for this meeting was about the Hoffman children of yesterday. Why did they not bring this up before I brought it up, and now, why are they not letting me finish my story before jumping in with their questions? They did not have the courage or nerve to start with the real reason for this meeting. What a bunch of twofaced people!

"Sorry, Mrs Ferreira", I said, "She came and said she's coming to fetch the children and that she had been sent by the police to fetch the children, not to come and breastfeed the child".

Mrs Ferreira ignored what I had just said and continued, "So they are waiting for me now to tell them what to do. Will there be a problem if she goes and breastfeed the baby?"

"I don't see a problem if she goes and feeds the baby. The baby is actually not a baby anymore. He is over a year old".

"But she is still breastfeeding", says Mrs Ferreira.

"As long as she is sober, Mrs. Ferreira. I don't allow drunk people ..." I try to tell her as the mother arrived drunk when she came to collect the children.

"OK. The smaller one, was he also involved on the abuse?", she asks.

"Yes", I tell her.

"Isn't it possible that you give the child back to his mother?", Mrs Ferreira asks me.

My head spins. Is this how the system works. The mother is charged with child abuse. The Child Care Act states that siblings are to be kept together. There is a police docket opened against the mother. The case has not been heard by the magistrate. The social worker has not investigated the circumstances and yet the supervisor, Mrs Ferreira, asks me if it is not possible to give the child back to the mother? It is mind boggling when for the last two hours they have been giving me hell over whether or not I may or may not sign Form 4s or whether or not I may be caring for too many children?

I ask her: "What are you saying Mrs. Ferreira, is this baby going to be safe if she did what she has done?"

She replies, "I don't have all the details...only what you have told us now".

But at that point, I had told them very little about the case.

"Yes, you don't have all the details. The police were supposed to investigate the case. In fact the investigating officer is Sergeant Pongolo. So the police must tell you whether they think that the child is safe and if it is going to be in the best interest of the child", I retorted.

"The Social Workers can also investigate and not the police", said Mrs Ferreira.

Mr Mata said, "I have read the Form 4 to you and you know what it states, Mrs Ferreira".

What Mrs Ferreira had said is, in fact, incorrect. A social worker can investigate the circumstances of the child's family and environment, but cannot investigate cases of child abuse when a complaint has been made with the police. This is a criminal matter and can only be investigated by the police services.

"What I'm saying, Mr Mata, is that according to the way I see it I have followed the procedures as best I could", I said.

Mrs Ferreira said, "OK".

"With all due respect, Superintendent Kakuiyu, I do not believe that you really know what is going on in your own police station", I stated.

He was so taken aback by what I had said that his chair moved backwards with his body movement.

"Yes. You, Mrs. Lang, I actually don't want to fight with you. But what I just want to put something clear. I think all the people of Middleburg or half of the community knows it that if you have such problems and you are a member of the CPF that you should go to the Station Commissioner...me! I am available twenty four hours that you should bring these things under my attention and we should here open another investigation and if there would be any problem on the police side I would have investigate and act upon it.

"Would we have been here Mr. Chair?"

"Yes. We would have been here, because you know that out of that meeting we said that we should be meeting with the role-players to clear the air and to see how best we can accommodate each other. From my side I think there is a lot of clearance now between you and everybody. The listeners who listen to this heard what was said. If there would be other question to put to Mrs. Lang. I think we should proceed now".

"Yes", said Mr Mata. "I have a question to the Social Workers. I was also aware that all these Social Workers of the ACVV, BADISA, after I was appointing Mrs. Lang. It is been done and of most of the problems is been done. Members of the NGO were appointed to the Form 4. What problems do you foresee with this appointment, because there are. I encourage her to liaise with Social Development up to signing the Form 4 to bring that immediately to the office?

"In principle I don't have a problem with the procedure after that", stated Mrs Ferreira. "If we could clear that and make sure that everybody complies with that, then I cannot foresee a problem. I have got a request also that we don't "sommer" (just) issue form 4 because a form 4 is... when you read the act, is for a child when a child's life in danger. The other thing I wanted to say is that Johan Pienaar (Chief Social Worker) informed me that the form 4 that was sent to him, there is an insight agreement between the Department and ours that if any correspondence should go via a lay person. So that is my request. Let we just follow the right channels of communication".

"I don't think that she is a lay person now that she is appointed. It was the correspondence from her that obviously your Department misplaced it. The child for whom she signed the Form 4 is really in need for that", Mr Mata responded.

"Can I just take it from there?", asked Mrs Ferreira. "When we started here I was referring to the Child Care Control Unit. That is why I'm asking that anything they take up with you please refer it, as it was done in the past by your predecessor, to our Child Care Control Unit in Cradock. We will decide it from there otherwise we don't have any control."

Cradock is a town 105 km away from Middelburg, which means that if they have all the control over the children in Middelburg, despite the fact that the Justice Department in Middelburg has control over the children in Middelburg, children's court cases are delayed for obvious reasons.

"Are the lines of communication not that its from here to your local Branch and your Local Branch ass it on to you?", asked Mr Mata.

"You see the District office is in Cradock", replied Mrs Ferreira.

"This office has jurisdiction so therefore these people must pass it on to you?", (in Cradock) asked Mr Mata, incredulously.

"Perhaps we are missing each other here. We got the instruction from Head Office how to do this and it is that it must go via Child Care Control Unit. There is not a problem it lands over to you. You understand? Not at all, because you are going to look into it and you'll decide if this is a valid reason to do this. After that you must communicate with us and we'll refer it from there. Perhaps I must also explain to you how it works with the other Social Workers. If it is not a case of life or death at that moment then fax the form 4 to me and I'll take to the Child Care Control Unit and they'll put a covering on it and then refer it to you", explained Mrs Ferreira.

"That is basically what I have encouraged" said Mr Mata.

I had a burning question that I had to ask. And I had to ask it in front of the magistrate. "I understand that the form 4 is there for when a child's life in danger. If a child is kicked in the stomach by an adult, isn't that child's life in danger? As far as I'm concern, yes.", I asked Mrs Ferreira. This is exactly the reason I had written down on the Form

4 in the Hoffman children case. And she had asked me if I would consider letting the baby be returned to the mother. I waited for her answer.

"I think I did say this", she said. I wanted to push her some more. I wanted clarity on what she considered a life or death situation with regard to a child. From my experience of social workers and children, I had yet to come across anything that was considered a life and death situation. Rape, sodomy, stabbing, beating, starvation, neglect, sale of children, hands being boiled on stoves... none of these were ever considered severe enough to require a Form 4 removal to a place of safety.

"But Mrs. Ferreira, all these cases here are children's whose lives are in danger", pointing to a pile of files on the floor. "I thought that by taking all this to a Social Worker that the Social Worker will complete the Form 4 properly and send it to your office and bring it to the Magistrate, but that has not been done. All this information I took to Pumza Mobo and Johan Pienaar. They told me that they have got too much work to do and that they would source it to other Social Workers. As far as I am concerned that was done, but they still are illegally with me. These ones," I way, pointing to another pile of files lying on the floor, "are the ones where there are pending criminal cases of child abuse outstanding. If they are illegally with me, that means that the Social Worker or the alleged abuser can just come in and take control".

"I just wanna ask something", said Mrs Ferreira. "Because they are illegally there? Just a minute. The children of which there are cases pending of those who are in place of safety and those reports have been forwarded to court".

"Not as far as I know", I said.

"Yes", said Mrs Ferreira.

"No", I said, "I have them all here".

Superintendent Kakuiyu was listening. "How many cases were taken to court or which are outstanding?", he wanted to know of the child abuse cases.

"I don't know, I said. "Maybe twenty-eight or thirty".

"I didn't know", said Mrs Ferreira.

"Thirty cases?" said Superintendent Kakuiyu. "I think this should be brought under the attention of the Commissioner of the Children Court."

"This has been reported to the Commissioner of the Children Court", said Mr Mata.

"I have reported it, and all the people in the Community Police Forum knows about it, Captain Colyn knows about it, your Inspectors know about it, your Detectives know it. Superintendent, in the meeting we had it was also brought up that cases were all outstanding. And I am concerned that we have all these child abuse cases outstanding", I said.

"Yes, can just I'm asking a favour here as the chairperson. I said this meeting was to clear the air and the way forward. Do you concur with me? And there are up to two cases. In other words, twenty- two cases we should be know about it and, really I am the Station Commissioner and we have meetings every morning on that cases, and I don't want to bring this up now because I have got a lot of Form 4 in my possession and if that link to this I want to call Captain Meiring because I said he must here at 11h30 and he is not here. I just want to call him so that he must come and hear if there are twenty-two cases and why doesn't the Station Commissioner know about it, Social Workers don't know them. Then we have a problem with the police. And it is my component. Then we must talk about this and our legal officer will give us a way forward on how we will handle this", said Superintendent Kakuiyu.

Superintendent Van Loggenberg, who had been a silent observer up to this point, stated, "I've been listening to everything that has been said and fortunately I do have a little bit of background now. Is the principle clear now for the reason for signing the form 4? Your last comment to me was that you know".

"Correct and if they haven't done that the state can be sued", said Mr Mata.

Superintendent Van Loggenburg asked, "Why if there is a concern for Mrs. Lang signing the Form 4?".

"I think there are a consolation because she is a custodian to keep the children there for herself. I think that is the only concern", replied Mr Mata. Superintendent Van

Loggenburg turned to me and said, "Concentrate on not compromising. I think Mrs. Lang is the only one to make that decision. I think what you should be concern on this. Do not go to Inspector Jenner if you have a problem. He is only one police official. I know he is actively involved in this trust".

"But he is our Management Committee Chairperson", I say.

"Yes I know", continued Superintendent Van Loggenburg, "But I think for your own credibility you should not call him. If you have phoned me yesterday when you had this problem I give the insurance I don't think that this should have happened. Secondly, it's his responsibility to give you guidance. I think that is a matter of concern that you should take on. The very reason what should have been done was to take a statement from the complainant, registering the case and then it is a police matter. You do not have the components and the skills. The parties that should have been involved in this is, Department of Social Development and the police. If I was you I would have gone to the police and said that the department doesn't want to assist me. With the appointment of Mrs. Lang, I cannot foresee a problem. If the department or the NGO are not available she's just another check to help. I think we shouldn't try to stop her from doing this. We should guard the credibility of her by ensuring that the police and the Department of Social Development do their responsibilities in order to get everything in place. In short, Mr Chair, I don't know what the problem is because these are the minor problems. We shouldn't have to deal with this part, but there cannot be, if we take legislation in account, there cannot be a problem, if we do our duties by referring these problems. However we must mark the credibility of Mrs Lang. Based on the situation Mr. Chair, what happened yesterday, there's nothing wrong. What has been done from yesterday to today? Has the complainant given a statement? Was an assessment done? That is the main problem. You must do that."

Mrs Niemand, who had up until this time remained quiet stated: "Can I react on that? I also think that the Social Worker, as you said the police do assessments, should also do the investigation of the situation. My question, my suggestion is...if the Social Worker was involved in any of these cases not only or seeking out one specific case they have to assist the situation. My observation would be or if I hear that someone abuse a small child, my first observation would be that that child is in danger and we have to do something to protect that child. The Social Worker that is to assess this situation might have done something else to protect this child but without issue the Form 4 and for that reason I would again strongly recommend and bring it under your attention once again that you should make use of the Social Workers because they commit themselves and don't get anything extra for themselves. (Was she suggesting I get something extra for myself? The LRC would eventually assist us in applying to the Supreme Court to get the Department of Social Development to pay Safety Fees of R12.00 per day per child in 2007) They do it out of the seriousness of the situation to see these cases before a Form 4 is issued. For a Social Worker there is many Form 4 issued in a community, and that is a problem, and issuing these Form 4s is not going to solve this problem. But why does?

Another question that come to my mind is: why does one person get so many references and there is five Social Workers in the community and they are unaware of these cases?

"May I answer that?", I asked. "The reason why I know about these cases is because I have lived in the Townships for two years prior to living in town and that's how I started looking after children. I have lived in Kwanonzame. When you live in a Township you become part of a Township. A Social Worker is an outsider. I am not. I lived with the community. I am part of them. I speak their language. I understand their customs. I grew up in the Transkei. The children trust me because I am not a policeman and I am not a Social worker. Much more information comes to me for this reason. Another reason is because I am not habituated to the suffering of the children as most of the townspeople are, and that includes the social workers and policemen".

"You cannot take a child from his home", stated Mrs Niemand flatly.

"If a child is abused or has no home? And if there's a case open, a child is being abused, neglected, raped? Are we going to leave that child in that environment so she can look at her alleged rapist everyday she goes to school?", I ask angrily.

"Mrs. Lang... Mrs. Lang...", says Superintendent Kakuiyu, shaking his head.

What is this? Don't they want to know the harsh realities of life? Do they prefer to sit at their desks thinking that everyone is just fine in the township?

"Mr Chairman", I say. "Just one more thing! About the compromising of my position: These are my financial statements", as I put them on the desk, "because it seems that people are thinking..." I leave the sentence unsaid but the implication is clear. "I am not furthering myself by having these children. These are my financial statements; these are my rejections for funding. And that will show everybody that I look after these children with my own money".

"OK. Just a moment before we come to that", says the chairperson.

Superintendent van Loggenberg reiterates what he said before. "The protecting of the children will still maintain. She shouldn't be placed in a position to compromise herself".

"I agree. I agree. I will not phone Mr. Jenner if there's a problem with any of these cases, but I would like to also add, Superintendent, that there are problems in this town. I was signing those Form 4s yesterday because there is a problem with the service delivery of both the Departments", I said.

'Mr Chair, another point I want to raise is that... that child who was abused, was the case registered?", asked Superintendent Van Loggenburg.

"Yes", I said.

"Was the child taken to the doctor?", he asked.

"No", I replied.

"That is my concern. Firstly I don't think that you've been gathering evidence. I think you realize that these are problems".

"Yes I do".

"And I would like to ask you to not gather evidence because you will testify for that", Superintendent Van Loggenburg said.

"I will take it back to the police", I responded.

"I just want to reiterate on that. Firstly it says that parties due to the facts and that the Magistrate will not take your statement due to your no medical qualifications. Secondly, I think that it might be that prosecution can't be reached on taking private pictures of injuries of people. You must remember in future in any case reported that the police must register the docket and it must be referred. We are paying for that medical bill. We are paying for that so we are going to send that child or the victim or the complainant and send the evidence that we have to the police. The police need further guidance on this. I don't say the Department of Social Development they must be involved. I don't say that, but I think that they must acknowledge that they are in the wrong end. I think they are confusing all these problems", said Superintendent Van Loggenburg.

By now Superintendent Kakuiyu had really had enough and was adamant that he was getting his five minute break. In fact, during this time he called for back up from his station so that he could answer some of the questions regarding the unresolved dockets on child abuse.

"Can we break for five minutes just to relax and then come back? There are still of the...that's why the Form 4 was issued and I said I don't know about twenty-two cases. There might be other cases of which I don't know and maybe these cases were not registered".

After a short break we were joined by Captain Meiring, the Second in Command to the Station Commissioner and the Head of the Detective Branch. All other members of the meeting were still there. Superintendent Kakuiyu got straight to the point by telling Captain Meiring that he had been called to confirm that there were twenty- two cases.

"Yes" said Captain Meiring, "There are twenty-two cases. Inspector Liz McEwan is busy with the investigation. Then when the Public Prosecutor decides to prosecute, the twenty-two different dockets are going to be opened, but all twenty-two statements are there in this one docket".

"OK. When did this happen?", asked Superintendent Kakuiyu.

"April", Captain Meiring and I said at the same time.

"April?", Superintendent Kakuiyu asked.

"The dockets were originally investigated by Inspector Potgieter and then it was handed over to Inspector McEewan because she was the appropriate person for the investigation seeing that she is a woman and easy to work with", said Captain Meiring.

"Inspector Fredericks has also got some of our cases", I said.

"One case? All and all now we have about three cases", says Superintendent Kakuiyu.

Oh, Lord, I am losing the thread again. Why do numbers jumble this man so.

"In one docket", says Captian Meiring.

"In one docket yes. If you include the one of yesterday or yesterday before, when was that?", he asks.

With incredible patience, Captain Meiring says "Day before yesterday".

"Day before yesterdays' in other words then?", the Superintendent asks again.

"The first appearance was today", answers Captain Meiring.

I am developing respect for this Captain as well. Respect for his patience.

Superintendent Kakuiyu was off on a tangent again. "Yes. OK. No. Thank you. Thank you people. There it is. It's on the table now. I think the way forward now. I ask a question of... we still do have forty eight children except for those who were registered with form 4 who were who are legally now according."

"I have reunified one of the children with his family", I said.

"And there was another one pending for reunification", said Mrs Ferreira.

"That one, Mrs Ferreira, we started with the reunification with the parents and Pumza...it was her case. She tried to investigate but she was too busy. So, I did not get to see the parents before and when they arrived to get the children, they were drunk".

"OK, I think I will refer to my next question to the legal advisors here and to you. I want to know how are we going to do this because according to Captain Meiring, there are this one docket with twenty-two cases and its being investigated and I think those children are still in the care of Mrs Lang. What are we going to do? How I just want to know. I just want to handle those forty eight cases. The way forward for them. I just want to roughly your mind now. What is the way forward as from today?", said Mrs Ferreira.

"Sorry, Mr Chair, just before they answer can I tell you what I have done", I said. "Mrs. Robinson is the Cluster Head of Magistrates in this area. She suggested that we write out the Form 4 just so that they are legally in my care. They are illegally in my care, which is true because the form 4 has not been completed, due to the social workers not doing their work, and there is also that there's a rumour going around that I have children illegally in my care. I submitted only two to the clerk of the court, with as much information, the case numbers, and everything else. These two are outstanding ones. I submitted them. They were sent back to me by Mr Mata because Social Development confirmed and Johan Pienaar said that the Form 4's were already issued for these two. I phone them and said... how can you tell the Magistrate that this has been done? There are two dockets". I bend down to the pile of files to look for the two dockets. "Sorry, I've got a lot of children. I just need to find it. It is Thembakazi and Gcobani. These are the two. I think there's a misunderstanding. Although they are in the social development books, the Form 4's have not been issued. These are ones I do not have". I find the two files and open them. I point to each file as I say, "This one here, is with Pumza Mobo, and this one here is with Johan Pienaar and they both told Mr. Mata that the Form 4s were issued".

"You see that's what I said earlier on. It's the Magistrates office responsibility when this is issued", said Mrs Ferreira.

"Except that the Social Worker asked me if I can please photo copy these files for her because she didn't have any information after she told Mr. Mata that a form 4 was issued", I said.

Mr Mata replied, "I think she called, that girl, yesterday informing the clerk of the Children Court that she had made a mistake. There is no form 4 signed for this child".

"Could I suggest something? Lets start the ball rolling. These twenty-two cases, Mrs Lang, that are under investigation, could we have those names so that we can attend to this and when I got the names and the addresses we will give to the Social Workers because everybody is working in a certain area. Middelburg and Kwanonzame, and Midros people are Diakonale Dienste and then Rosmead calling to that for starters", suggested Mrs Ferreira, mentioning the various areas.

Mrs Smith said, "May I make a suggestion? She says its forty-eight cases which are not placed with Form 4. Can we gather these names for starting point to do the investigation, and if its necessary we fill in the Form 4 and place them legally with Mrs Lang".

Had they forgotten so quickly that all the children had Form 4's and were already linked to a social worker, and that the social workers had not done their work? All that was needed was that the social workers do the investigations, write the reports and take the children to children's court to have them legally placed. This was a requirement of every social worker according to the Child Care Act and neither I, as an officer of the court, nor a police officer could continue the process after a Form 4 was signed.

"Let's get all their names if it's indicated to us where there are similar criminal cases pending to them. I must mention something else before I forget this. Both Social Workers at BADISA (Another government funded social charity) are leaving at the end of this month. So there is still three Social Workers in this town. How soon can we have those names?" asked Mrs Ferreira.

"Johan Pienaar and Pumza Mobo have got all the names but I will do that for you and Mr Mata can also have a list of the names. The police already have a list", I said.

"Mrs Lang, will you do it?", asked Superintendent Kakuiyu. The man was really an idiot.

"Yes, I will do it", I said. "I just need to say a few things. Mrs Ferreira, please stop telling people or letting your social workers tell people that I am keeping children illegally, because the community keep coming there saying I'm taking their children when there are outstanding criminal cases against them. It is causing a problem and the community just say that I have the children illegally. The police are also saying that I have the children illegally. I understand that theoretically its illegal, but this is because social welfare are not doing their work fast enough, and neither are the police. However, once the child is past my doorstep, it is my responsibility to ensure his safety. That too, is in the Child Care Act".

"But I hope its not true", she said.

"It is", I answer.

"Because I haven't done it", says Mrs Ferreira.

"Its not from my office", says Mrs Smith.

"But it will in any case be prevented", Mrs Ferreira said.

"Is there anyone who wants to say something before we come to a conclusion?", asked Superintendent Kakuiyu.

"Just one remark" said Superintended Van Loggenburg. "What seems to be the matter is that the SAPS must be motivated in signing the Form 4, and you as the Station Commissioner, *will* see to that".

I went home after the meeting, which ended long after lunch time. In some ways I felt it was a waste of time, and in other ways I felt that I had not allowed them to smash me down. I had stood up to them. That sentence that I had used on the station commissioner: "With all due respects, Superintendent, it appears you don't know what is going on in your own station", played over and over in my mind, giving me strength and courage.

I have never stood up to someone in authority in that way before. I had looked "Idi Amini" in the eye and told him what I thought of him and I was proud of myself. Yes! Yes! Yes! I thought. I did it! That man is such a pompous arse. They had tried to screw me over, but that one sentence had me buoyed for the rest of the day and evening. Standing up to him filled me with energy, and for the first time in a week I had the energy to get all the children together after supper and go for a long walk, singing all the way. The children naturally have wonderful rhythm and voices, and we have used dance, walking and singing as a means of bringing joy and happiness to an otherwise sad and agonizing world. Instead of focusing on death, we have focused on life. AIDS is part of life in South Africa, and without the drugs to control HIV, death is at our door every day - singing and dancing is our medicine. We walked, we danced and we sang around the streets of the town. When we got home, we were all on a high.

Sadly, I did not know that what I thought I had gained was just a hollow victory and the children, the staff and I still had a long, painful and weary path to tread.

Kayla and Shudan

The Department of Social Development did not leave the Hoffman children, who had caused the Friday 13th August court house meeting, alone. They seemed determined to remove them from the safety of our home. Kayla, a 4 year-old girl, had been kicked and beaten over a long period of time. The neighbours were more than willing to go to court as witnesses to the abuse. They were also willing to state that the children were often left outside the house to sleep at night because the mother was drunk most of the time, and became violent when drunk. Kayla's brother, Shudan, was 15 months old and suffering from foetal alcohol syndrome, from being carried through a pregnancy by an alcoholic mother. Shudan was being breastfed, although he was also on sold food and could drink from a cup. His eating habits were an important factor in what happened next.

The Children's Home had strict visiting hours for parents and family members. Visiting hours were on Saturday afternoons from 14h00 to 17h00 and again on Sunday afternoons from 14h00 to 17h00. We also did not allow parents and visitors to bring food or sweets into the home, as it caused problems for the other children who did not get visitors. If any sweets or biscuits brought into the home by visitors had to be shared by all the children. However, any other gifts such as clothing, shoes, school fees, toiletries were encouraged.

Kayla and Shudan's mother would visit any time of the day, in all kinds of conditions. When she arrived drunk, we would not allow her into the house. She would then stand at the door shouting abuse at the staff and the children. At other times, she would come into the house, relatively sober, with sweets for the children. When we requested her not to bring sweets for the children as it was unfair to the others in the house, she set up such a racket of screaming and abuse that we had to forcibly remove her from the home. She was the most unpleasant and abusive person we ever had to deal with. It was a sad situation as she is a young woman with much potential, but the alcohol and drug abuse had ruined her life and it was threatening to ruin the lives of her two young children.

She would arrive at the home with a number of her drunken friends and start shouting abuse, swearing and accusing us of stealing her baby. She was not interested in Kayla at all and when she did visit she would not speak to or look at Kayla. It was only about 10 days after the Friday 13th meeting when the Chief Social Worker, Johan Pienaar, arranged a court appearance to return the children to the mother. I was seething with anger at the audacity of the social workers, who were quite prepared to return the two children to their abusive mother when there was a criminal docket opened for child abuse against her. I took the children to court and fortunately managed to convince the magistrate, who also acts as Commissioner of Child Welfare, that there was an outstanding investigation of child abuse against the mother, and that it would not be in the best interests of the children to be returned to the mother. I reminded the Commissioner of Child Welfare that it contravened the Criminal Procedures Act to return the children to a person who had an outstanding investigation of abuse still pending.

While at court, I got to speak with the children's grandmother, Emma. Emma, too, was very hostile towards me, but with a gentle approach I managed to engage her in conversation. I found out her circumstances. She had just lost her husband and had been away in Cape Town for a number of months. She had returned to Middelburg and found that her daughter was completely uncontrollable, drinking and going out all hours of the night, and leaving her children alone in the house. She had also heard that her daughter had been abusive to her granddaughter. I asked her whether she thought she might be able to care for her grandchildren and she was overjoyed.

I invited her to spend time with the children at the Children's Home to establish a bond between herself and the children. I organized with the social worker that I had a possible family member as a place of safety and requested that an investigation be done, a report be submitted, and a court date set so that the children could be placed in the care of their grandmother. During this time, the mother continued to harass us relentlessly. She would arrive at any time of the day or night, blind drunk and demand her baby to be returned to her (she never asked for Kayla). Her swearing was worse than any drunken sailor. This was very upsetting for the children at the home. We asked the police to do something about her trespassing on our property, but they did nothing about it. I discussed the issue of the mother being abusive in Emma's home should the Commissioner of Child Welfare put the children into her care, but Emma said that she would be able to cope with it. I made it clear to Emma that once the children were put into her care, she would then be totally responsible for their safety, and that should her daughter try to harm the children, she would have to call the police and she would have to lay a charge against her own daughter. Emma understood the implications of taking the children and being solely responsible for their safety. Emma and I became good friends and we often spent time spring cleaning the houses, putting up curtains, climbing ladders and decorating the children's bedrooms, while we waited for the social workers to do their investigations, write their reports and finally to get us a Children's Court Hearing.

Eventually the day of court arrived. Off we went, Emma, the children and I. They were taken out of my care and put into Emma's care. The Commissioner of Child Welfare reiterated what I had said about her being solely responsible for the welfare and safety of the children, and that should the mother threaten, abuse or interfere with the children, Emma would then be bound by law to report the abuse to the police.

I felt like I had done a good job. There were two children safe with their grandmother who loved them. And with my hectic life, and not seeing Emma anymore, I soon forgot about them.

About a month later I got a phone call from a very distraught Emma. She told me that she could not cope with her daughter. She was continuously drunk, coming into her home, demanding to remove the children, swearing and cursing, and abusing the children and hitting Emma herself. Emma told me that the mother had abducted Shudan two days before and she had not returned with him. I immediately called Johan Pienaar, the Chief Social Worker who was assigned to the case, and told him the story. He said that he was very busy and could not deal with the problem at that time. I offered to collect Emma and Kayla and bring them to his office. He agreed, and said that he would advise the grandmother to get a domestic violence restraining order against the daughter.

"Johan, if the children are not safe with Emma, then it is no longer a place of safety for the children", I said. "Why don't the children come back in to us until the protection order is in place", I asked him.

"We have to educate our people", he said. "This is the way to do it".

"But Johan, the child has been abducted from a place of safety. This means that the place is no longer safe for the child", I pleaded.

Again, Johan said that he would tell Emma how to go about getting a Domestic Violence Restraining Order. My mind boggled that he was going to "educate" his people at the expense of another abused child. I sent one of my staff members to collect Emma and Kayla and had them delivered to Johan. There was little more that I could do.

Four days later, Emma brought Shudan back to the Children's Home. She said that she could not keep him safe from his mother. I notified Johan Pienaar immediately and followed it up with a hand-delivered letter and copied the letter to the Commissioner of Child Welfare. I asked

Johan Pienaar to reverse the Place of Safety Order, and place Shudan back in our care. I sent a copy to the Commissioner of Child Welfare. This I did every two weeks from March 2004 to December 2005. The child was never placed legally in our care.

In April 2005, we changed the trading name of the organization from the SA CARE Trust to the Dianne Lang Foundation so that we could trade on my name to improve our chances of raising funds after I won the FairLady/Clarins Woman of the Year. When this became known, I receiveda letter from the Commissioner of Child Welfare, withdrawing my appointment as an officer of the court with the explanation that I no longer represented the SA CARE Trust. Despite a response letter explaining that the legalities of the foundation remaining the same, my letter was never answered. This put us into a quandary when Shudan became desperately ill. Legalizing his stay with us became imperative. We again made urgent application for his Form 4 to be changed from his grandmother to us, but still nothing was done. Fortunately, Shudan recovered, but had he not, we would have been held for culpable homicide because Shudan was not legally placed in our care, through lack of service delivery by the Department of Social Services.

On 7 December 2005, Johan Pienaar arrived to remove Shudan from our care and placed him in the care of his grandmother. We never received the Form 5 that should have accompanied his stay with us. This also means that without the Form 5, we cannot claim safety fees for him for the period that he stayed with us. The reason that Shudan was removed from us is because the Department of Social Development suddenly decided that they were removing as many children from our care as they could because I could not provide each child with 5m² floor sleeping space.

Again, this was not in the interests of the child, but another form of harassment towards me. The floor sleeping space would later become a thorn in my side as I would fight another losing battle against social workers who would prefer children sleeping on the street than children sleeping in double bunk beds.

Shudan's mother was never charged with child abuse. The Public Prosecutor refused to prosecute for lack of evidence. However, the police never took any statements from those who were prepared to give evidence, neither from any witnesses to the continued child abuse.

While still writing to the Department of Social Development for an independent investigation into service delivery in our area, I was totally unaware of what was taking place behind my back. The meeting of Friday 13 August had got the knives out for me. After all the experiences that I had had of how the authorities operated, I should not have been surprised, nor should I have let my guard down. However, I took people at face value and did not expect people to go behind my back to try and break down something that I perceived as being a benign way of helping the children in South Africa. I should have known better. Do not trample on a lion's tail. He is likely to turn around and bite you. And I had trampled hard on the tail during Friday the 13th. I had not submitted quietly to their attack on what I was doing to help the children. Another thing that I did not realize was that if you show up a person for not knowing his job, he will become extremely vindictive. I had made myself a lot of enemies on that day.

Luke

I woke up with a jerk. Someone was yelling.

"Mama D. Mama D. Luke is getting bad. Come quickly".

I jumped out of bed and ran down the passage. Luke was ashen, lying with his big eyes looking at Amore as she held him. Amore was one of the many young people that I had gathered around me during my life. I always seemed to have with me a young person who was troubled. She had come with me to Middelburg because she had problems with her family, and although she did not take Patience's place, she did have a very special place in my heart.

Luke had the most beautiful eyelashes and eyes I have ever seen on any child. Luke was eighteen months old and dying of AIDS. He had been living with us for almost ten months. When his mother brought him to us to take care of, the doctor told us that he did not have long to live, and the best that we could do for him was to make him comfortable. But we never believed doctors. We lived as though there were no tomorrow. Luke had been sick before and we had managed to get him well again. He had even managed to go through the baby stages, getting teeth, sitting up, trying to stand and walk, all the things that he was not able to do when he arrived. For some reason, we just all believed that Luke would be like all the rest. He would just grow up and be like all the other kids. Whenever the children got too sick, they would be brought into my bedroom and there they would stay until they were well enough to join the others. When they got really ill, I would put their little bodies against my chest, wrap a

147

baby blanket or towel around the two of us, and let the baby feel my heartbeat. I would not put them down other than to change their nappies or to feed them, and then back they would go, tied to my chest. And time and again, they would get better. Now was the time for Luke to come to my bedroom.

When Luke became ill this time, Amore asked me if she could take care of him. I agreed, but I did warn her that it might be traumatic. Amore was only twenty at the time. She wanted to be with him 24 hours a day so that he would not be alone for one minute. I agreed, as I would be there as well.

Amore sat rigid in the chair, her eyes as wide as saucers. I could see she was afraid that Luke might be dying and she was scared of death. Luke was conscious but in pain. His frail little body was sore and as I gently took him from her arms, he moaned faintly. His breath was coming in short sharp intakes and the out breaths just left his chest without any effort on his part. His heart was racing. You could see how the artery was fluttering in his neck. He was looking past me as though he was seeing something there that we could not see.

"He will not die now Amore, but Luke is dying", I said gently. I knew that there was nothing more we could do for our little boy. He was beyond our help. This time we would not be able to save our boy.

"Nooooo!!!", she howled as she leaned over and put her head in her lap. Her body shook with grief and her anguish poured out of her in great big sobs. When Amore had calmed down a bit, I asked her, "Do you still want to be with Luke till the end?".

"Yes".

"Then come", I quietly encouraged her. I called the staff and told them that Luke did not have long to live and they went to break the news to the other children. The children were sad and crying, but they all came and said goodbye to Luke, some kissed him, others touched his forehead and others just stroked his little feet. The staff stood around and said a prayer. I called Father John and he came and baptized Luke and gave him the last rites.

Father John called me aside and said, "Dianne, you are forever calling me out to baptize your children at all hours of the day and night. I think you should now do it yourself. I can't always be coming out, day and night, whenever you think one of your children is going to die and then they don't. All you have to do is say, *I baptize you in the Name of the Father, and of the Son and of the Holy Spirit.* OK?".

"Yes, Father, thank you for coming", I said.

We sent word out to try and find Luke's mother, but she had gone to Cape Town. Amore and I sat with Luke. It took eighteen hours for him to die. He never lost consciousness. He was awake the whole time. He suffered for eighteen hours. His breathing became more and more erratic. He could not swallow. He could not pass urine. He could not cough. He would take a deep breath, exhale and then there would be no breath for a long time and then he would take another deep breath. And so it would go on. And on... and on... and on. Amore grew tired. I told her to go and have a sleep. I would wake her if there was any change. We were taking it in turns holding Luke in our arms, talking to him and singing to him all the time. Amore curled up on the couch with a blanket and was soon fast asleep. The emotions of the day were draining and she needed to rest. Who knew when this would end?

In the stillness of the night, Luke's breathing became more pronounced and his suffering became more evident. I longed for the suffering to end. This poor little mite was struggling to breathe for hour after hour. I had already phoned the pharmacist and asked her if there was anything that would ease his suffering, but she had told me that there was nothing. I knew from experience that there was nothing at the hospital. What could I do to help this little soul? The minutes ticked by so slowly. I kept looking at the clock. How much longer does this have to go on?

"Please God, stop this suffering. Take this child into your care now. This is enough. Don't let this carry on any longer. Please don't let him struggle for one more breath. Just let him stop breathing", I prayed.

But no one heard. The silence was made more deafening by the incessant struggle for the next breath from Luke. OK, I thought. I will do something now. Amore is asleep. No one will know what I am about to do. I will take a pillow and put it over his mouth and then he will stop breathing and it will be over. Not even God listens. To allow this to carry on is beyond cruel. I lean over and take the small pillow out of the pram. I hold it up in my right hand. Luke is lying in my left arm. He has stopped breathing. I don't have to do it.

"Thank you, God".

Then he struggles for the next breath. I have to do it. I hover with the pillow still in my hand. I hesitate, knowing that I have no right to take another's life, but at the same time consumed by the need to stop the suffering. I move the pillow closer to his head. Closer still... the pillow is now just above his face. And still I hesitate. Do I or don't I? I need to stop his suffering. I have an irresistible need to stop this awful breathing that is filling my brain and my mind and my soul with anguish and the suffering of hell. He looks at me. Those big eyes of his, look at me. What is he trying to tell me? Help me? But how? The pillow goes down on his face. Gently. My hand holds the pillow gently on his face.

I pull the pillow away from his face and fling it across the room. I can't do it. I have failed him.

"Oh, Luke, my darling, darling little Luke, I am so sorry, boy. I am so sorry I could not make you well. I did my best, but you must go now my love. Please go now. Don't stay any longer". "Amore", I call, "wake up, and come and hold Luke".

She stretches and comes over. I put Luke into her arms. He is still struggling to breathe. I tell her to tell him it is OK for him to leave us now. She does. It is not long and she screams and throws Luke at me. I catch him in my arms.

He has stopped breathing. He will never breathe again. Our baby is dead. I phone the hospital and tell them that our baby is dead.

"What must I do?", I ask.

"You must phone the police", they tell me. "Because if someone dies at home, it could mean that it is a homicide".

I phone the police and tell them that our baby has died. Two police officers arrive within minutes. They call the mortuary van over the radio. The mortuary man arrives and takes Luke. He opens the back door of the mortuary van and wants to put our tiny little Luke into the back of the cavernous vehicle.

"Please can't you take him in the front with you", I beg.

"OK", says the man, obviously seeing how distraught Amore and I are.

Luke leaves and our family mourns: the staff , the children, Amore, me. For the rest of the night, I cradled Amore in my arms. Little did we know what the next day would bring. I had never had to bury someone before so I was learning the steps as I was going along. There was much to organize to bury Luke. There was a coffin to buy, a plot to purchase, and a funeral to organize. Amore and I went off to the funeral parlour to discuss the cost of a funeral and realized that we could not afford it at all. When I told them that we would bury Luke ourselves we were promptly told that we would not be allowed to do that because we would not be given a death certificate.

"Thank you very much", I said as we sailed out of the funeral parlour.

By this stage, I did not trust anything anyone in Middelburg told me and this smelled like a racket to me. Was this a way to get poor people locked into expensive funerals? Where were our constitutional rights? I needed to go back to my books and back to the telephone to find out how to go about getting a death certificate without going through a funeral parlour. After numerous telephone calls I discovered that the death certificate story that I had been given was a scam that all the funeral parlours were using to ensure that they got all the business. No wonder no one buried their own family. All I had to do was go to the police station and get a burial order. It was that simple. Next was the purchase of a coffin. We went to three funeral parlours to find the cheapest coffin. They were all out of our price range, although at that point, any coffin was out of our price range.

We were struggling to keep food on the table and had not paid the school fees yet. The end of the month was coming up and staff salaries had to be paid. On top of that, it was only two months to Christmas. Eventually, I asked a funeral parlour if they did not have a damaged coffin or one lying around that could not be sold that we could repair. The lady obviously took pity on us and went out into the back yard to take a look. She came back with a little white coffin that was damaged and falling apart. It was dirty and weathered from lying outside, obviously exposed to the elements for a long time.

"Perfect", I said, "how much?"

"What about R100?"

The deal was made and we left with the coffin. Amore was still so afraid of death or anything connected to it that she would not even carry the coffin. With bravado, I picked it up and carried it across the street and put it into the 4 x 4. With a little bit of paint, nails and screws, the coffin looked much better. The children painted pictures on the coffin and it looked quite festive - a sarcophagus fit for a boy prince. All the preparations for Luke's funeral kept us busy and focused, and I had little time for grief. The staff were very unhappy about us having a funeral without a funeral parlour.

"What will the community think of us? They will think we are poor and will look down on us. It is our culture to use funeral parlours. We must also provide food for everyone who attends the funeral and there will be lots who will come because they want to see what goes on in the Children's Home. We must also have all the dishes outside so that after the service at the grave, everyone can wash their hands before coming inside".

These arguments were disruptive to the children's home and they would not be placated. One of the many problems that have frustrated me over the years of working in the community has been the use of the word culture. Having grown up in the Transkei, I know the customs and culture of the Xhosa people. Using funeral parlours was definitely not part of the culture. I remember a workshop that I had taught where I had used an example of the necessity of using a seat belt in a car. One of the delegates told me that he would not use a seat belt because it was not part of his culture.

"And using a vehicle is not part of your culture either. You should be riding
a horse", I retorted.

The delegates howled with laughter. I have found that many people use the word "culture" as an excuse for doing or not doing something. Culture is also often used as another word for racism. And the annoying thing is that those who use this word so indiscriminately are those who have never grown up in a tribal system, but have grown up in cities and in a western environment. What they know about tribal culture is dangerous. Culture is often used to further their own ends, or to line their own pockets. It was time for a serious talk to the staff regarding more than just culture and funeral arrangements. I needed to impress on them once and for all the dire financial situation we were in. For some reason, they were under the impression that I was a never-ending source and supply of all things, because whenever we needed something, I always seemed to come up with what it was we needed, when we needed it. However, it was more due to providence and good fortune that we always seemed to just make it.

I brought out our bank statement and showed them that we had a total of R1800,19 in the bank. I showed them my private banking account with an overdraft of

R50 000,00 which had been keeping us afloat. I showed them the total monthly expenses. Not all of them grasped the seriousness of the situation, but they took it that I was not a never-ending supply of money and that I did not have any money to spare. I also had to tell them that I had sold my own home in Port Elizabeth and that all the proceeds of the sale of the home had gone into keeping us afloat. I had no other means of getting more money into our project.

"Funeral parlours are not part of the custom", I said.

Nonqaba agreed by saying "Ewe, Njalo". (Yes, that is true) She is the only staff member who had grown up in the Transkei and, being the oldest member of staff, everyone had to concede to her superior knowledge.

I continued, "What we are going to do is bury Luke ourselves. The community did not care for him. They did not step in and offer any help. They have not assisted us in any way at all. In fact, no one did anything for the children before we came here and we are not here to put on any show for anyone. Apart from trying to locate Luke's mother to get her to attend, we are not advertising this funeral. If we had money we would have been able to buy the drugs for Luke and he would not be dead. We do not have the money for a big funeral. We will do what we can with what we have. There will be no more talking about big funerals".

After more discussions, it was decided to have a short service at the Catholic Church, and then we would walk to the nearest cemetery where we would bury Luke. After that, we would come home, have lunch and then have a video afternoon for the rest of the children. Organizing the church service with Father John was just a phone call. Organizing the grave site was another matter altogether.

To purchase a burial plot, I had to go to the Municipal Health Department. Amore and Jackson came with me. Jackson was one of the first HIV and AIDS Trainers that I had trained, and he had been a volunteer for a long time before he joined me in caring for the children. I asked them for a burial plot for a baby.

"That will cost R60,00".

"That's fine. Is that in the town cemetery?", I asked.

"What colour is the baby?"

"What difference does that make?" I was shocked by the question.

"The town cemetery is for whites only".

To say I was taken aback is to put it mildly. Here we were, almost 10 years into the new South Africa, and we were still talking about cemeteries for white people. Had Middelburg not heard that there had been a take over by the ANC? And that apartheid was gone?

"What did you say?", I asked.

"It is a white cemetery", the lady behind the desk said again.

I had wanted to bury Luke in the town cemetery because it was the nearest cemetery. We only had one vehicle which could carry eight children at a push, and therefore everything we did outside the home had to be within walking distance. The other two cemeteries were too far away for the smaller children to walk to. During the previous government, one cemetery had been for blacks, one for whites, and the third for coloured people. The only reason I had chosen the "white" cemetery was because it was closest to where we lived. Now, the cemetery became an issue for me. It had to be that particular cemetery, not because it was the closest one anymore, but because I was told that it was a white cemetery and Luke was a black baby and he could not be buried there. Was this another one of the new South Africa's sick jokes?

"That is bullshit, utter bullshit. This is the new South Africa. There is no such thing as a white cemetery. I want a plot in that cemetery and I don't care what you have to do to get it for me. You had better pick up that phone and phone your superiors and clear it with them now, because I am not walking out of here until you give me the receipt that I have paid for a plot in the white cemetery for my black baby".

My voice was raised; those waiting around to be served had stopped talking and were waiting to hear what would happen next. Amore was pulling me by the arm and telling me to calm down. Jackson was standing there with his chest stuck out a mile, looking pleased as punch and strutting around while bending his head in my direction every now and then when someone looked in my direction. Jackson is one of my biggest fans, and he loves

158

it when I get mad and give the authorities hell on some human rights issue. This was just up his alley.

The little lady behind the window at the desk was busy on the telephone. Comments started being made by those waiting to see various people in the department.

"She will never get a plot in the white cemetery".

"Yes, she will. You watch and see", said Jackson.

Other comments were made and Jackson was strutting his stuff, proud as
punch to be the centre of attention. I was shaking with anger. Amore kept rubbing my arm up and down and telling me "Calm down Mom", but I was beyond being calmed down. The lady came back to the office window.

"This has never been done before. I can't get hold of anyone".

"If it has not been done before, it does not mean it cannot be done now. Either you sell me that plot in the town cemetery, or you get hold of someone who will authorize you to do so. I have told you that I will not leave here until you do so", I repeated.

Back she went to the telephone, this time clearly flustered. The consternation that was going on in the Health Department had drawn other staff members into the office behind the glass window and they too were having their comments and opinions. In the meantime, I remembered that I had the telephone number of Mr Kelvin Claasen,

Head of the Health Department in Cradock and called him while waiting at the glass window.

"Kelvin, this is Dianne. I have a problem here. One of my children has died and your department won't let me bury him in the white cemetery. I thought this apartheid bullshit was over. Can you please tell them to cut their crap and give me a plot?", I said as I banged on the window and handed my mobile through to the lady.

"Here, take this call. It is Mr Claasen".

I watched her face. She said nothing. She nodded, and then nodded some more.Then she said "Yes, Mr Claasen".

And that was it. "The plot will cost you R285,00" she said.

"Why does it cost more than the original quote?"

"Because you want a white cemetery", she replied.
"This too is utter bullshit. The white cemetery costs more than the black cemetery? Does the ground cost more?" I asked as I paid. "Will the Health Department dig the grave?", I asked.

"No", she fumed. "OK, we will do it ourselves. Thank you for all your help", I said sarcastically as we left.

Jackson was in his element. As we went through the door, Jackson could not help himself. He had to put his head back in to say "I told you so" to the gathered audience.

Saving Mandela's Children

We woke up to a perfectly brilliant sunshine day - a perfect day for digging a grave. Surely not such a big job for Jackson, Amore, the kids and I? We had a pick and two spades so it would be fairly easy. It had to be done today because the funeral was tomorrow. We would cover the grave overnight with plastic, just in case it rained. Just after noon, the three of us took the plastic, pick, spades and water bottles to the cemetery. We found the grave site fairly easily. The Department of Health had drawn an outline of the size of the grave into the hard earth. Starting with the two spades, we dug around the marked areas. This is where we encountered our first problem. The earth was so hard that the spades bounced back up from the ground when we thrust them into the ground. We tried jumping onto the spades so that the shock of the bouncing would be less on our arms. When this seemed like a losing battle, we resorted to the pick. Amore and I had tried the spades, so now it was Jackson's turn with the pick. He would pick at the earth and we would use the spades to move the earth out of the hole. It was slow going. Even the pick was making very little difference in the earth. The sun was streaming down and in very little time, the sweat was pouring off of us and we were huffing and puffing.

An hour and a half had gone past and we had gone down 4 inches. We needed to get to five feet. The earth was hard, dry clay. We could not stop. We took it in turns with the pick and the spade and made slow progress. We stopped talking. It was too hot and we were too tired to talk. We just wanted to get the job done. The only sounds were the sounds of the pick and the spade on the hard baked earth and our panting. There was not a breath of wind. Three hours later, we were down to three feet, but now we could not use the pick. The area of the small grave was too small to stand in and swing the pick. It was spades only and we were getting nowhere.

"Let's go and get the big boys to come and help us", I said.

"What we need here are some metal tins to use to scrape the ground out and they will be small enough to get into the grave and do it".

By now the wind had started to pick up and there were dark clouds brewing in the south, a sure sign of a summer storm. We would have to move fast.

When Matthew, Mark, William and John arrived with their mbozo's (tins), they got into the grave and started working on clearing the ground. It was hard work for them as well. We tried to stack all the ground that we were taking out up on the one side of the grave so that it would be easier to fill in after the burial. This would also make it easier for us to get the coffin into the grave. While they were working and we were encouraging them, the rain started coming down, so I rushed over to the van and got the plastic sheet. We all huddled under the plastic sheet, the boys in the grave and the three adults sitting around it while the storm got worse and worse. The wind buffeted the plastic sheet and it took all the adult strength to keep it from flying away. As fast as the storm had arrived, it stopped. Off came the plastic sheet and back to work we went.

The cemetery is bordered by a well-used road that runs parallel with the fence and leads to the predominantly coloured area called Midros. Seeing this group of blacks and only one white woman sparked something in the people who were driving past and they started shouting obscenities at us. Some told us to get out of the white cemetery. Whites drove past and shouted "Wat maak julle daar? Kom daar uit!" (What are you doing there? Get out of there!)

At three and a half feet, the rain came down in buckets again. Again we sheltered under our plastic cover, but we were wet and cold. When the rain stopped, we would dig again. And so the afternoon continued. Digging, raining, sheltering, people shouting at us, digging, sheltering - it seemed never to stop.

"Will they know if we don't dig all the way to five feet?" asked Amore.

"No, but I think we should continue", I said, having visions of a flood and this coffin floating out of the ground.

This was the first grave I was digging and I did not want to get it wrong. Looking back on this now, I wonder why I never doubted myself, what made me just go ahead as though nothing was impossible? It was dark and still we had not reached five feet. This called for torches, and so we continued to dig with tins while using torches to light our way. Eventually we finished at about nine that night.

"I hope no one else dies because I am not digging any more graves", said Matthew as we got home.

I hugged him and thought, "Yes boy, I hope we never have to dig another grave".

The next day, I went to fetch Luke from the mortuary and Amore and I dressed him in "our" favourite clothes. We wrapped him in his favourite blanket and put him in his specially designed coffin. We all left for church at the same time, with Jackson carrying the coffin at the front of the line. The children were all walking behind the coffin, walking slowly behind, two by two, holding hands. After the service, we walked to the cemetery. There were no other guests who attended. It was only Luke's family - us who loved him. Luke's funeral that day was simple, beautiful and a celebration of his life. It was also a time to remember how grateful and honoured we were to have loved Luke and to have been with him for those many months. The funeral service at the Catholic Church was sad, with the children singing hymns. I sobbed when they sang "Goodbye goodbye" to Luke. I sat there remembering how Luke got one tooth at the bottom first, then one at the top. Then he got another at the bottom and then another at the top. He only ever had four front teeth. He loved his milk biscuits and Vienna sausages that Amore gave him. He loved to be pushed around fast in his pram by the other children and squealed with delight when tickled. We never did get to find his mother before he died, but heard later that she too was so ill that she would not have been able to come to Luke even had she wanted to. Luke's mother died four months after Luke. There was no money to bury her. She lay in the municipal mortuary for five months before she was given a pauper's funeral.

The smaller children still ask me when we go past the cemetery, "Mama D, can't we wake Luke up now? He has been sleeping long enough".

They do not understand the concept of death. The 'white' cemetery is no longer 'white'. Everyone can be buried under the beautiful trees in the most beautiful cemetery in Middelburg. Many people of colour are buried there today. I doubt if they spare a thought for the little black boy who was the first to lie amongst the fancy marble headstones of the apartheid whites only area, or a thought for the woman who fought so hard for that plot, or the rag tag band who dug the grave with jam tins.

Chicken run children

It had been a long day in May 2003. We had all worked really hard at scrubbing, scraping, cleaning, painting and sanding our little house in Middelburg. Our support group home was nearing completion. We were proud of what we had achieved. There was a home based care worker on every street. We had peer educators in the high school. We had street drama performers. Our trainers were training Aids awareness workshops. We had had our first AIDS concert. Things were buzzing. Our support groups were well attended. What more did we need to achieve? The HIV trainers and Home Based Care Workers had gone home early as it was freezing cold. I had warmed up some tomato soup and was sitting on the floor in the lounge, sipping at it and eating dry bread, contemplating whether I had the strength to boil the kettle at least three times to have a bath or whether I should leave it until the morning. We did not have a bath, only a toilet in the little house. I had borrowed an oval tin bath that needed at least four kettles of water to get a good wash. I could just put my bum into it and with my knees around my ears. I was filthy and covered in splashes of paint and if I patted my head, the dust flew. No, I thought, I will have to brave the bath, even though the temperature was moving to below zero. I wearily stood up and as I did so, I heard a knock on the door. It was about 21h00.

I was a little afraid of opening the door at that time of the night so I shouted out "Who is it?"

"Welile", came the answer.

Saving Mandela's Children

Welile worked with the street children at a shelter up the road and I had often spoken to him. He was an outcast in the community because he had such a strange head. It pointed upwards in a Mr Spock look-a-like, and because he always had a number of boy children walking around with him, the community made fun of him. However, I would always make a point of collecting second-hand clothing and blankets for his children and his shelter. He was helped by Father John of the Catholic Church. I immediately opened the door to him.

"Dianne, I need your help. I have found these three children in a chicken run and I can't look after them because the one is a baby and the other two are girls. Can you take them please?".

And before I could say anything, he was gone. I think he must have known that I would have found a million excuses to say I could not take them. I did not even like children. I had had my fair share of children, having brought up my own children as a single parent. In all the time that I had been doing AIDS awareness workshops, Trainer workshops and home-based care workshops in Middelburg, I had not once taken any notice of the children. Children were not part of my conscious awareness. And now there I was with three children on my doorstep, in the middle of winter, with a temperature dropping to below zero, at night and with no knowledge of what to do with them, or even wanting to help them. But I was stuck with them. I could not close the door on them. Welile was nowhere to be found. And looking up at me were these three little children. Two girls aged about 10 years and a little boy no older than two and a half. They looked at me and I looked at them for what seemed an eternity but I am sure it was only a moment or two. I opened the door wider and said "Ghena". (Come in).

In the light of the passage, I was appalled by what I saw. One girl had a nasty burn from a fire on her leg, did not know what her name was or how old she was. She was dressed in rags with no shoes on her feet and was shivering from the cold. She said that she could not remember how long she had been in the chicken run, but that sometimes people would throw food at her. I asked her what name she would like if she could choose any name. She said "Patricia". So this little girl became known as Patricia. She had been badly abused, had a number of scars on her body, was extremely thin and told me that she had been raped "lots of times". She had not developed at all so she was definitely pre-teen. She was extremely nervous and constantly moved her hands and feet around. Her attention span was very short and she had never been to school. When I looked closely at her, I thought that I recognized her. I asked her if she sometimes walked around with the street boys, and she said yes. I took out my photographs and checked the pictures I had of Welile and the street boys and true enough, there was Patricia, a small, pathetic little thing, dressed like a boy, standing between two bigger boys.

"Why do you dress like a boy Patricia?", I asked.

So they don't "racher" (rape) me", she answered.

"Have you been "rachererd" a lot?, I asked her.

"Lots of times", she said.

Patricia was covered in scabies and her hair was full of lice.

While I was asking the children these questions and trying to make them feel at home, I was heating up some tomato soup and cutting bread. We did not have a bread knife so the bread was being 'sawed' with an ordinary butter knife. Soon the children were sitting on the floor eating as though they had not seen food in years.

"When did you last eat?", I asked them.

In between mouthfuls of food, they told me that they had eaten a piece of bread two days ago.

The other little girl told me that her name was Blou (blue) and that the little boy was her brother. He did not have a name so she just called him Boetie (brother). Blou had a huge haematoma on her head where she had been kicked by a group of older boys and numerous lacerations on her body. She also had a very painful vagina and could not walk or sit properly. When I asked her about her painful vagina she said that four men had "rachered" her and, when she tried to run away, they had kicked her on her head. From her description, she had been raped four days previously. She had been sleeping in the chicken run when the big boys came back and did it to her again. She was also covered in scabies, lice, dressed in rags, had no shoes and was extremely traumatized. She had virtually no facial expressions while Patricia did all the talking. She told me that Blou had also never been to school.

The little boy, Boetie, was a pathetic sight. He could not even feed himself and I had to spoon the food into his mouth. He was running a very high temperature, was dressed in a thin shirt and shorts with no shoes, and also had scabies and lice. He was pathetically thin and the glands in his neck were standing out like golf balls. He had sores on his lips and thrush in his mouth. He was coughing badly and looked about 18 months old although he had a mouth full of teeth.

Once I had fed the children and covered them with odd towels and blankets, I boiled the kettle and got the tin bath out. With a bottle of disinfectant thrown in, I bathed Boetie and then got Patricia into the water. The water was so dirty after that, I had to do it all over again for Blou. With the children clean, the next issue to deal with was what to put them into. They looked quite ridiculous in my clothes. Since there was only one bed in the house, I put all three of them into the bed, after giving Boetie and Blou some pain killers and Boetie some cough mixture. Their heads had not hit the pillow when they were fast asleep. Then I sat down and tried to figure out what to do.

"OK", I thought, "I don't like children. I don't like animals. So, if these were puppies, I would take them to the SPCA or the vet tomorrow. So, I will take them to the welfare tomorrow and they will find them homes. Simple".

With the problem solved in my head, I took one of the pillows, one of the blankets and camped down on the floor next to the bed. After breakfast the next morning, Jackson was the first volunteer to arrive.

"Look what we have here, Jackson", I said. "A little group of kids. Come with me to the welfare so we can get them some homes".

He looked at me as if I had gone off my head, but I took no notice and with the three children in the 4x4, with Boetie on Jackson's lap, I drove to the Department of Social Welfare.

"I have three children here that need homes", I said to the social worker.

She too looked at me as though I had lost my mind. "We don't have homes for them. They are street children", she said.

"Well, what am I to do with them?", I asked incredulously.

"Put them back where you found them", she said.

"I found them on my doorstep", I said.

"Well, they are street children, so they must go back to the street. We don't have any homes for them", she said.
I walked out of their offices and put the children back into the vehicle. I was fuming. Jackson was amazed at my reaction. He could not understand why I was so angry.

"This is the way it is", he said.

"Well, this is bullshit. Even dogs and cats have a place that finds homes for them. What the fuck is the welfare doing? We can't put these children back on the street. They are sick. They have been raped. Look at them! For fuck's sake Jackson, this is unacceptable. I am taking them to the doctor and then we will find homes for them".

How naïve I was. How naïve I have always been throughout my journey with the children. I made an appointment with the local doctor. He examined the children and told me that Boetie had full blown AIDS, that the girls had HIV and that without medication, none of the children would live very long. He said that Boetie would probably not live longer than a week and the girls a couple of weeks. He gave me antibiotics for all three children, cough mixture for Boetie, something for pain for all three of them, something for their scabies and something to get rid of the lice. It cost a small fortune, considering we were living on a shoestring. Next it was a stop at the local cheap clothing store. Three sets of clothing for each child, including underwear, pyjamas and shoes. And then it was back home again to get them lice and scabies free and to get them into clean clothes, medicated and fed. The lice was so bad in the children's hair that I had to send Jackson out to buy a razor so that we could shave their hair off. We just had no choice. When the children were clean, medicated and fed and were settled down looking at books, Jackson and I had to decide what to do about the children.

"Look, Jackson, we can't put these kids back on the street. It is cruel and barbaric. I would not even do it to a dog, let alone a child. The doctor said they are not going to live very long, so why don't we just keep them until they die? You come in every day from now on, I give you a stipend to help me with the children, and then we will see how it goes. I will have to stay here as long as I can and if I have to go to Port Elizabeth, then you sleep here and look after the children. Is that OK?".

"Mama D, if that is what you want, it is OK by me, but we don't have a choice now. You have made up your mind and when you do that, you don't change it. This is the way it will be".

And that was that.

One of the first things we did was to give the children better names. We asked Blou if she wanted to choose another name for herself. Since she was starting a new life and she was going to now live with us, we wondered if she would like a new name. Without hesitation she said, "Betty". So, Blou became Betty. Boetie could not be called "Brother". He too, had to have a name and since he was Betty's little brother, we asked her what name she would like him to have and again, without hesitation, she said, "Sam". Betty then told us that Sam's father used to throw him around and beat him with a belt. So now we had a little family of children, Patricia, Betty and Sam.

Our first priority was to try to find the children's families. We got hold of Welile to assist us in finding the children's families, and the word got out that we wanted to know who the children belonged to.

Patricia had no known relatives and there was no clue as to a birth date. Because she did not know what her name was, we could not look up the hospital records. All we did know is that she did not have a mother, that she had been on the streets for at least six years, and that she did have a father who was in jail in George although no one knew what his name was.

We found that Betty had a clinic card but no birth certificate. She was born at home and was visited by the clinic staff on the 7 August 1992, her weight being 5kg. She was therefore born prior to that date. Her name on the card was Nobomi Tom, although she did not know this information. Sam is the half-brother of Betty, sharing the same father but not the mother. Sam's mother has been missing (presumed dead) since Sam was two months old. The father is an abusive alcoholic without employment and does not want his child. Investigations have shown that Sam slept in various shelters of all kinds as his father was often missing for weeks on end. We found a clinic card with no name in it, but believed to belong to Sam, showing his date of birth to be 30 January 2000. If this is the true clinic card, Sam would have been about three and a half years old at the time he came to us. This may have been correct as Sam could hold a fairly good conversation and he had a mouth full of teeth, even though he looked like he was 18 months old.

It soon became obvious that all three children had very different personalities. Patricia was a wild child who could not be still for a moment. She would also speak incessantly. Within a short time, she started communicating well and smiled easily. Betty was afraid of adults and men in general, although it did not take long for her to befriend Jackson. Any other man was a threat to her. Betty did not communicate unless she was spoken to and then she would give one word answers. She also did not smile easily. Sam was a moody child. He would alternate between screaming with laughter or having a sullen face, and nothing you could do would make him speak or smile.

One thing we were sure of. These children were not going to die alone, afraid, cold and hungry. We would love them and care for them and they would die a dignified death. We fed the children, we medicated them, we entertained them, we cared for them...and then Sam got very, very ill. By this stage, we had beds for Betty, Patricia, Jackson, Sam and me. I took Sam into my bed with me. I watched over him every minute. I gave him his medicine but nothing seemed to be helping. I took him back to the doctor but was told there was nothing that could be done.

Well, I thought, the whole idea was to look after the children until they died and Sam was going to be the first one. We all knew that. But Sam was not just a kid any more. He had somehow crept into my heart. I lifted him up into my arms and sat on the chair with him. His breathing was rasping in his chest. He had not eaten the whole day. We could not coax him with anything. He just lay in my arms listless. The fever was burning him up. We had given him all the medication as prescribed. He would not drink anything. I would drop water into his mouth with a dropper. His eyes would slowly open, take in his surroundings and then close again. Everyone was quietly praying for him. We were burning a white candle on the table. The house was quiet. The door would open and close at regular intervals as HIV trainers and Home Base Care workers would come and go, visiting and paying their respects.

Still Sam hung in there. The day wore on and on. Sam showed no improvement. As evening came, his breathing became worse. He would take a deep breath and with no effort at all, the breath would be out. A few seconds of silence and no chest movement would follow and then again, another deep breath and with no effort at all, the breath would be out. And then it happened. He never took another breath. I waited for it but it did not come.

I grabbed Sam under the arms, held him up in the air and screamed, "Sam, Sam, breathe, breathe, Sam breathe", as I shook him vigorously backwards and forwards.

My heart was thumping in my chest. My mind was screaming "Don't die, for God's sake, don't die, I love you". Suddenly, Sam started breathing. The tears flowed down my cheeks as I hugged him to my chest. It was in that moment that I knew that there was no turning back for me. I loved Sam with all my heart and I would do everything in my power to make sure that he lived. Not only would I do everything in my power to save Sam, but I would do everything in my power to care for Betty and Patricia as well. They were my children and I loved them passionately, protectively, completely. I did not know how I would do it, but these were my children now and there was no turning back. I would do whatever had to be done to keep these children safe from harm and out of the jaws of death.

No rainbow nation

Life became a round of caring for sick children, doing workshops, running support groups, listening to the agonies and traumas of the people in the townships and trying to help the community on all levels. I was going back to Port Elizabeth less and less and my practice as a therapist was suffering. Less and less money was coming in and I was starting to dig deeper and deeper into my savings. Sam got better and started having fewer of his bad moods. Betty started talking and responding more to us and Patricia was still a rather wild child. Despite all this, we were a happy family. Jackson had now moved in as a permanent member of the family and I honestly don't know how I would have managed without him. Jackson was HIV+ and we had had his CD4 count taken and according to the results, he should have already been dead. But with the love, good food and the feeling of being needed, he was blossoming with health and his CD4 count was climbing. And we did not have access to ARV.

There were always people in and out of the house, HIV+ people, trainers, home based care workers and people needing advice. It was a very busy little house. We only had two bedrooms, a kitchen, a lounge but a rather quaint back yard with an ancient grapevine growing over a pagoda, which made for a wonderful meeting place in the summer.

Middelburg is demarcated into racially geographical areas through freeways that cut through the town. On one side is Kwa-nonzame, which is the area where all the black population live, on the other side is the predominantly coloured area and in the town live the predominantly white population.

Our little house was in the "white" area. Having being brought up in the Transkei, a part of South Africa that had been independent since 1976 and self-governing since the early '60's, I had not been subjected to the apartheid system. When I left the Transkei as an adult, I was disgusted by the separation of the races, and was soon carrying my banned ANC card, working for the Black Sash and carrying information for the ANC, dodging the security police and enjoying every moment of it. I felt that apartheid was disgusting and I would do what I could, in my small way, to see that it was abolished. I was therefore overjoyed when the referendum came in with a resounding YES vote to give all people the vote. Now I was to experience racism in all its forms. I certainly was not ready for what was about to happen.

I was busy with the children, settling them down for the morning with puzzles and books when there was a knock on the door. I went to open the door and was pleasantly surprised to see a well-dressed white woman at the door. Thinking this was my first real visitor, I opened the door with a friendly, "Good morning, come inside". She stepped inside the door without a smile. "My name is Dianne", I said.

"I know who you are", she said. "I have just come to tell you to get your kaffirs out of town and to warn you that if you don't, we will come and burn your house and you out of town".

With that, she turned on her heel and walked out.

"Jackson", I called, "come here quickly. Who is that woman?", I asked. "Oh, that is Jane Roux, the doctor at Grootfontein's wife", he said.

"Do you know what she has just said to me?". I told him what had happened. "This is unacceptable Jackson, get the kids ready, we are going to lay a charge against her at the police station". We went to the police station and laid a charge against her for intimidation, racism and for threatening to burn our house down. The police thought it was very funny. Needless to say, the docket never even got to the Public Prosecutor.

It was a beautiful afternoon and the children and I were going for a walk when a white woman who was watering her garden called out to me "Jy is 'n fokken kaffir". (You are a fucking kaffir).

There were about seven children with me at the time and they all asked me what a "kaffir" was. I don't bring my children up with words like that so they wanted to know what it meant. I just told them that it was a very ugly word that the woman had used. Again, I reported the incident, but this time the police returned to me to tell me that the woman had only said "Waar is my fokken kat?" (Where is my fucking cat?) When I told the police that seven children could bear witness to what she had said, the police told me that children could not be used as witnesses. Obviously at the time, I was still too inexperienced to take them to task on these issues, and believed that the South African Police knew what they were doing. After all, they were there to protect and serve

179

the public. This same woman, who lives directly opposite the children's home, has caused a lot of trouble for us with her racism.

One Christmas, we were practicing our Christmas carols as we were the official church choir for the Catholic Church that year. By this stage, there were around 60 children and we had three homes in the street although the largest home was used for all the activities, including the meals. The two other homes were used for sleeping purposes only. We were singing "Oh! Come all ye faithful", when there was a loud knock on the door. When I opened it, there were two large burly policemen standing there.

"Can I help you?", I asked.

"There is a report that you are making too much noise. Can you please keep quiet", the one policeman said.

"Why don't you come inside and join our singing?", I asked him. "It is Christmas time and it is a time for good will. Whoever has reported us for making a noise surely cannot tell the difference between beautiful singing and noise", I said as I pulled them inside.

The children took their cue from me and within seconds, little hands were pulling the policemen inside. We continued our singing and the policemen started smiling. They left, shaking their heads, muttering to themselves that the woman across the road was full of shit.

On another occasion, I had phoned down to the main children's home to tell the staff to get the children ready, lined up two by two outside the house as I was going to take them for a walk. It was a beautiful evening and a walk was just what we all needed. I had taken the office keys with me so that I could collect a hammer that I needed to do some work with back at one of the other homes after the walk, so I stopped at the office on my way down to collect the hammer. All the homes are in the same street. As I was locking the office, I looked across the road to see the objectionable woman standing in the middle of the street screaming at my children. I could not hear what she was saying, but from the manner in which she was standing and the sound of her voice, I knew that she was threatening my children. They were all standing on the pavement in their normal two by two hand-holding formation. I ran down towards her, my hammer flying by my side.

"Wat is jou probleem, mevrou?" (What is your problem madam?) I asked her.

Just then, a police vehicle came flying down the road and stopped inches from the two of us. She told the policemen in the vehicle to arrest me for an "onwettige optog" (illegal demonstration). The anger rose in my chest and I could feel my blood boiling. There were my children, standing in a row, waiting for me to take them for a walk, singing quietly while they waited, and she had the nerve to phone the police to come and arrest me for an illegal demonstration.

There is still a law that prohibits more than a certain number of people being in one place that may constitute a demonstration, but this was ridiculous. This was a group of children, from a children's home waiting for their "mother" to take them for a walk. My hammer was still in my hand and I was holding it in a very threatening manner. I could feel my grip on the hammer get tighter. I could feel my months of frustration against this woman rise in my throat. I wanted to take that hammer to her head. The policeman told me to take my children back into the house.

"No, I won't do that. This is not an *onwettige optog*. We are going for a walk. Tell this bitch to get out of my way", I shouted.

She had by now positioned herself between me and my children. The children had stopped singing. There was silence in the street other than what was going on between this white woman, myself and the policeman. His vehicle was parked right in the middle of the street.

Again I said to the policeman, " Tell this bitch to get out of my way", as I tried to move around her to get to my children.

She took a step sideways to block my way. I lifted my hammer into the air and in a split second help came from God. There was no conscious thought. I took another step sideways and started singing a freedom song, using my hammer as a baton and, as if we had practiced it for years, the children started singing on cue. I pushed her out of the way and walked straight to the head of the line of children.

"Let us go", I shouted and we walked, singing as loudly as we could, our heads held high.

Saving Mandela's Children

But my heart was thumping in my throat. I wondered what would happen now. Would I be arrested? Would the police follow me? Would they take this as an "onwettige optog"? We walked the streets, up and down, the hammer now a baton. Every now and again we could see the police vehicle trailing us. I was sure they were wandering what to do about us, or they were waiting for instructions from their superiors. Eventually it was time to go home. We were all exhausted by the time we got there. We were exhausted by the walk, and by the excitement of the encounter with the woman across the road and the policemen.

On Christmas Eve, we walked to the hospital and sang Christmas carols for the patients, and also went to the Police Station to sing Christmas carols for them. We have done this every year since. However, the first year we did it, I was given a surprise visit from the police. I was told that I could not go out with all my children and sing while we were walking because it was upsetting to the white community, and it could be construed as an unlawful demonstration; and if I insisted on doing so, then they would have no alternative but to arrest me. I told them that they were more than welcome to try to arrest me because should they do so, they would have their arses in the Constitutional Court before they could say "how do you do". I told them that I had no intention of stopping walking and singing with the children. I also told them that if they should try to arrest me, that they should buy themselves a vehicle with seats, because I would not get into their vans which were meant for transporting goods and live stock. On that issue, I would have them taken to the constitutional court. It would be a violation of my human rights. I further informed them that since they could only house four people per cell, how were they going to house me with my children, because by law they had to take me with my babies and I had eleven babies at the time. This again would contravene my human rights. From that time on, the police left me to walk and sing all over the town with my children.

Another racial problem we encountered was finding a church that would accept us all. In one church the children would be accepted, but I would not, in another I would be accepted but the children would not. In the end, we went to the Catholic Church in town. It was the nearest church to walk to, and we were the only members of the congregation.

Racism is something one normally thinks of as being a dislike of black of white or white of black. I experienced racism in the oddest form. Never in my life had I experienced racism, nor did I have a racist bone in my body. People are people to me, but my experience of caring for the children had changed my views of racism completely. One can become a victim of racism, not by another racial group, but by one's own racial group. This phenomenon has been an eye-opener to me and one that has been very hurtful. There does not seem to be an explanation for it. It is easier to understand that a white person or a black person can dislike or hate a person of a different colour because people generalize others of colour. But the racism that I have experienced has not come only from members of different racial groups, but most surprising, from members of my own racial group.

I was walking along the shop fronts towards the children's home when I passed two white gentlemen. They did not even wait until I was out of earshot when I overheard them say: "Dis daardie snaakse wit vrou wat saam met die kaffirs woon". (This is the strange white woman that lives with the kaffirs). I also found it strange that even though I would be first in line to be served in the shops, the white assistant would serve everyone (black and coloured) before I was served. If I greeted a white person, they would not greet me. This continued for years before I managed to get some of them to greet me. Even though they refused to greet me, I continued to look at them and greet them in Afrikaans. Of course, my Afrikaans was not as good as it could have been, but by working in the area, it soon came up to scratch. Naturally, when I got angry, my Afrikaans was as good as the next Afrikaner. I remember walking past two white men who said to me "Jy is 'n kaffir boetie" (you are a kaffir brother), to which I replied, "Nee meneer, jy het dit verkeerd. Ek is eintlik 'n kaffir susie". (No, sir, you have it wrong. I am actually a kaffir sister)

One night I received a telephone call from a very distraught sister from the hospital who was being beaten by her boyfriend. She was begging me to come and help her. I told her to phone the police.

"I can't", she said, "he is a policeman".

"Then come to me", I told her. She arrived very distraught with her little son in tow. I calmed her down and advised her to call the police and lay a charge of assault against the man. This was domestic violence, and whether the man is question was a policeman or not was beside the point. The police duly came and took her to the police station to make a statement while I looked after her son. When she came back, I settled her down and soon she and her son were fast asleep. Her name coincidentally was Diana. I could not sleep. I was too upset by what had happened. This town was filled with domestic abuse, alcohol abuse, rape, sodomy and crime and there seemed to be no end to it. When a policeman beats up his common law wife, during a year when the Minister of Safety and Security is making it the Year for Non-Violence against Women and Children, we were in a pretty poor state. I wondered whether she would withdraw the case the next day. On average, a woman is beaten 57 times before she finally goes to court. This was her first time and it would not have surprised me if she withdrew the case the next morning.

The night was very quiet and I was lying in my bed thinking. The streets of Middelburg are very quiet at night, especially after midnight, so it was strange to hear a vehicle going up and down the street. I got up and went to the window and looked out. There was a red 4x4 belonging to the stock theft police, driving slowly past the house. What was it doing riding up and down the street, I wondered? Then I thought that it may have been the boyfriend of the woman who I was protecting. I lay down again. The lights were all off, so the driver of the vehicle could not have seen me. He drove on and did not come back for a long time. I must have drifted off, because I woke up with a jolt. There was a noise outside the window. The window was right on the pavement as there was no front yard. My vehicle was parked right against the pavement. As I jumped up to look out of the window, the red 4x4 drove fast down the road. Strange, I thought, and then I saw the two youngsters from down the road walking home. I turned over and went to sleep.

The next morning the tyres on my vehicle had been slashed. They had not been deflated. They had been slashed with a knife. I phoned 10111, the police number, and asked them to come as my tyres had been slashed and it was malicious damage to property. The policeman in the radio room said that he would send the van around immediately. Half an hour later, I again phoned the radio room. I was told that a van was on its way. An hour later, I phoned the radio room again, and was told again that a van was on its way. Two hours later, I was angry. I phoned the radio room again and asked the policeman if someone was going to be sent or not. He then told me that he had sent Inspector du Plessis three times and that he had refused to attend to the complaint.

I asked him to put me through to his superior, Captain Meiring. When I got through to Captain Meiring, I told him that Inspector du Plessis had been asked to attend to my complaint three times and that he had refused to do so.

"Mrs Lang, the police don't like you. You can't expect them to just come and attend to your complaints", he said.

"Then you had better send me some black policemen because they don't have a problem with me. And furthermore, Captain, the police are civil servants, paid by the tax payer and whether they like me or not, they have to do their job. I certainly hope that you will reprimand that Inspector", I said.

Two black policemen were at my door within three minutes to attend to my complaint. They were courteous, friendly and professional. However, no investigation was done and no one was prosecuted for the crime.

One evening after supper, the children were sitting around the dining room tables doing their homework, while the smaller children were being put to bed by the staff. It was just an ordinary evening, a still and beautiful summer evening. The front and back doors were open although the front door has a security gate on it. The need for a security gate on the front door is to stop drunken friends or family members walking in whenever they want and disrupting our family. There was nothing untoward about the evening. The children were doing their homework, and now and then you could hear one ask another for help with something they did not understand.

All of a sudden, something was thrown into the front door, through the security gate, and the smell was something that could not be described. The children's eyes started burning and they started coughing, they started crying and screaming from the pain in their eyes. The staff came running and they too succumbed to the pain in their eyes and the burning in the chest. I shouted to everyone to leave the house via the back door. It was bedlam as no one could see where they were going. I knew that someone had thrown teargas into the house. It took a good five or six minutes to get everyone out of the house and then to get the hose and start hosing everyone's eyes out. We left all the windows and doors open for a long time before we ventured back inside. We called the police and gave them the "evidence" of what had been thrown into the house. They took it away and said that they would have it analyzed. To date, it has never been analyzed.

Since that incident, we have a next-to-perfect fire drill that will take us all to get out the house within 32 seconds, whether it is fire, teargas or any other outside or inside threat. Our "fire" alarm is the banging of pots, and depending on where the pots are being banged, that is the area where you will leave the house.

What depth of hate and depravity must one have, to go around collecting dog shit to throw at someone? Imagine walking around from one house that has a dog to the next, looking for piles of dog shit and then picking it up and putting it in packets. Imagine how the whites hated what we stood for, what we represented, the true democracy, that they had to collect dog shit, climb onto an open vehicle and drive past us and throw dog shit at our houses? This was done a number of times. By this stage, we did not bother to report it to the police because nothing would have been done about it anyway.

As the months and years dragged by, a few whites slowly started greeting me and serving me in the shops, although they always made sure that they greeted me when there were no other whites to witness their friendliness towards me.

The sale of a child

Patricia, Betty and Sam had settled in well in their new surroundings and were the stars of the township. Everyone was amazed at what these street children had turned out to be. Jackson was now their unofficial teacher, and we had got all their teaching material from the local school, so that we could help the children catch up with their schooling so that the following year they could go to normal government school in an age-appropriate grade. We were still doing HIV awareness workshops, but now with trained HIV Trainers we were letting them get on with the job. We were coordinating and mentoring them. Our hands were full with children now. I had forgotten how much work there was bringing up children. By now, Patricia, Betty and Sam had been joined by Jane and Kelly. With the ongoing HIV training, Home Based Care workshops, drama groups and peer educator groups, I had my hands full.

I asked Nonqaba to join us as a volunteer. Both Nonqaba and Jackson were essentially volunteers, but they were receiving a stipend every month. Poverty was rife and I could not expect them to help me without giving them some money to take home. With no funding coming from the PCRD, I was getting desperate about obtaining money to keep this little family going. I was also not going back to Port Elizabeth very often to run my practice and as a result, the practice and, of course, my income, was suffering badly. I was only just making the payments on my bond and there was no income at all.

I started sending out e-mails to all the people and friends I knew, asking for donations of food and clothing, which helped a great deal, but this still did not cover our costs. We were also embroiled in trying to get milk formula for the HIV mothers for their babies, and our little home was abuzz with activity. There were medical supplies to get for the Home Based Care workers and support had to be given to them as well. I was getting desperate. I wanted to continue doing what I was doing, but without money it was becoming impossible. I thought of all kinds of alternatives, but the only one that I had was to sell my home in Port Elizabeth. I loved my home on the beach. It was the first home that I owned and I loved it. It was mine and I had worked very hard for it. I still had a bond on it, but it was negligible to what I could sell it for. I had a huge decision to make. Give up my home and do this work that had taken such a hold over me, or give up the work, go home and pretend that life was the same as it was before.

But what to do with Sam, Patricia, Betty, Kelly and Jane? There was no alternative home for them. The alternative to me was the streets, and I loved these children now. I approached the Commissioner of Child Welfare and asked whether it would be possible for me to take the children with me to Port Elizabeth. Unfortunately, it was not possible as the children could not be moved from the jurisdiction of the Middelburg district. The children had to stay in Middelburg, so I had to stay in Middelburg. By now, the children saw me as their mother and they were calling me Mama D. How could I abandon them and put them back on the street, but how could I keep them and still keep my home?

While I was still pondering on this dilemma of mine, Nonqaba came to work in the morning and told me that there was a baby girl for sale for R50.00. By now, I knew the abuse of children was rife in Middelburg, and I thought that this would be a good chance to catch someone selling a child. I would set a trap and at least one person could be arrested and punished for the crime.

That afternoon, Nonqaba and I went to the house of the woman who was selling the little girl. It was in one of the houses that the government had built - a two room house that had one bedroom and a toilet with a kitchen that served as a lounge. It was no more than 20 square metres. There were about five small children playing in the dusty yard, all fairly adequately dressed for the cold weather and all eating a piece of bread.

Inside the house, in the kitchen was an open primus stove. Sitting naked on a hand towel inches away from the primus stove was a little girl. She was so thin that her entire skeleton was visible through her almost translucent skin. She looked no more than 8 months old. Her skin was parched and she looked like one of the children you see in National Geographic Magazine from Biafra or in refugee camps in the Sudan. I was horrified. If she had moved her hand three inches forward, it would have been in the open flame.

"Is this the child you want to sell?", I asked.

The woman standing at the door replied in the affirmative.

"Why do you want to sell her?", I asked.

"Because she is a foster child and I have not received a foster grant for her for three months so I don't want her", she said.

"Why does she look like this?", I asked.

"Because I am not going to use my money to feed her", she answered.

"Look, I will buy her from you but I will take her now. She looks like she is going to die so if she is still alive tomorrow at twelve o'clock, you can come to my house and get the R50.00. I am not going to buy a baby that dies. Is that OK?" I asked.

"Sure", she replied.

I picked up that little scrap of humanity and gave her to Nonqaba. We climbed into the 4x4 and drove home.

"Why did you not pay her", Nonqaba asked.

"I have my plan", I said.

I drove straight to the hospital with the baby. Sister Diana Jagers was on duty. She became a close friend after she came to me for protection when her policeman boyfriend beat her. She told me that the baby was dying. She was dehydrated, malnourished and there was very little chance of her living.

"Why don't you leave her here", she said.

"No, I will take her home and nurse her there", I said.

When we got home, I bathed the baby, called Father John to baptize her "Mary", and fed her with drops of water into her mouth. She could not even swallow so it was a very slow process of getting liquids into her mouth. I phoned the police and told them to come to my house at noon the next day because someone was selling a baby for R50.00. I also phoned the social worker and told them to come to my house because a baby was going to be sold for R50.00. I thought by doing this, the woman would be prosecuted for child neglect and for selling a child.

The next day, the police, social worker and the woman arrived. After I told the police and social worker the story, they just shrugged their shoulders and told me that if I wanted the child then I should pay the money. I was flabbergasted.

"Are you serious", I asked.

"Yes", they said, absolutely serious.

I paid. They all left. This is the way things get done in Africa. If I did not pay for Mary, she would have been taken away and she would have had no chance of survival. It took many, many weeks before Mary started getting better. She was so dehydrated that she did not urinate for seven days. Slowly, we got her to swallow, drink water, then milk and then we put her on baby porridge. She weighed 5.7 kg. She was three years old. Mary could not stand and her legs were bent inwards in a cross legged position.

Between Jackson and Nonqaba, we did our research into Mary's past. How did she land up in a foster home where the foster mother failed to feed her because her foster grant had not come through yet? Who was Mary's mother and why had she been removed from her mother? Which social worker had removed Mary from the mother? And if Mary had been placed in foster care, then no services had been rendered by the social worker, or else the social worker would have known that Mary was in an abusive situation. All these questions we wanted to know.

What we did find out about Mary was that she really was 3 years old. Her mother was a prostitute, and when the mother was plying her trade Mary would be locked up in a small cupboard for hours at a time (the reason for her bent legs). The social workers were from the Department of Social Development. They had never followed up or rendered any service to the new foster mother or to Mary. The foster mother was not unemployed, but worked for the municipality, earning a good wage.

It took three months for Mary to laugh and four months for Mary to crawl and another three months for Mary to walk. Mary started talking seven months later. Although Mary has caught up with her peers, her poor start in life has left its mark on her. She is a dwarf. In all other areas of her life, she is very advanced and intelligent. She thinks she is the senior staff member, because when I walk into the Children's Home she is the first to come and tell me if she thinks there is anything wrong in the home.

I remember one time when she took me by the hand and said: "Look here, Mama D, the staff are not doing their work properly", while moving her index finger along the fridge, bringing it up proudly with some dust.

Because Mary is small for her age, the other children tend to baby her, and she gets very frustrated with them. She does however, have quite a mouth on her so she needs no protection.

Betty and Patricia were telling me one day about the Restaurant. This is the rubbish dump where the street children go to try to find something to eat. For some reason that even today I don't understand, I asked them to take me to the Restaurant. We went in the 4x4 and what I saw there was unbelievably sad. There were children living in old broken cars, making fires to keep themselves warm, and scratching through rubbish looking for something to eat. Oh, God, what more is going on in this place, I thought. The children saw me and tried to hide. Patricia and Betty called them and told them I would not hurt them and they could come and talk to me. There were about 20 children there between the ages of 3 and 16, all living alone and without any adults. Most of them were sniffing glue from empty milk cartons. They told me that it kept them from getting cold and hungry.

All of a sudden I heard a baby crying from inside one of the old cars.

"Is that a baby?", I asked the others.

One of the older boys ran to the car and brought back a screaming baby in his arms. It was covered in a dirty towel and had the biggest mop of unruly back hair I had ever seen. It could not have been more than six months old.

"Where is this baby's mother?", I asked.

Nobody knew.

"Where does the baby come from?", I asked.

"He was crawling along the road here from the brickworks long ago and we have been looking after him", they said.

"Can I take him and look after him?", I asked.

With that, they passed the bundle into my arms.

"Does he have a name?"

"We call him Donovan", they said.

And with that, I had another child. We were now a family of seven. Little did I know that when I got home, little squint-eyed Shaun was waiting for me, making our family eight. And in our little house, we were becoming a little pressed for space. I called a carpenter in and between the two of us, we put up bunk beds, four up on two sides of the one bedroom, giving us an extra eight beds. The big children on the top and the little ones at the bottom.

My dilemma about the funding of this new family of mine was becoming more and more stressful, as I now had to borrow on my bond to keep us in food and the necessities of life. I was spending so little time in Port Elizabeth that my practice was now non-existent. I had to make the decision. It was a heart-breaking decision to make. Not only was I leaving the one home that I had ever owned, but I was leaving the sea, I was leaving my memorial garden for Patience, I was leaving my family and I was leaving my sanctuary.

I tried to find foster parents for the children, but in the poverty stricken area, foster parents did it for the money and not for the interests of the children. I asked the welfare if they would consider adoption outside of Middelburg and they would not. I again asked the Commissioner of Child Welfare if he would allow me to take the children to Port Elizabeth, and he said it was against the law. I had two choices, and neither of them was good. I could put the children back on the street, or I could sell my home and use the proceeds to keep us going for a year or so. The decision gave me sleepless nights. I spoke to my friends and family. They were dead against me selling my home, and all told me that the Department of Social Development was the one to care for the children and it was not my business to do so. While I agreed with them, the reality was that the Department of Social Development did nothing for the children. And in fact, the more I had to do with the Department of Social Development, the more I realized that they were further violating the children's rights by their poor and often non-service delivery as far as the children were concerned. I felt sick about the decision I had to take.

Evelyn, Pretty and Louis

It was the 26 June 2003 and it had been raining all night. There was a leak in the bedroom. Water was still pouring out over the gutters. The gutters needed to be cleaned out. The pine trees surrounding the property had done their work and the gutters were clogged. There was only one thing for it. We had to get them cleaned out. Without a ladder, things were going to be a little difficult. Jackson is a skinny fellow, so I was a little weary of him holding me while I climbed onto the wall of the veranda and then up onto the roof, but the process was not so difficult. He handed me a broom and the gutters got a good cleaning. I walked over the zinc roof and found that a roof nail had lifted, leaving quite a hole where it was leaking into the bedroom.

"Right, Jackson", I shouted, "You take some money out my purse and go to Build-It and buy some roof sealer and some of that material stuff that you put on the roof. I will wait here".

I sat down on the roof and watched him walk up the road. Just then I saw a young woman walk up the road in the opposite direction towards the house. She had a small baby on her back. Two small children were walking behind her. They were about 2 and 3 years old. She came up to the house and knocked. Nonqaba answered the door. I could hear them talking inside.

A little while later, Nonqaba came outside and shouted up at me, "This woman has no food for these children and she does not want them".

"Tell her to wait, I am fixing the roof first. Feed the children, Nonqaba".

Jackson came down the road with the roofing material and climbed up onto the roof with me.

"We got problems down there, Jackson", I said. "Two more kids. What we going to do?"

"Take them", he said.

I read the directions on the roof paint, but saw that we needed a pair of scissors. Down Jackson went again to get a pair of scissors to cut the fibre glass. We patched the roof and then it was down to the problem in the house. The woman's name was Regina Jantjies. She looked tired and beaten and had a black eye. She told me that she was bringing these two children to me to look after because she had no food to feed them and she already had one child that she was breastfeeding. The boy was five years old and the girl was three, although they both looked much younger than their ages. Their names were Louis and Pretty.

The next day, we got a Form 4 signed at the police station, delivered one copy to the Clerk of the Court for the Commissioner of Child Welfare and delivered another to the Department of Social Development. The children settled down quickly and soon started to pick up weight. They were no problem, except that both children wet their beds. Soon they were part of the family. Every seven days, we notified the Clerk of the Court that a Form 5 had not been issued and that a Children's Court enquiry had not been held. We heard nothing from either the Children's Court or the Social Workers.

On 14th August, Patrick Diamond arrived, claiming that he was the father of the children, and that he had been sent by Johan Pienaar of the Department of Social Development to collect them. We refused to allow him to take the children as the matter had not been attended to by the Children's Court. We told him to go back to Johan Pienaar for a court order to remove the children from our care.

Two days later, the mother, Regina, arrived and told us that she and her elder daughter, Evelyn (ten years of age), had been beaten badly by the father and we were under no circumstances to give Louis and Pretty to Patrick Diamond. I immediately sent a letter to Social Development with a copies to Mrs Ferreira, the State Prosecutor and the police to look into the abuse of the child, Evelyn. Nothing was done.

On 12 November I received an anonymous telephone call to tell me that Evelyn had been raped and that I could check out the validity of the story by contacting the hospital. I was given the hospital admission number. I contacted the hospital and was told that she had been admitted with stomach ache and discharged after two days.

I contacted Pumza Mobo, the social worker, and notified her that the child had been raped. Two days later, I again asked Pumza Mobo, to investigate the situation of Evelyn.

Still nothing happened. On 20 November, I telephoned Mrs Ferreira and told her about the situation. "Mrs Lang, we will not jump when you tell us to jump", she said.

And that was the end of the conversation and her concern for the child. I was by now so concerned about Louis and Pretty's sister that I asked Fikile to come with me to visit Evelyn's home. By now, I had three helpers, Jackson, Nonqaba and Fikile. When we got there, we asked Patrick Diamond, Evelyn's father, if it was true that Evelyn had been raped.

"Yes, but she went to hospital and the damage was not great. In any case, the rapist has paid me so the case is closed", he said.

Both Patrick and Regina were as drunk as lords. Evelyn looked traumatized and neglected. Early the next morning, I went back to Evelyn's home. I was hoping to catch the parents a little sober. I spoke to Patrick and convinced him that Evelyn would be better off staying with her brother and sister. I don't know how I managed to do it, but I did, and I put little Evelyn in my 4x4 and drove her home.

One of the saddest things about neglected and abused children in the township is the terrible names that the parents, care givers and community give them. When I asked Evelyn what her name was, she told me that her name was Papsak. A "papsak" in Middelburg is the plastic bag that contains wine that is sold cheaply by the liquor outlets. I asked her what she would like to be called and she gave herself the name of Evelyn. She told me that her mother and father called her Ndutsu. "Ndutsu" means arsehole.

Leaving her in the capable care of Nonqaba, I went off to the police to report the case. I got a Form 4 signed by the police, delivered it to the Clerk of the Court and the Department of Social Development, and faxed it to Mrs Ferreira. That afternoon, I got an appointment for her with Dr Leeuwner, and he said that rape or vaginal abuse had taken place and he gave us medicine. However, he said that he did not want to get involved in any rape case.

I called Evelyn's teacher in and she had a chat to Evelyn. Evelyn told her about the rape. During the week of 25 November, Detective Lesley, Detective Pyper and one other male police officer tried to take a statement from Evelyn. She started telling them and then would not say another word. I requested a female detective to take the statement. On the 26 November, I telephoned Mr Makasi, Mrs Ferreira's superior, and notified him of the situation. On 2 December I again requested a female officer to take a statement from Evelyn. On 3 December Mr Makasi phoned me to tell me that there was no evidence of rape. On 4 December, Pumza Mobo, the social worker in Middelburg, phoned me and told me that Evelyn had not been raped.

Eventually, after a long struggle, Pumza Mobo took the case of Louis and Pretty to court and placed them in the care of Amore, one of my volunteers who was by now living with us, on 24 December 2003. This was done because I was not allowed by law to care for more than six children, even though I was still caring for all of them. It was merely a formality. The parents had been found to be incapable of caring for the children. However, the case of their sister, Evelyn, was still outstanding. The parents had been found to be unfit to care for Louis and Pretty, but not to be unfit to care for Evelyn.

On 8 January 2004 I went to the offices of the Department of Social Development to request them to put Evelyn into our care. They promised to do so. From the 19th January through to 13 December 2005, I requested again and again for Evelyn to be put into the Children' Home. She remained an "illegal" child for the entire time, until I went directly to a stand-in Commissioner of Child Welfare and put my case to him, She was then placed legally in the Children's Home. During her "illegal" status, I re-signed a Form 4 so that she could have her teeth out under a general anaesthetic.

Despite having Evelyn's evidence, the teacher's evidence, the father's admission to the rape and Fikile and my witness to that admission, and despite having opened a docket at the police, the prosecutor refused to prosecute for lack of evidence.

In March 2004 I found out that the parents had received a back pay in child support grant of R6000,00 for Louis and Pretty from the Department of Social Development. The grant had already been spent. The father arrived at the Children's Home under the influence of alcohol and told us that Pumza Mobo of the Department of Social Development had sent them to collect Pretty and Louis. As no documentation accompanied the parents, I refused to hand over the children. I contacted Pumza Mobo and asked her to investigate the circumstances, and if the children were to be returned, I insisted that an integration back into the family should be done in such a way that unnecessary stress was not placed on the children. I recommended that the parents visit the children regularly during visiting hours, and that they should arrive sober. I also requested her to give the parents the necessary counselling regarding alcohol abuse. I told her that the parents had only visited the children once in 7 months.

In the meantime, Regina, the mother, came to tell us not to let the father take the children under any circumstances because she was worried what he would do to them. I also told Pumza Mobo about the mother's visit.

As arranged with Pumza Mobo, the parents collected Louis and Pretty for the weekend. They failed to bring the children back on the Sunday afternoon. I got the police to fetch them the next day. The children were crying, dirty and hungry and the parents were drunk. When I told Pumza Mobo about the situation, she agreed that the parents would not be taking the children until they had received counselling from her.

Weeks went by and we heard nothing from the social workers or the parents of Louis and Pretty. We assumed that nothing was going to happen about the children. The parents did not visit the children nor did the social worker contact us regarding the re-unification of the children with the parents. Life went on as normal.

We had been extremely fortunate in that my friends had started assisting me by contributing clothing for the children, beds and cots starting arriving. We received donations of nappies, pots and pans, cutlery and bedding. But food was always a problem. We were always in need of food. I was borrowing heavily on my bond and my overdraft by this stage, as my savings were completely dried up. However, the joy of working with the children completely overshadowed my worry about my finances. I looked to the abundance of the universe for my income. However, things were not looking good on the financial side of things. It was only when I went to bed that I would worry and fret about the money, but when I was awake and busy during the day and much of the evening, I did not have the time to worry about the money. There was always so much to do with the children, with the Home Based Care Workers, with the community and with our volunteer work.

We were still doing our hospital cleaning and, by now, we were so much part of the hospital life that we knew who was alone and dying. We took it in turns to be with the dying patients so that no one died alone. And of course, there were Mary and Sam, who needed constant care. Mary spent most of her time on Nonqaba's back and Sam needed constant care. Either Nonqaba or Jackson would spend the night with me to help me take care of the children. We were becoming such a large family, and there were so many children to care for, that one person could not do it alone. It was bottles and sterilizing, it was changing of nappies, it was teaching older children to read and write, it was entertaining children and rocking others to sleep. It was cooking and cleaning. All washing was being done by hand as we had no washing machine. It was a round the clock nursery. But always, there was laughter, there was singing and there was joy.

We were bursting out at the seams. The house was too small for us. We would have to convert the dining room into another bedroom. With some wood and a door, we put up a partition between the lounge and the dining room and we had another bedroom. The lounge now became the dining room as well as the general play area. There were twelve children and three adults in a very small house. And the children kept coming. One morning Nonqaba came in with a ragamuffin in tow. She was a dirty but feisty little girl of about two years of age.

"And this, Nonquaba?", I asked, pointing to the child.

"She has been living on the streets for ages, so I found her mother and asked her what she thought she was doing leaving her child to wander the streets, and she said she did not want her and her boyfriend shouted that the child must voetsek (go away) and die, so I brought her to you", she said.

"Oh, right", I said, thinking that one more would make no difference and, in any event, by now I could not turn a child away.

Before I could even go to the phone to call the social worker I heard Nonqaba say, "I will fetch her brother this afternoon".

For some reason that is still unfathomable to me, the social worker had no problem with placing those two children, six-year old Michael and his three-year old sister, Zimkita, with us. With Zimkita's arrival, all hell broke loose. As gentle and as quiet as Michael was, Zimkita was hell on wheels. She was into everything. She touched everything, wanted to taste everything, fiddled with everything and got on everyone's nerves. If Zimkita was not within your field of vision, you were sure that she was up to something she should not have been doing. She would be tucking into the dry porridge, or she would be unwinding the toilet paper: she would have the hosepipe on in the middle of winter and be saturated or she would be scaling the fence. She was totally undisciplined. She would not listen and would want to have the last say on everything. She interfered in the other children's games, teased them unmercifully, pulled their hair, and if she did not get what she wanted, she would just take it anyway. Within a short space of time, we were all running around Madam Zimkita. It was time for family conference. What to do about Zimkita!

We tried positive reinforcement, we tried ignoring her, we tried one-on-ne attention, we tried it all, but Zimkita is Zimkita and even today, after her second year of school, she is still much the same. She has the last word on everything, still interferes in everybody's business, and tries to tell everyone what to do. She is the leader of the pack in her age group and what she says goes. Even her teachers throw up their arms in despair of her behaviour. We all know Zimkita now as the child with the wild spirit, and we also know that her bossy behaviour is tempered by a very kind heart. She is the first to go running when someone is hurt or crying, and she is the first to confront any bully at school. She is very protective over her "family". She has a fiercely independent spirit and for that I admire her. I just wish she would be quiet in church! Michael, on the other hand, is the quiet child, although with a sister like Zimkita he does not manage to get a word in edgeways. He has grown into a beautiful-looking boy with dimples when he smiles. He is a friend to all the children in the home and is an exceptionally good gumboot dancer with a flair for drama. Michael has a passion for my mother. He calls her magogo, meaning grandmother. They are great friends and when my mom comes to visit, Michael is always on her lap.

Dancing and singing were becoming more and more part of our daily routine, and the Township Prophets would now come and teach our children the art of dancing and performing. We would now go with them when they were performing, and the little ones would go on stage as well for their five minutes of fame. It was the 10 September 2004, and I was with some of the children in Noupoort doing a gumboot dance show for the Drug Addicts Centre, when I was phoned by Pumza Mobo. She told me that she was in possession of a court order, and that I was to bring Louis and Pretty to her office immediately for return to their parents. I was in a state of shock. We had not been to court. How could she be in possession of a court order? As soon as the performance was over, I drove back to Middelburg and collected Louis and Pretty from home and went to Pumza Mobo's office. She handed me the Court Order and told me to leave the children in her office.

I looked at the court order. It was dated 2 June 2004. What game had she been playing with me? What game had she been playing with the lives of Louis and Pretty?

"This court order is dated 2 June 2004", I said.

"I know. Now leave the children here and go", she said.

Pretty was holding my hand and Louis had hold of my trousers. I looked down at them. They did not know what was going on.

"But Pumza, these children don't know what is going on. They have not been informed or made ready to go back to their parents", I said.

"You have known long enough that they were going back. Now please leave them and go home", she said sternly.

There were two chairs against the wall in her office. I took the children and put them on a chair each. They looked up at me.

"I have to leave you here, my darlings. Your mommy and daddy are coming to fetch you", I said, trying to keep my tears back while my heart was thundering in my chest.

I wanted to take the children and drive away. I wanted to grab Pumza Mobo by the throat and shake her and ask her if she knew what the hell she was doing? If she was removing Louis and Pretty, then why leave Evelyn with me? Why had there been no communication with us for months? Why had the parents never visited the children from the time they had taken them home for the weekend and had not returned them and we had found them drunk? Why had no family services been rendered? Pretty started to cry and then Louis followed suit.

"Don't cry. Please don't cry. Be brave. You are going to see your mommy and daddy and you will have a nice time with your little brother. And I will come and visit you", I said. "And you can ask Mommy and Daddy to bring you to us to visit. OK?", I said, but my voice was wobbly.

If I did not leave soon, I too would be crying in front of the children.

"You can leave now please", said Pumza.

I turned around and without looking back, I left her office, walked down the passage and out of the building, hearing the cries of the children. I got into my 4x4 and drove home in complete shock. I could not believe what had just happened. Back home it was like another two deaths. Gone without a goodbye. Gone without any preparation. Gone without the rights of the child being taken into account. Just gone. They come, we love them and then the power of the social worker can just wipe it all away. I have driven past Louis and Pretty's house twice since. I can't go again.

They are neglected, dirty and thin. Louis should have started school last year. He did not. Pretty should have started school this year. She did not. If the social workers were concerned, they would know that the children are not even going to school, despite the fact that the parents are receiving state grants for those children. Pumza Mobo has not done any follow up on the children that she threw away that day in September in 2004.

Mala Fide

The decision to sell my house to keep the children was ultimately taken out of my hands by the arrival of the Department of Social Development. Without any advance warning, Mrs Ferreira, Head of Social Development in Cradock, and Mr Johan Pienaar, Chief Social Worker in Middelburg, arrived at our little home. I knew there was going to be trouble by their demeanour.

I introduced myself and when Mrs Ferreira said "I know who you are", I thought, "Here comes big shit".

"Who are you then?", I asked.

"I am Mrs Iza Ferreira, Deputy Director of the Department of Social Development of the Cradock Office and this is Mr Johan Pienaar, Chief Social Worker here in Middelburg. We have come to tell you that you may not have these children. This is illegal".

"Are you telling me that you are here to take them away from me? I asked.

"Yes", she said.

"But you can't do that! Where are you going to take them?"

"Back to where they came from", she said.

"But they came from the street!", I almost shouted.

"Well, you are not allowed to have them. It is against the law", she said in a frosty voice, her eyes as cold as ice.

Johan Pienaar just stood there, breathing heavily, his huge body taking up most of the wall space between the filing cabinet and the doorway. I was aghast, petrified, horrified, and terrified for the children and for me. I loved the children and now she was coming here to take them back to... where, for God's sake? Was this a human being I was dealing with? I can't antagonize her, I thought. If I am going to save these children, I had better lick her arse. I had better do whatever it is I need to do to save these children. She has their lives in her hands and I had better toe the line. I will whine and plead. I will do anything to save these children.

"Please Mrs Ferreira, I love these children. Tell me what I can do to keep them", I pleaded.

Silence. Deathly silence. I tried again.

"Please Mrs Ferreira, help me. I love these children. What can I do to keep them?".

"Well... well, you can foster them if you like, but you can only foster five. So choose five", she said.

Choose five? Choose five? How the hell do you choose five children when you love eight? My mind went through each one of the children, one by one, and I could not choose just five of them.

"Please, Mrs Ferrera, please can you make an exception?"

"No, choose five. What you have done is illegal. You can't just go on to the street and just take children. You can go to jail for what you have done", she said.

Mr Pienaar just stood there, leaning against the wall, and nodding his agreement with everything this woman had to say. I tried again. I was desperate.

"Please sit down Mrs Ferreira, and let us talk about a solution to this", I pleaded. I pulled out a chair for her and she sat down. I pulled out another for Johan Pienaar and he sat down, his huge stomach making it impossible for him to close his legs. He seemed to be either nodding off to sleep, or not be part of the proceedings. I tried again.

"Mrs Ferreira, would it not be possible for me to foster some of the children, and for Amore to foster the others?" I asked.

"Yes", she said, "that's possible". My heart leaped with joy. We could keep the children. There would be no problem.

"Oh, thank you, thank you, Mrs Ferreira. Thank you so much", I bubbled. "But you can't keep them together in this house", she said with a smirk.

"Why not?", I asked.

"Because you must give every child five square metres sleeping space", she said.

My mind raced. How could I do that? I would have to buy another house. Would she give me some time to find another house? Would she take the children away from me now? Would she let me keep the children? I begged and pleaded to keep the children. I bargained and negotiated. I cajoled, sweet-talked and persuaded. Eventually, she said that I could foster half the children and Amore could foster the other half, but that I would have to split the children up into two different houses because the children would be fostered by two different people. It did not matter to her that I would be still taking care of them, that I would be paying for them and maintaining them. As far as she was concerned, the law was the law, and I was not allowed to look after the children. What I had done was against the law, and I could be arrested for taking the children off the street. She was doing me a huge favour by allowing me to foster the children. Johan Pienaar would bring the necessary papers the next day so that the legality of the children could be sorted out.

The next day I put my home in Port Elizabeth on the market. I also e-mailed all my friends and asked them to e-mail everyone they knew for assistance with funds, so that I could purchase and furnish a home big enough to keep all the children together. Donations from friends and friends of friends started coming in. Boxes of clothes and linen started arriving. Second-hand kitchen utensils, old towels, babies-clothes, children's books and toys started arriving every day. We were overjoyed by the donations. I still had no idea that what I was doing was against the law. All I was concerned about was taking in the children that were being neglected, abandoned, orphaned or abused and caring for them. They were on the street, no one was looking after them, so I was doing it. What was wrong with that? Days went by, and then weeks went by, without Johan Pienaar coming anywhere near us with the foster care papers.

In the meantime, more and more children were arriving. Some children were brought in by adults who had found the children wandering around and had heard that I looked after abandoned children. Some children came in on their own, and said they did not want to live on the street anymore. We were bulging at the seams, and we needed more space and we needed more staff. I could not get anyone to volunteer without some sort of wage. With such poverty in the area, it was understandable that people would work only for money. However, I could not pay good salaries, and in the beginning, the volunteers were given a stipend in lieu of a wage. At least it was something to take home and kept those families in food. After Jackson and Nonqaba, Fikile and Niel joined me. They had been on the AIDS awareness workshops and had also gone on to become HIV Trainers and Home Based Care Workers.

I kept on phoning Johan at the Department of Social Development about the foster parent papers for the children. He would then ask us to find out information about the children, how old they were, who the parents were, where did they come from, and where were their birth certificates. We were trying our best to get this information for him, but at the time we did not realize that this was his job and not ours. Without this information, he could not process the foster parent papers. Of course, he now knew that we had more children than we were now allowed to foster, so he was putting pressure on us to put them back on the street. Eventually, we were able to give him as much information as we could about the first eight children, and those children were put into the names of Amore and myself. We were now officially their foster others. The other children were now at risk of being put back onto the street.

My home was sold, and we had some money to live on after I had paid off the bond that I had borrowed against to keep us going. I had hired a large house across the road from the one we were in and it had ample space for all the children, even at five square meters per child. Still, we had to watch every penny. The children were often ill and medications were costly. We had to pay for electricity, rent, telephone, internet, the wages (no matter how small they still had to be paid), the food, the clothing and shoes, the school fees, the school clothes, the school books - the list was never ending. And of course, we were still doing our home based care work, our drama performances and our AIDS awareness workshops, all of which were eating holes into the bit of money that I had.

The sale of my beautiful home on the beach did not happen without a lot of sadness for me. It was the first home that I had ever owned and I had always thought that I would never leave there. I had spent so many happy hours and days and years there and, of course, my memory garden of Patience was there as well. I could sit out on the deck and watch the waves roll on to the beach. I would watch the most beautiful sunsets and feel at peace with the world. It was my sacred space, the place that I called home, the place that made my spirit soar and my creativity run free. Everything that was in my home I brought back to Middelburg for the children to use in the big house. But my beautiful garden, my view, my home were gone forever. I was deeply, deeply sad, but had to think of the lives of the children that I was saving in place of the home I was giving up.

By now, I had realized that I would have to do things legally. I could not carry on doing things the way that I was. Everything I was doing was brand new to me. I had never done anything like this in my life. I had never opened a children's home. I had never registered a trust, or a non-profit organization, or run a children's home. I was doing things for the first time and I was learning as I was going.

I approached some really good male friends whom I knew and asked them if they would be trustees in a non-profit organization to care for children. They agreed. We registered a trust and registered as a non-profit organization. Now we were a legal entity. I could now write funding proposals and send them out. Writing a funding proposal was a mission in itself. I had never done anything like it before, and it took me days and days on the computer looking at other funding proposals and trying to work out budgets and forecasts. I then sent out funding proposals to every major business in Port Elizabeth, as well as sending them via e-mail to my friends and asking them to forward the proposal to anyone they knew who may be able to help us.

I also applied to be registered as a Children's Home. The process was made extremely difficult by Mrs Ferreira. She stalled every step of the process. She blocked and hedged and opposed every part of the procedure. What could have taken two to three weeks took months to achieve. We had to get the Environmental Health Officer to evaluate the homes to see whether they could be used as a Children's Home and as a Place of Safety. There were a few odds and ends that we had to do to come up to scratch, which we did. We also had to put a hand basin in the kitchen, so that the kitchen staff could wash their hands in a hand basin, and not at the sink. There were a number of items that had to be repaired. Eventually all that was put right, and the Environmental Officer gave the go-ahead to care for twenty-six children in the Children's Home. This certificate was faxed to Mrs Ferreira, but she put every obstruction she could in our way. She never received the fax, then she lost the fax, then someone mislaid the fax and she continued to hedge. The Social Workers came to do a report on the Children's Home and that too was also submitted to her, but still she hedged. I eventually had no alternative but to appeal to the Director of Social Development for a Children's Home certificate. After almost nine months, the Children's Home Certificate was supplied.

We received a telephone call one day from a lady who worked for Delphi Components. She said that a group of them were coming up to Middelburg with a truck and trailer to bring us cots and mattresses, linen, blankets and clothing. They were going to arrive on the Saturday. We were so excited. They arrived as promised with the jewels of a lifetime. Not only did they bring all they had promised, but they gave us fifty thousand rand to buy the house. What a celebration we had that weekend.

Having a Children's Home Certificate, a registered trust and a registered Non-Profit Organization did nothing to help us keep the children. The Department of Social Development would not put the children into the name of the children's home. They would not cooperate with us at all. We would go to the social worker with a child who was abandoned, abused, neglected or orphaned, and the social worker would tell us that they would ask Mrs Ferreira what to do. We would go back and ask the social worker again and they would tell us that Mrs Ferreira had not got back to them. This would happen time and time again.

By this stage, I was starting to realize that if I did not start learning the Child Care Act and the Constitution, not only the children would be in trouble, but I would be as well. I went to see the attorney I had chosen to represent us in Middelburg, Andre van Lingen, who kindly gave me a copy of both the Child Care Act and the Constitution. I got to work. I sat up until all hours of the night studying the Act. If the Department of Social Development was not going to help me with the children, then I was going to do it myself. Since the social workers were not helping me put the children into the Children's Home through the Children's Court, I needed to do something about it on my own.

When a child is removed from an abusive parent, a social worker, police officer or an officer of the court must sign a Form 4, get the parent to sign acknowledgement of the Form 4, and then Form 4 must be given to the Commissioner of Child Welfare as soon as possible thereafter. A copy must also be given to the social worker, so that she or he can investigate the circumstances of the case and present it to the Commissioner of Child Welfare. This must be done within forty-eight hours of the removal of the child and the signing of the Form 4. Once the Commissioner of Child Welfare has heard the case, he or she will place the child in temporary care on a Form 5 for a maximum period of eight weeks. During this time, the Social Worker is to investigate the case thoroughly and present a report to the Children's Court placing the child either in Foster Care, a Children's Home, for adoption, or replacing the child back with the parent if the parent has been found fit to care for the child.

The situation I found myself in was that an abused child would be brought to me and I would notify the social worker. The social worker would not sign the Form 4 because he or she would wait for Mrs Ferreira to give consent. Without the Form 4, the child would then be "illegally" in my care. Mrs Ferreira would not give consent even though, in many cases, the police had brought the child to me and the parent had been charged with abuse and arrested.

In this manner, Mrs Ferreira could say that I had the child "illegally" in my care, even though it was through her instructions or lack of diligence that the Form 4 was not signed. In addition to this, even if a Form 4 was signed by a police officer and I had delivered the Form 4 to the Commissioner of Child Welfare as well as to the Department of Social Development, the social worker would not write the report, so the Form 4 would lapse. The law also states that should a Form 5 not be given within seven days, the person in whose care the child has been placed is to notify the Clerk of the Court in writing.

This I would do every seven days, over and over again, and still nothing would be done. Again, I was caring for a child "illegally".

There were also cases where a child was put into the Children's Home on a Form 5 but only after I had to fight for the child's rights. We would go to Children's Court, the social worker would present her recommendation to the Commissioner of Child Welfare that the child be returned to his or her parents, and I would have to tell the Commissioner that the child's parents were still under investigation for child abuse and that, according to the Criminal Procedures Act, the child could not be placed back with the parent. The social worker was only intent on removing the child from our care, unconcerned about the interests of the child.

These situations happened so many times that I wrote to the Member of the Executive Council of the Department of Social Development and asked for an independent investigation into the poor service delivery of the department with regard to children in the Middelburg area. I received no response, so I wrote again asking for an investigation into their service delivery. When I got no response again, I wrote to the Public Protector and asked for an independent investigation into the poor service delivery of the Department of Social Development with regard to children in the Middelburg area, citing examples of cases where children's rights were being further violated by non-service delivery by the department, sending a copy to the Member of the Executive Council (MEC).

Saving Mandela's Children

I was unwittingly making myself an enemy of the Department of Social Development while I was trying to protect the children's rights.

Tide turns against us

On the 25 August 2004 at 10h30 in the morning, I received a telephone call from Mrs Ferreira's office to tell me that an investigation team would be visiting me from the provincial office at 11h00. This was two weeks after Friday, 13th horrid meeting. It meant that the MEC's office was responding to my letter requesting an investigation into the non-service delivery for children in the area.

However, I by now knew how these people operated. There would never be reconciliation or a working together for the good of the child. This would be a case of "Let's see what we can find wrong with the Children's Home, and that way we will look as though we are doing our work". I had already experienced this kind of thing in the Magistrates Court when the Police and the Department of Social Development had their meeting with me. I was not feeling very confident.

For the thousandth time, my heart was beating wildly in my chest. I did not know from where or how the next attack would be. Anything was possible with the Department of Social Development. Would they come and remove the children and put them back in the street as they had threatened to do once before? Would they be coming to arrest me for having more than my quota of children, thereby contravening the Child Care Act, as they had threatened?

There had to be something sinister if I was only being given a half hour notice and the team was coming from more than 500 km away. I had spoken to the Director

224

Makasi on the telephone the day before, and he had not mentioned anything. So why the sudden investigation? If these people were up front, surely he could have mentioned it, since he was also part of the investigation team. What was I dealing with here? The FBI? The Secret Service? The old regime and their security police? This did not bode well for me.

I called my lawyer, Andre Van der Lingen, and told him what was happening. He told me to calm down and to call him when they arrived. It seemed a very short time before there were three vehicles pulled up outside my door and people were climbing out of them. I went outside where they introduced themselves to me as The Investigation Team.

"What are you investigating?", I asked. "That is not for us to reveal to you", I was told.

I called the lawyer on my mobile and he arrived within minutes. He asked them who the leader of the team was. He was told it was the Director of Social Development, Mr Maxegcwana.

"Well, where is he?", Andre asked.

"He is at the Magistrates Court, discussing this investigation", replied one of the team members, Mrs Matthews.

Andre called me aside. "Look", he said, "These people cannot, by law, institute an investigation into you or your project without first notifying you in writing, giving you fourteen days notice. Do you want me to use my legal status to get them to leave?"

I was so confused, anxious and shocked by what was happening, I did not know what to answer.

Andre continued, "Do you have anything to hide?", he asked.

"No", I answered.

"Well, then I think you should let them go ahead and investigate all they want. I am going to the Magistrates Court to see what is going on there. Do you want to come with me, or do you want to stay here and watch what they are doing?", he asked.

"I want to come with you", I said.

I invited all the team into the house and got Jackson to make them all a cup of tea. The atmosphere was tense and hostile. There was not a friendly face among them. There were no smiles. I knew that they were there with some prior agenda that I was not aware of. Nothing was making sense. I felt like I had woken up in a nightmare where everyone was speaking a foreign language, and that there was danger around, but I was left on the outside and was desperately trying to understand the language that was being spoken. I told them that I would be back as soon as possible as I was going to the Magistrate's Court to find out what was going on.

"But we don't have time for all of this", said Mrs Matthews. "We have a lot to do and we have an investigation to complete by tomorrow afternoon. After all, you called for this investigation", she said with a good measure of antagonism.

"Mrs Matthews", I said, hearing my voice shake with emotion, "if this was the investigation I had asked for, it is hardly independent since all of you are from the department that needs to be investigated. I am not the one you should be investigating. You should be investigating the poor service delivery of your own offices in this area".

I had done it again. My mouth had made it worse for me and the situation. They all started talking to me at once and when Andre, who was standing just outside the door, heard all the commotion, he came rushing into the house and got me by the arm and almost dragged me out and into the vehicle. Before I knew it we were in the Magistrate's office.

The Magistrate was behind his desk and sitting in front of him were two gentlemen. One was Mr Maxegcwana, a large imposing man with small beady eyes and the other was Mr Mjamba, a middle aged man with a beard, who is the District Coordinator of Social Development. Mr Mjamba was the man I had spoken to on many occasions on the telephone, and I had always found him very friendly. I was therefore shocked by his icy attitude towards me when I greeted him. Andre greeted the magistrate, Mr Mata, who being the only magistrate in Middelburg, acts in all capacities. Before anything else could be said, Mr

Maxecgwana said that I should leave the room because a delicate matter was being discussed.

"Your Honour, I am Mrs Lang's attorney in this matter. Since the matter under discussion is regarding investigation into her and or her project, I feel that she has every right to be here", stated Andre.

"Yes, you are right", concurred Mr Mata.

"As I was saying", said Mr Maxecgwana, "certain allegations have been made that Mrs Lang has children in her care who are there illegally. Other allegations have been made by the social services. We are here because she asked for the investigation".

My mind went vacant. What was this? The social services were making allegations about me and at the same time they were here at my request? Was I going mad? While I was in this strange state of mind, I could hear Andre speaking to the other gentlemen, but I could not comprehend what they were saying. All I could think about was that they must be here to close the Children's Home down, and put the children back on the street. I was also afraid of their arrogance, as well as the power and authority that they wielded. It would be easy for them to find something to nail me on. They could trump up anything on me and have me arrested and the children taken from me. I felt insecure and frightened. My bravado had left me and I was a shaking, gibbering wreck. It seemed that the "meeting" was going to take a long time, so Andre told me to go back and let the other investigators get on with their investigation.

Since I had gone with Andre in his vehicle to the Magistrate's Court, I walked home, shaking and crying all the way. I tried desperately hard to pull myself together before I got there so as not to look like a whipped puppy. I had to stand up for what I believed in, no matter what was going to happen. But I did feel very threatened and fearful. Walking back into the lion's den, which had just an hour ago, been a sanctuary of peace, love and laughter, it was evident that the attitude of the investigators had not changed.

"Where would you like to start your investigation?", I asked.

"We don't have much time, so three of us will go through your files, two of us will speak with your staff and some of us will go to each of the houses that you keep the children in", Mrs Matthews said.

Oh, God, I thought, I have not even had time to warn the staff. I would not even be able to be with these people when they go through everything. I wouldn't be there to answer questions or defend myself. I didn't know what the staff would tell them. Would the staff be intimidated by them as I was? My emotions were oscillating between fear and anger. The fear was coming from the power these people had to do as they pleased, regardless of the consequences to the lives of the children. Often in the past decisions were made regardless of the law, my fear was also of the disregard they had of the law.

I was somewhat comforted by the fact that Andre was around. The anger was whirling around inside me at the audacity of these people who were invading my space, coming and investigating me when I had been asking them for an independent investigation of their own department. I had been caring for these children without any financial help from them, and yet they could come here and wield their power over me. They made me feel powerless, and from that place of powerlessness, the anger raged. This was, yet again, another attempt by the authorities to stop me from caring for the children. Why, I wondered. Was it because I was showing them up by doing what I was doing? Did what I was doing make them look like they were not doing their jobs? Was I a threat to them because I had not kept my mouth shut? Were they protecting their positions and jobs by turning the tables on me?

There was nothing I could do now. They were here to investigate me. The team dispersed to the various houses, leaving Mrs Matthews and two other investigators with me. I pulled out all the files on the children as well as all the financial statements.

"You have children here that are illegally in your care", said Mrs Matthews, "please show us their files".

"No child is here illegally, Mrs Matthews", I said.

"You have children here who are not placed on a form 4 and who do not have a social worker", she said.

God, here we go again. Do we have to repeat the whole saga of Friday, 13th, I wondered. "Mrs Matthews, here is an example of all the so called "illegal" children. A Form 4 was signed by the police. It was delivered to the Social

Development Office and the Clerk of the Court. When nothing was done about it, a letter was written to Social Development. On advice from Mrs Robertson, head of Magistrates in Grahamstown, a duplicate Form 4 was signed by the police and with a covering letter. It was delivered to the Social Development Offices as well as to the Clerk of the Court. Again, when nothing was done about it by your department, I applied to the Commissioner of Child Welfare to be made an Authorized Officer of the Court. Once this was approved, I again signed duplicate copies of the Form 4 as well as Form 4A, and together with another covering letter, submitted it to the Social Development Office and again to the Clerk of the Court. As you can see from this file, there are a number of letters that were also written to Mrs Ferreira at your district office in Cradock in this regard. Therefore, the fact that these children are still considered "illegally" placed is certainly no fault of mine, but due to poor service delivery from your department", I said. I handed heaps of files to each of them.

"Oh", said Mrs Matthews.

The other two just raised their eyebrows. It appeared that this is not what they had expected to hear and it certainly was not what they wanted to hear either. There was silence for a long while as they started reading the files. As they read the files, I could see their arrogance and self-importance start to deflate. And as their self-confidence started to deflate, mine started to return.
"Now do you see the reason for requesting an independent investigation into the service delivery of social services? Why are you looking into what I am doing

231

instead of dealing with your own department's poor service delivery?" I asked.

"You have this all wrong, Mrs Lang, we are here to do an independent investigation", said Mrs Matthews.

"You cannot investigate your own department and remain objective", I said, by now so angry the tears were filling my eyes.

"Please don't get upset, Mrs Lang", she started to say.

"I *am* upset, I am not *getting* upset. In fact, I am angry, *very* angry", I stated, emphasising my words. "I have had enough of the way I have been treated by your department. Your people have deliberately hindered me from caring for the children. I have no idea why you have a problem with me. These children should be taken care of by the government, not by me, but I am doing it because you are not. These children are our children. They are not my children. They are *our* children. And the worst thing about it is that the children who are supposed to be protected by these departments are actually having their right violated. Does nobody care? What is the alternative to what I am providing? Back to the streets where they are dying of hunger and AIDS? Where they have to exchange sexual favours for food? Where they are being abused and neglected?" I continued, the tears now streaming down my cheeks.

I did not care what I looked like. I did not care that I had let my guard down in front of these hypocritical, self-important and heartless people. What did it matter that they saw me in tears? They were unmoved by the pain and suffering of the children. They had nice jobs, were paid by the state every month, worked an eight-hour day, got bonuses and holidays. What did it matter to them that millions of children were starving, being abused or neglected? They thought they were doing their jobs by attending meeting after meeting to arrange meetings to set up meetings to decide on what time to have a meeting. Nothing was ever done other than having one meeting after another or attending one conference after another. I had been to enough of them to know exactly how the system operated. No matter how many of these meetings or conferences these people attended, nothing changed for the people or the children on the ground.

"Have any of you or any of your social workers ever fed one of these children, or taken them into your homes, or nursed a dying baby in your arms?" I continued. I left the question hanging.

The silence was deafening.

"Well, that is what I do", I said quietly. "I care for the children that nobody else wants".

"We do have laws that have to be abided by and we cannot just look after children without going through the necessary legal channels, Mrs Lang", stated Mrs Matthews. "According to your Children's Home Certificate, you are only allowed to have twenty-six children. You have too many children here".

So now that they cannot get me on the "illegal" children issue, they are going to go for another issue. I was right. They were here to harass me and to show me up to the Minister of Social Development in their report. Thus, the independent investigation would show that I was the problem and not the poor service delivery in the area. They were still trying desperately to turn the tables on me.

"Do you know on what basis I am only allowed twenty-six children, Mrs Matthews?" I asked.

"No" she replied.

Dear God, I thought. All the letters, all the faxes, all the telephone calls that I had made, all the explaining that I had done had fallen on deaf ears. Did these people not read their correspondence? Were they so biased that they were here just on what they had been told by their local department? This being the case, they definitely were here just to harass me and were not here to do an independent investigation, despite what they professed and despite their assurances. They were not to be trusted. Their smiles were those of someone who was trying to lull me into a false sense of security in the hope of catching me off guard. This was a cat and mouse game and I was the mouse. I needed to be on guard all the ime. There were three cats in the room and they were smart. Or were they? Did they really not know why I was only allowed twenty-six children or were they playing dumb? Why had they not done their homework before they arrived? There must have been piles of correspondence from me to their department, since I had a huge file of the copies that I had sent them about all this.

Saving Mandela's Children

Thoughts were flying through my head at a rate of knots while I was formulating how I was to answer the question. Answering the question in itself was not the problem. That was a simple statement of truth. The problem I was facing was one of emotion - how to control my emotion that was raging between anger, frustration and wanting to scream. On one hand I was thinking, who the fuck do these people think they are, and on the other I was wanting to tell them to take over and see if they could do the job better than I could and that I had had enough of their bullshit.

After all, was this not the job of the government to care for the children? I was doing their work and they were not assisting me. They were harassing me and I had had enough. What did I have to lose by telling them exactly what I thought? The children may be put back on the street, but I, me, I would lose nothing. What could they do to me that they had not already done? Nothing. What could I lose that I had not already lost? Nothing. Absolutely nothing. Thinking this, I felt less afraid, less anxious and more powerful. With that power came the ability to answer the question calmly.

"Well", I started explaining, as though I was speaking to a class of twelve year-olds, "the number of children or people allowed in a children's home or residential home is based on five square metres sleeping space per child or person. I have been to all the old age homes, the hospital, the boarding schools in the area and the children's homes in Port Elizabeth and, not one complies with this law and yet you have issued them with certificates to accommodate far more people or children. What this means is that you are not treating me with fair and equal treatment and that is against the constitution. And, what is more, I bought two more houses, applied to have more children and have been waiting to hear how many more children can be accommodated. And although Mrs Ferreira tells me that I can have more children, she cannot tell me how many. Tell me how competent is that?"

The other two investigators sat quietly, observing, making notes and occasionally whispering to one another. Mrs Matthews moved her glasses up on her face and stared at me.

I continued, "Now, this law is as old as the hills and comes from long before our new government. The law is completely outdated. If this law were to be applied uniformly throughout all institutions, I would be happy to comply, although I would still lobby government to change it as it no longer applies in the changing times in South Africa where we have such huge numbers of vulnerable and orphaned children. But, Mrs Matthews, if you want to nail me on this one, you will have to do it in the Constitutional Court".

Utter shock registered on all three of their faces. They could not believe what they had just heard. If they had thought that I was an easy target that they could just push over, they were having the surprise of their lives. Did they think they were dealing with a simpleton?

My mind wandered back to the beginning of my journey with the children, when I knew so little about the child care laws, the Constitution or the policing of the Child Care Act that I took every official's word at face value. I was completely taken in by what they told me, but at the same time incredulous that we would have laws that did not protect the children. All I knew back then, is what made common sense, and what I was being told by these people in authority, did not make common sense. It was through much pain, tears, heartache, frustration, anger and seeing social workers take children from me and return them to the same abusive and often life-threatening situations, that made me start studying the Child Care Act and the Constitution, often until the early hours of the morning. Without any legal background some of the law was difficult to read and understand. Often I would have to read and then re-read sections. And on top of that there were more often than not amendments to amendments that confused the issue even more. Getting hold of the relevant reading material and books was also a problem. Living in such a small town away from all the luxuries that one takes for granted in a large city has its limitations. Books had to be borrowed and photocopied, the internet had to be surfed and books ordered.

Every time I was faced with a situation regarding a child and the welfare, I would refer to the Child Care Act and then use that in their defence. No longer did I meekly accept their word. I refused to allow them to remove children without a court order. I insisted on being present at court hearings. Whenever I had to deal with an abused child and had to call the police, I would check on the policing of children and tell them what to do.
Over weeks and months and eventually years, my late-night learning was paying off, or at least that is what I had thought. Unfortunately, my hard-gained knowledge was making me more an enemy than an ally.

I handed her another two files, marked Jonathan and Lionel. These two children's cases had been going on a long time and nothing was being done about it. They had been placed by social services in foster care, but when they came to live with us, they had been living on the streets for months. While I was on a funding trip overseas, the boys were removed from our care and placed in a correctional facility. I had unsuccessfully tried to get them back for months. However, there was a sinister twist to how social services had managed to convince the various authorities why the boys should be removed from my care and how they managed to do it. I explained the entire case to the three investigators and made a copy of all the relevant documentation. They promised to look into the case, which they never did. (This story and the tragic consequences of their lack of concern is told later in the book)

They asked questions. I answered. It carried on and on. I told them the stories of some of the children. I showed them the evidence. I showed them the photographs of when the children arrived and what they looked like after a few weeks. They went through my finances. They asked to see my Non Profit Organization Certificate. They asked to see my Trust Documents. They wanted to know how many local people were involved in the "project". They asked me where my grants were that I was getting from the department for the children. Could they not have checked that on their own computers before they came to investigate? When I told them that I was not getting any grants they wanted to know why not. How was I to tell them why not? They should have told me why they were not giving me funds or grants for the children. I did not even bother to reply as I showed them a letter that I had received from their department stating that I would not be getting any funding due to a lack of funds. It would be a joke if it were not so tragic.

Every day the news was filled with government department corruption. There were even advertisements on the radio telling the public to phone in to a number if they knew of anyone who was defrauding the system by claiming grants or subsidies from the social welfare if they were not entitled to it. It was ludicrous: advertisements going out to the public to report fraud, when the fraud within the system was not being stopped. The loopholes within the system, the corruption and the incompetence, were all contributing to millions of rands going down the drain, while our children were dying of hunger, let alone dying of AIDS. It was a runaway train. How could there be no funds when millions were going missing every month? Why was the corruption and fraud continuing despite the media coverage of the ghost pensions that were being paid out monthly? People who were dead and buried were still being paid monthly grants. Foster grants were paid out in cases where children were on the street.

On numerous occasions I had notified the Social Development Department, the Justice Department and the Police about cases where parents and/or foster parents were claiming grants for children who were not living with them. These people were very seldom prosecuted, and it was months and often more than two years before the grants were stopped, and then only because I was continually on their case about it. I remembered one case where the public prosecutor refused to prosecute because he said that the high unemployment rate meant that people relied on child grants to survive, and therefore he did not want to prosecute. This decision was taken despite the fact that the child was living on the street and the money was being used for alcohol.

The three ladies were still going through the files when the other investigators returned. However, Mr Maxecgwana and Mr Mjamba had not put in an appearance since I had last seen them at the court house.

"Well?", I asked, my stomach knotting as I saw their faces.

"Why have you not trained your staff? None of them have any qualifications to care for children. You have not sent them on any child care courses. What provision have you made to remedy this?", they demanded.

Jesus Christ, I thought, what next? I could feel the heat coming up from some place deep inside, the heat of blind anger. Today was a day of riding the waves of emotion: one moment calm, the next feeling confident, the next anxious, the next fear, and then the next, blind and raging anger. I started to take deep breaths. Count to ten Dianne, I said to myself. Just count to ten. I could hear my heart pounding in my ears. Fuck you, I thought, I have had enough of your stupidity, your arrogance, your lack of compassion, your utter incompetence. Fuck you, fuck you, fuck you! You low down miserable piece of shit. I could hear myself talking, punctuating my words, emphasizing others, but no thought was going into it and no sound came from me.

"Listen to me", I said. "I do not get government funding, despite the fact that you don't even know that. I rely solely on private donations from friends here in South Africa and from the United Kingdom. These donations are small and we struggle to make ends meet each month. The first eighteen months I funded this project myself from the sale of my home in Port Elizabeth. My priority is first to feed the children, second to see to their medical needs and thirdly to see that they get an education. There is no money left over to send the staff to a city for weeks or months on end and pay for courses and accommodation for them to get child care certificates or diplomas. All the staff are qualified HIV and AIDS trainers and Home Based Care Workers and above all, they love the children. And for me... that is enough. If you had a choice between feeding the children or training the staff, which one would you choose?", I continued.

"We have a certain standard to maintain in Children's Homes and staff has to be trained as Child Care Workers", I was told.

"And when your department funds us, the staff will be sent on the courses", I retaliated.

In an area where 98% of the population is unemployed, I was providing employment for eleven people, most who had never been employed before. From the eleven employed people, seventy-six people were extended family of the employees and they were being supported each month. Half of those employed were HIV+ and one of the staff members had been given less than six weeks to live more than two years ago. Two of the staff members were illiterate. These were the facts and the reality of living in Middelburg. The staff had also completed and qualified as HIV and AIDS trainers, done basic hospital training, voluntary counselling, qualified as Home Based Care Workers, and done numerous hours of staff training in child care. They were dedicated, motivated, enthusiastic, protective and above all, they loved and cared for the children as though they were their own.

My antagonists left, informing me that they would be back later. I immediately telephoned Andre to find out what had taken place at the magistrate's office. He told me that they were doing an "independent" investigation, and that since I had nothing to hide I had nothing to worry about. Again, I reiterated that there was no such thing as an "independent" investigation and told him what had taken place during the day. He said we should wait and see what happened next. Andre was very calm. It must be something that lawyers learn at law school. His constant style is calm. "They" never came back that day.

Early the next morning, the whole entourage was there, including the team leader, Mr Maxcegwana, the local police station commissioner, Superintendent Kakuiyu "Idi Amin", followed by Andre. "Here comes big shit", I thought, "especially with this idiot of a police commissioner in tow".

He marched in first, huffing and puffing like a great big orangutan, police hat in hand and uninvited, plunked himself down. He had this supercilious grin on his face as though he had finally got his way with me. Everyone else followed and stood around until I invited them to take a seat. Mr Maxcegwana refused a seat and stood. There was silence until Andre took charge and asked what the outcome of the investigation was, particularly in respect of the SA CARE Trust and me.

"We cannot really say right now. We have to go back and write individual reports. We will then have to gather all the information. A report will be sent to you within ten days. With regard to Mrs Lang, it must be noted that her staff have not been adequately trained for the positions that they hold".

And that was that. No report ever came. I asked for the report on many occasions, telephonically and in writing, but to no avail. At the time of writing this book, it has still not materialized.

Lindelwa – the face of courage

I was busy sending and answering emails when Jackson told me that there were police at the door with a child. I went to the door and the two policemen left a ten year-old girl with me saying that she had been raped and that I must take care of her. I asked them to sign a Form 4 and to deliver it to the Department of Social Development. It was the 22nd December 2003.

Lindelwa was dressed in a filthy little summer dress and a dirty jersey with sleeves that only reached her elbows. She held her arms protectively around herself. Her hair was long and bushy, and she was not only dirty but dusty as well. She looked as though she could be dusted off with a feather duster. She stood in my office, eyeing me out of the corner or her eyes.

"Hello Lindelwa, how are you?" I said.

"Molo Mama, ndiphilile", she replied. (Hello Mama, I am fine).

"Do you know why you are here, my child?", I asked her in isi-Xhosa.

"Yes, I know", she replied.

"Do you want to tell me what happened", I asked her, while asking Jackson to make her a sandwich and to bring her some cool drink. I gestured for her to come and sit on my lap.

"We were playing in the street. My father's friend, Dati (who is fifty-five) called us to come and see something in his house. He lives at 55 Meitjie Street. Everyone was in the kitchen and then he called me into the bedroom. He told me to climb on the bed and took my panties off. I started to cry. He climbed on top of me. He held my legs apart. When I started crying louder, he started beating me with his fist. Then he put his thing inside of me and I screamed. When he was finished, I went out of the bedroom back to the kitchen. My friends asked me what was wrong when they saw the blood coming out of me and running down my legs. My friends said that they were going to phone the police. The police came to the house and took the old man. They also took me to the police station and the hospital. My father was drunk when this happened so he didn't care", she told me between sobbing.

"My mother who is not my mother but my father's new wife puts my hands in a pot of boiling water every time she is cross. She holds the pot on the stove and holds my hands in the hot water. She is always drunk", she continued, the tears running down her dusty cheeks, leaving two clean lines from her eyes to her chin. My grandmother hits my sister and me with her fist or with her shoes. She also stabbed me in my left hand one day. My grandmother drinks all the time. She drinks jabula. Sometimes she chases me and locks me out the house and then I have to sleep outside. My sister has also been raped. I know who raped her but I don't know his name. I can show you where he lives. I was raped before too but those two men were not so old. Their names are Mbuzo and Kali. I don't want to go back to the township. I want to stay here with you because there are no bad people here".

Lindelwa's hands were badly scarred and her fingers were pulled up towards her wrist, and her nails were little blobs on the ends of her fingers from being in boiling water so many times. There was also a visible scar on her left hand where she had been stabbed. Lindelwa then pulled up her dress and showed me where she had also been stabbed in her stomach by her grandmother. I pulled her towards me and gave her a hug.

"Who have you been living with Lindelwa?", I asked.

"I have been living with my grandmother", she said.

"So it will be alright for you to live here with us and the rest of the children", I asked.

"Oh, yes", she said, her face breaking into a huge smile. "I have been wanting to live here for my whole life", she stated, exaggerating.

"Well, then this is no problem because you are going to stay with us now and no one is going to hurt you any more".

With that she jumped off my lap and tucked into the sandwiches and cool drink. My heart felt squeezed. What this child had lived through and what little she asked for in return. When Jackson returned to collect the plate and cup, she spoke to him in Afrikaans. I was amazed.

"Do you speak Afrikaans as well, Lindelwa?", I asked.

"Ja, and I can speak English too", she said in English.

We had a bright one on our hands.

"Can you read and write in all these languages too?", I wanted to know, and with that she jumped up and grabbed one of the papers on my desk and started to read to me in English.

Because we now had fifty-two children, we had eleven staff members. I put Lindelwa in Monea's care and continued with my work. Monea would go through the clothing donation boxes and find Lindelwa clothes, kit her out for school, Jackson would take her to school in the morning and tell the headmaster that there was another child that belonged to us, and find out about overdue school fees, Nonqaba would deal with the sleeping arrangements and Nombasa would introduce her to her age group and her dormitory friends. She would also be kitted out with towel, face cloth, toothbrush and the other necessities.

It was around 11pm that evening when I was called for an emergency with Lindelwa. She could not urinate. No matter what we did, running the water, making shhhh sounds, there was no way we could get her to urinate and she was in pain. So, it was a trip to the hospital in the middle of the night. The nurses phoned the doctor who prescribed a mild tranquilizer for her and within a half an hour she was urinating.

Back home we went. All was well until the next day after school. She saw the man that had raped her. He was still walking about around town. She stopped urinating again. Back to the hospital and the doctor we went again. Another tranquilizer and she could urinate again. Now it was a serious situation.

I called the police and asked them why the rapist was still on the street and why nothing was being done about the situation. They said that they were still investigating. I took Lindelwa to the private doctor and he prescribed mild tranquilizers for her. We did not see her rapist again for a couple of months. Lindelwa settled down quickly and her school marks improved dramatically. She was a happy and well-adjusted child in no time. However, she did not cope well if she was near a male, so we made sure that the male staff stayed away from her until she made the move towards them first.

One of the problems, as usual, was with the social workers. They had done nothing about taking Lindelwa to Children's Court. The Form 4 had expired as it was only valid for forty eight hours. The Form 5 was supposed to be issued immediately thereafter and is only valid for sixty days. Thereafter a Form 8 places the child in the Children's Home permanently. I continually wrote, phoned and faxed the social worker, but nothing was being done. I did the same to Mrs Ferreira in the District office but, again nothing was done. After much fighting, Lindelwa was eventually placed on a Form 5 on 18 June 2004, six months late and eventually in the Children's Home on 19 January 2006, two years late!

A couple of months after Lindelwa was with us, her rapist was back on the streets of Middelburg and we had the same problem again with her urinating. Lindelwa is on permanent medication so that she can urinate.

One 18 January 2006, the Public Prosecutor sent us notification that he was not going to prosecute in the rape case of Lindelwa. I have taken this refusal to prosecute further, and am demanding to know the reasons behind the decision. Letters are still being written to the Head of Public Prosecutions in Queenstown today requesting an explanation into the reasons behind the refusal to prosecute in Lindelwa's case.

Once children are placed on a Form 5, the court order stipulates that the Department of Social Development pay the person who is caring for them R12,00 per day. From the time that we have been caring for the children, we have battled to get payment from the welfare of this R12,00 per day. There is a particular internal departmental procedure that has to be followed to apply for this safety fee of R12,00 per day per child. However, the social worker and the social worker's supervisor have to sign the application form, together with the applicant. When we first tried to apply for this safety fee, Mrs Ferreira would not supply us with the application forms. The next time she said that there were no funds available for safety fees. The following time we tried to apply for safety fees, Mrs Ferreira said that she would not sign for any safety fees. And so it went on and on.

Eventually, Mrs Ferreira left her post, and Mrs Levani took over. Mrs Levani provided us with the forms, but she did not know how they were to be completed and she would not sign them until she had inspected the home. We made arrangements for her to come and inspect the Children's Home, but then she telephoned us to say the Department of Social Development had no vehicles, so we drove to Cradock, collected her so she could do her inspection, and then drove her back to Cradock. She then gave us the forms to take back and to complete, which we did. She wanted us to drive back to Cradock the following week and to bring the forms with us. Again we complied.

When we arrived in Cradock, she told us that she would not sign the forms because she did not know whether we were cheating or not, so we would have to leave the forms with her but when we were in Cradock again, we could pick them up and take them back to Middelburg for the Middelburg social worker to sign them. Again, we went to fetch the safety fee application forms and gave them to the social worker in Middelburg. We were then told that we could not claim the safety fees for the children for the entire period but only for the previous two months. The social worker then showed us a different way to claim for the safety fees, and told us that we could not claim safety fees for any other period, despite the fact that it was a court order.

Eventually, safety fees for some children for two months were sent to a bank for withdrawal, not by us, but by one of our ex-employees. We notified the Department of Social Development that the money was made out to someone else and not to us, and notified the bank not to pay it out to someone who was not entitled to it. We also had a meeting about this with the local, regional and provincial

Department of Social Development, this time taking the LRC lawyer, Ruth Williams, a Canadian, with us. The Head of Department, Mr Webb, of the Department of Social Development said that he would see that the situation was rectified, but this was never done. Despite numerous appeals and letters to Mr Webb from the LRC, no response was received.

In 2007, the LRC in Grahamstown assisted us in making application to the Supreme Court of South Africa against the Department of Social Development, and the court ordered the payment of safety fees and costs to us. However, all further applications for safety fees has met with no response.

Our intelligent and special Lindelwa in the meantime has been promoted to a higher grade and beyond her peers. She is a very gifted child, particularly in languages and mathematics. She wants to be a magistrate when she grows up. When you ask her why, she says she wants to put all rapists in jail. I believe she will.

Walking on high heels

By the time we had opened up the big house, the children were pouring in, and at one point, we had seventy-two children. Of course, this meant that we had to have more staff to take care of the children. Some children had to be home-schooled because they had never attended school.

This was one of the tragedies of the New South Africa. Whereas schooling had been free during the Apartheid era, we were now faced with school fees, paying for school books, and having to have uniforms or the children would be sent home from schools. With such extreme poverty, many children did not attend school. If the parents or guardians could not pay the school fees, the children just did not attend school. There was a growing generation of illiterate people.

The red tape was also making life extremely difficult in the area of education. We were not allowed to home-school the children, but the teenage children refused to go to school with the five and six year olds. The only thing we could do was to home-school them and try to assist them as much as we could, so that they could catch up with their peers and go to school when they could attend a class that was more age-appropriate. This we did illegally. We employed a retired teacher for the twelve children who were too old to attend baby classes. These children could neither read nor write, let alone do basic arithmetic. The only skills they had were for survival on the streets.

One of the problems we had was that we needed the curriculum that was being taught as the schools, so that these children would be able to adapt to the class environment when they got to school. My plan was to get them past at least three grades in a year so that they would be able to catch up to their peers. In order to make them feel that they were in school each day, I bought them their own "Care House" uniforms which they had to put on in the mornings to attend school. I negotiated with another non-profit organization to use one of their buildings to have school there so that these children could also feel that they were attending a "real" school. Fortunately, I had made friends with a primary school teacher, and she gave me the text books that I could photocopy for the children. We were ready for school. Of course, all this was highly illegal, but there was no other way to get the children educated and to get them back into mainstream schooling.

I had written to the Education Department for specialized schooling for the children on numerous occasions, explaining the problem in the area, but they did not seem interested. When I told them that I was going to run my own school for the children, I was told that I could not do it as it was illegal and that I would have to register as a school, employ teachers and provide a set number of classrooms. Their list was so long that I would have had to be a millionaire a couple of times over to get these dozen children educated. Again, I went where no one else was prepared to go. I went ahead and did what I thought was best for the children in my care.

It is a conundrum that although the Department of Social Development was adamant that the children were illegally in my care, the Child Care Act stated that once a child went over your threshold, they were then your responsibility, and if you abandoned them or neglected them you could be held liable and could be convicted of a criminal offence. It was this little part of the Child Care Act that I kept in my head as a defence against them, although in my mind and in my heart I was doing what was right and just and no one could stop me. So, my children went to school – those who had never been to school and were too old or too sick to attend normal schooling. And they were happy and they were motivated and eager to learn. And that is all that mattered to me.

The other school-going children were attending regular school and were doing well. At the end of their first year at school, we had a one hundred percent pass and our little home school children had managed to get through three grades of schooling. We put together a huge prize giving at home, letting the children dress up in their best, with prizes and certificates being handed out to everyone, including certificates for those who had shown the most perseverance, the neatest child in the home, the most helpful child and the most loving child. We managed to find something good in every child and a certificate was given to everyone.

Unknown to the staff, I had made a certificate for each one of them as well, praising them in areas that they were particularly good. We had sweets and cakes for after the presentation, and then the normal and joyful activities started as we brought out our old drum that we had made and started beating it. The children soon joined in with dancing and singing. What a wonderful and happy night we had.

Someone had donated a digital camera to us and very soon afterwards someone else donated a colour printer. This was just what I wanted. I took photographs of all the children, printed out colour A4 pictures and had the pictures laminated. The children and I had great fun putting the pictures and the certificates up around the dining room walls.

Our second home was enormous, covering more than three hundred square meters. We had enough room for all our children, together with the first house we had. We used the first house as an office and the second house as the central home. However, with the number of children we now had, we were exceeding the regulated five square metres per child sleeping space. Something had to be done. Just up the road I found another house that was vacant and looking rather dilapidated. I made enquiries and found that it was on the market. Again, without thinking, I put an offer in on the house, applied for a bond and before I knew it, I was the owner of another house in the same street. Now we had three houses in the same street and we would be able to accommodate the children as per the five square metre sleeping space.

I notified the Department of Social Development of the new premises and asked them to review the number of children we were now allowed to accept. Needless to say, it took them two and a half years to review that certificate and only after a high court application was it finally issued.

With more children and more houses, we needed more beds, more linen, more towels, more tables and chairs. I was still virtually on my own, without any moral, emotional or administrative assistance. My staff were helpful with the children, but without any of them having finished schooling, they were unable to assist me with getting funding, ordering food, sorting out the Department of Social Development, going to Children's Court, taking the children to the doctor or the hospital, organizing or delegating workloads. They could only follow orders and had no initiative whatsoever. I could not blame them at all for this, as this was the first employment any of them had ever had. It would take a lot of training and motivation to get them to where I needed them to be. Some of the staff were illiterate, they could not take a temperature, and I would even have to read the instructions on the medicine bottles and physically show all of them what medications were for what children and label everything in colour codes for each child. There were no qualified child care workers in the area, and I could not afford to employ anyone who was more educated.

I was in a catch 22 situation. The people who were working with me were also HIV+, and they felt they were needed and the salaries they were earning was keeping their extended families in food and shelter. They too were throw-away people and I felt a fierce loyalty to them. I would often find myself working sixteen to eighteen hours a day. Just about everything other than actually cooking the food, washing the clothes and physically caring for the children was my responsibility. I missed Patience desperately. I was tired and exhausted and I felt I was on a treadmill that I could not get off.

The trustees could do little to help me. They were involved with their own lives and careers. Without sufficient funds, we were unable to pay for the necessary staff to alleviate my workload. Apart from the mandatory quarterly trustee meetings when I would most times have to go to Port Elizabeth and report on what was going on, there was not much the trustees could do. But one trustee, Stuart, knew the circumstances of my finances and would send me parcels of luxury items that I could use for myself. The parcels would arrive and it would be like a double Christmas and birthday for me. There would be magazines, bath bubbles, olives, tuna, ready meals and luxury soaps. He would send me parcels of food at least twice a month for years. The heat was killing in the Karoo and he and Dave, another trustee, sent me two portable air-conditioners for the office. Trevor, our other trustee, organized cartons of antibiotics for the children. The trustees were always at the end of the telephone, but I was in the middle of things.

Furnishing the houses did not turn out to be such a major problem after all. I was nominated and won the Fairlady Clarins Eau Dynamisante 2004 Woman of the Year Award for working with children affected and infected with HIV and AIDS, and with it came a whopping amount of one hundred thousand rand. Now we could do something about the condition of the big house and furnish the homes. I had sent out a wish list to all my e-mail contacts, and we were fortunate to get all the linen donated to us for all the beds. With the money, I was able to carpet the big house, buy tables and chairs for all the children, double bunks for everyone, another stove, fridge, deep freeze, industrial washing machine, industrial tumble dryer, whirly wash lines and pay for a number of other maintenance jobs that were in dire need of being done. Now we had a first-class home.

No longer did we have to sit on the floor to eat our meals. No longer did we have to share beds. Now we could learn table manners and everyone had knives and forks and spoons. What a joy it was, and how much fun we had learning table manners. My heart would swell with pride as I would watch the children at the tables, eating their meals. The little ones in their high chairs, all the others sitting at the tables, with the tables set, the salt and pepper cellars in the middle of the table. Then it was time to learn to say grace.

"Cimela Amethlo", Jackson would say and all the children would close their eyes, the little ones putting their hands over their eyes. All the bigger children would remove their caps as Jackson would remove his.

"Masi Thandazela", he would say as we would begin to pray. "Bless us, oh Lord, and these thy gifts, which we are about to receive, from thou bounty, through Christ, our Lord, Amen".

In the beginning, all we would hear from the children would be "Bless us, oh Lord" and then a huge big "Amen" would come from them and then the clatter of the lifting of the knives and forks. As time went on, they would learn more and more of the blessing, until they could all say the entire grace, including the little ones, although the pronunciation from the little ones left a lot of smiles on our faces. I am sure that the Lord found it funny as well.

Learning to say the Lord's prayer must have been another incident that made God laugh, as it certainly had me in fits of laughter, although I had to pretend to be serious. After many months of learning to say the Lord's prayer in English, I thought I heard some strange words at the beginning of the prayers, so asked one of the older boys to say the Lord's prayer aloud for us all after reading the Bible before bedtime.

"Our Father, what are a lemon, hello, what is your name?..." said Nkosinathi, in all seriousness.

I had many amusing moments after that and cannot say the Lord's prayer without remembering Nkosinathi's rendering of his version. I had not realized the impact of teaching the children the morals and values of Christianity would have on their lives until the day I took them for the first time to the local restaurant for a milkshake. We had been given a donation for a treat for the children, and I thought that it would be a good idea to take them for a milkshake. None of the children had ever had a milkshake before, nor had they been to a restaurant. Having good table manners and being well behaved, this would be a good test of how they would behave in public as well as being a wonderful treat for all of us.

Off we went, walking in a long line, in what had become known as a "2x2", meaning that we would walk together in couples, each holding hands. Everyone was very excited, and we were all dressed for the occasion, with our best clothes on and faces clean and shiny, hair brushed and clean as pins. The faces of the waiters and manager at the restaurant was a sight to behold as their eyes stood out on stalks as almost fifty of us walked into their restaurant in the middle of the afternoon, taking up all the seats in the place.

I ordered a milkshake for everyone and asked that they make the milkshakes and then serve them all at the same time. The children sat very still, talking quietly amongst themselves. They were extremely well behaved. The manager came up to me and commented that he had never, in all the time that he had managed and worked in the restaurant trade, seen so many well behaved children. My chest expanded with pride. Eventually, the milkshakes arrived and each child had a large milkshake in front of them. They sat still, their eyes on the milkshakes.

"Come on", I said, "you can drink your milkshakes now".

They sat still, not moving.

"You can drink up now. What is wrong? Don't you like milkshakes?", I asked.

No one said a thing. Still they sat, as still as mice.

Eventually, a little voice piped up. "We have not said grace, Mama D".

I was humbled and ashamed and distraught. I had taught these children that food did not just land on your plate. We had to be grateful and give thanks for the food we ate, and here I was encouraging them to just drink their milkshakes without giving thanks.

"You are right", I said, "Close your eyes".

And we gave thanks for the milkshakes and for the joy of being together and for the love of one another and for life and for each other. When we had finished giving thanks to God, as if it had all been practiced beforehand, and in one coordinated movement they all took up their milkshakes and drank them down in seconds.

Not only was the giving of thanks a lesson to me, but the next thing the children did was another lesson to me. We had taught the children to take their plates and cutlery to the scullery after their meals, and that included the little ones of eighteen months, and even then the little ones would stand on the tips of their toes to get their plates into the sink. Again, in one movement, the children stood up, picked up their milkshake glasses and walked to the kitchen to deliver their glasses to the scullery. And that is when the waitresses, the waiters and the manager had tears in their eyes.

I was a very reluctant winner of the Clarins Fairlady Eau Dynamisante Woman of the Year. There were many reasons for this. The first reason was that I felt that I had not done enough to deserve the award. I had only helped a few children and there were millions of orphans in our country. Another reason was that I felt that I just could not go to Johannesburg to get the award. It was all just too much for me. I would have to drive to Port Elizabeth, get on a plane to Johannesburg, go to a function and then get all the way home. On top of that, I would have to make some sort of speech. The way I was feeling, I could just about do what I had to do, and to have to go to Johannesburg was too great a task for me.

I had been in this small town of Middelburg for so long that the idea of going to a city, to people I did not know, to a fancy function was terrifying. What would I wear? I was used to wearing t-shirts and denims and had one pair of shoes. There was no money for buying fancy clothes to attend functions, and I had lost track of what was fashionable. I felt completely out of my depth. I knew we needed the money that went with the award, but even that did not overcome the extreme reluctance and fear I had of going to Johannesburg to receive it. I was also suffering from exhaustion, from despair, and from severe stress resulting from the continual pressures from the Department of Social Development and the constant battle of caring for the children and the lack of funds. I was just about managing to do what I had to do, and this award loomed larger in my mind than what I thought I could cope with. I knew about it weeks before I had to go, but I put it off in my mind, thinking that I could refuse the award and give them a week's notice if I found I could not cope with it. I discussed it with my mother over and over and she kept on telling me that I should go, I deserved some recognition and that I could do it. The decision to go or not added to the stress that I felt. The time for my decision to let the organizers know whether I was going to attend or not came closer and after a final phone call to my mother, I decided to go. This decision was based, not on my feelings, but on the idea that this would give me the opportunity to speak on behalf of the children. I would accept the award on behalf of the children because I did not deserve it. They were the ones who were suffering, they were the ones who needed the money, and I would tell their story.

With much trepidation, I drove to Port Elizabeth to spend the night with my mother to catch the early flight to Johannesburg the next day. My mother and I went through her cupboard, looking for something appropriate for me to wear to the function, and although I took something of hers to wear, I found it totally inappropriate when I was met at the airport by the Clarins staff at the airport. They were dressed so beautifully, and here I was, with no makeup and wearing my usual dress code for caring for children in the Eastern Cape. I was devastated and did not want to appear at this function and let them down, knowing that they had chosen me to receive this award and I would be on the stage dressed like someone who had come from the bush (which I had).

I swallowed my pride, and confided in the lady who had been allocated to look after me that I had nothing appropriate to wear to the function, had no knowledge of what to wear, and also had no money to purchase the correct outfit. In no time at all, we were on a shopping spree and I had an outfit, earrings, and high heeled shoes to match. Next it was off to the hairdresser where I had my hair done. I was starting to be transformed. I did not even recognize myself in the mirror. I was whisked off for a pedicure and lunch, and then taken to a very luxurious hotel where I was told to rest and that someone would be along later to do my makeup.

I sat down in this most luxurious room. I had never seen anything like it in my life. The bathroom and bedroom had everything that opened and shut. It took me ages opening and shutting cupboards, fridges, flat screen televisions, DVDs, lights, shower doors, bath taps, and trying on bath robes and slippers. It was another world.

Now, I thought, it was time to practice wearing the high heeled shoes. I had about an hour and a half. I put them on and started walking up and down the room. First I wobbled my way across the room. Soon, I was able to do it without the wobble. Up and down the room I strutted. Then I sat and after a while, up I would get and do my thing, strutting up and down the room so that I could walk on those shoes without a wobble and as though I had done it all my life. I had never walked on high heeled shoes ever. They were beautiful sandals with silver diamante and about two and a half inches high. And I did look good in them. When I thought I had the whole shoe thing taped, I took them off, had a bath, dressed and waited for the makeup lady. After she had done the necessary, my face was transformed, and now I really did not recognize myself. From a bush baby in jeans and t-shirt, I was a lady, all dressed up in high heeled shoes with a smart hairdo and make up. I was ready to go, but as yet, I had no idea of what I would say when I received my award or any idea of how big or how enormous the function was going to be. I was out of my depth. I went downstairs to the hotel foyer and met the previous winners of the award and they all said to me that I should relax and just enjoy myself. They were very friendly.

We were all taken to the function together in a luxury vehicle, and when we got there, I had to consciously hold my mouth shut. Again, my senses were overwhelmed with what I saw. Never had I seen such luxury, such extravagance, so many people in one place for one reason and that reason was me. Never had I imagined that this function or this award was such a big event and had so much prestige, and that there would be so many press and television journalists there and that they would all want to talk to me. I was totally unprepared for it and completely overwhelmed. I was introduced to so many people who were apparently famous, but because I came from the "bush" and was too busy doing what I did best, the rich and famous did not make an impression on me, and because there was no money, I did not buy magazines or newspapers so I did not know who they were. I was therefore unimpressed by who they were. In retrospect, thank goodness, otherwise I would have been more nervous. The previous winners were whispering to me "But that is so-and-so" and I would just look at them and say "I have never heard of them". I must have seemed a complete idiot to all of them.

All this time, I had been on my feet, walking up and down on those high heeled shoes, being introduced to this one and that one; the only ones that really stood out were the French Ambassador and the French Chairperson of Clarins. There were just too many people. And my feet were hurting... badly.

Weeks before the event, a film team had been to visit us and had filmed the children and the work we were doing and, when the program for the evening started, which was during a scrumptious dinner with speeches, the film on our work was shown. I was so relieved to be sitting down as my feet were killing me. All my concentration up to that point was on my feet. Seeing the work I do on film for the first time and seeing my children brought tears to my eyes. It was an amazing feeling and it was then, for the first time, that I saw objectively that perhaps in some small way I was making a difference. The audience showed their appreciation of my work with the longest applause.

All too soon, I was called up on stage. I was handed my award, and now it was time to say something – to thank them for the honour, and I had to get my shoes back on because I had slipped them off my feet for some relief, before going to the stage. I put them on, feeling them bite into my feet as I did so. I stood up and all my brain could scream was "my feet". I walked up the three steps on to the stage and I knew that I could not think, I could not speak, I was a prisoner of those shoes. I could not do anything with those shoes on. There was no more pretending that I was anything else other than who I was. I was not the person who was dressed up like someone from Johannesburg's rich suburbs. I was not a famous person. I was not a rich person. I was just me. I was just Dianne, looking after children in the Eastern Cape. I was just the motivated, dedicated and passionate person caring for children that I loved.

I got on to the stage and said, "Now that you have seen how beautifully Clarins has dressed me and you have seen my shoes, please excuse me, but I cannot wear these anymore".

With that, I took off the shoes on the stage. Suddenly, there was a wild roar of applause and people started to laugh. The ice was broken. The tension was gone. And everyone was relaxed. They were in the palm of my hands. With the straps of my sandals over my hand, I graciously accepted the trophy and the envelope with the money in my other hand. I walked up to the podium, still without really knowing what I was going to say. There was deathly silence in the enormous room. Cameras were flashing. The films were rolling. And I stood there, taking a deep breath, hearing my heart beating in my ears. I thought suddenly of the enormity of the tsunami that we were all still reeling from and the frivolity of this event. What did it all mean? With a quick calculation, I began.

"I humbly accept this award on behalf of my children for it is not I who should be standing here, but them. They are the ones who have been through so much and yet have survived. We have just witnessed the most awful Tsumani where 35 000 people were killed in one day. The first people on the ground to help when the tsunami hit were the South Africans at the cost of 1.5 million rand. But in South Africa, we have a tsunami every six months and no one cares. 35 000 people die of AIDS every six months and no one makes a fuss. No one rushes to help.

"Our children are dying of AIDS because they have no medication. They are dying of hunger because they have no food. And no one cares. The social workers do not care. The Department of Social Development does not care and does not fund the children".

"We have the most wonderful Child Care Act and the most wonderful Constitution in the world, but for all it means to the children of this country, it may as well have been written on toilet paper. Children have no rights in this country. Children are left orphaned by HIV and AIDS, they are abused, abandoned and neglected, and the departments who are there to protect their rights are the very ones who violate their rights even further".

"I lay the blame for the state of our children at the feet of the Minister of Social Development. He needs to be taken to task over the total neglect of our children". I had to wait because the applause was deafening and the people were on their feet.

"In a country where no thought or care is given to the children, that country has no future, and unless we start to take care of our children, South Africa has no future. The children have no voice of their own. I am their voice. And I accept this award, with thanks, on their behalf".

I left the podium, with the shoes, the trophy and the envelope to a standing ovation. I had never realized that speaking from the heart was the right thing to do. By being who I really was, without the fancy clothes or the prepared speech – that was the person that they had chosen to receive the award. There were radio and television interviews and documentaries for days afterwards, and my private life became a public life. My life was never the same again, and I became a more ferocious advocate for the children. In that, I became, too, an enemy of the various government departments. The following year, at the award ceremony for the next Woman of the Year I was given another R25 000 to use for the children.

Jonathan

I flew back from Johannesburg to Port Elizabeth on a high, a complete opposite of how I had felt on my way there. When I landed in Port Elizabeth, I put my mobile phone back on and there was a message for me from the Erica Place of Safety. It could only mean one thing. I could go and fetch my boys and take them back home. These were the boys who had been removed from my care while I was on a funding trip to the UK. They had been put into a correctional facility by the social workers. What good timing, and what a grand finale to the Fairlady Clarins Eau Dynamisante Woman of the Year Award. Although it was February 2005, the award was for work done the previous year.

My mind wandered back to when I met Lionel and Jonathan for the first time. These two young teenagers, both thirteen at the time, were like chalk and cheese. Lionel was an ugly little boy, with a bad squint in the right eye, a coffee coloured child whom I could see was not very bright. He always looked dirty, no matter how hard we tried to scrub him clean, and continually had a beanie cap on his head. Lionel spoke Afrikaans, but Jonathan spoke perfect English to me and could speak Afrikaans and Xhosa with equal ease.

Jonathan was a beautiful looking child with long eyelashes that touched his eyebrows. He had hazel eyes, with a few freckles dotted around his nose. As ugly as Lionel was, Jonathan was beautiful. Jonathan always had a scarf tied around his neck in some gangster-type fashion, or around his head. While Lionel was dirty, Jonathan was always

269

impeccably clean and tidy. Jonathan was the more confident and well-articulated child.

My first introduction to Jonathan was when he was brought to me one night in December 2003 by the police. The policeman who brought him said that he had telephoned them himself saying that he had rights, he would not be beaten, and he wanted to be taken care of by Mama D. He had demanded that the police bring him to me. The policeman was quite amused, but I thought that the child was intelligent and courageous. He told me that he had for the umpteenth time been kicked out his home and that he had been living on the streets for months. It was a very cold night, so I just took him in for the night and thought I would deal with the issues of legality in the morning. I asked the policeman to sign a Form 4 for the child, but he refused. I established that Jonathan was an orphan. His mother, Anna, had died of AIDS. His father had come from the UK and had left Anna when Jonathan was a small boy, promising to come back and fetch him. He never did. Jonathan was put in an orphanage in Cape Town. His mother's brother was traced to Middelburg, and Jonathan was sent to Middelburg to his uncle. However, his uncle had other children and Jonathan was not treated the same as the others. He had also developed a relationship with a volunteer at the Cape Town orphanage, and the social worker in Middelburg would not allow him to make contact with that volunteer. He was terribly unhappy with his uncle and decided to go and live on the streets. His uncle had no problems with him living on the streets, despite the fact that the uncle was receiving a foster care grant for Jonathan. At the time that Jonathan came to see me, he had been living on the streets for four months and had not attended school. The social worker was from BADISA, a Christian-based non-profit, government funded organization. In March 2004, Jonathan brought Lionel to me.

"This is my friend who used to live with me on the streets", he said. "He is now ready to live like a real person. Can he also come and live with us?", he asked.

I found out that Lionel was also an orphan and that he was a foster child of a distant relation and he was often beaten, did not attend school, was often locked out of his home, was seldom given food, and he too had decided to live on the streets rather than endure the kind of home that he was being subjected to. He had been on the streets for about five months. The same social worker was involved in his case. I had made an appointment to see the social worker involved with Jonathan soon after he arrived, a Miss Lucinda Grootboom. I asked her about the child.

"Yes", she said, "I have him on file. He has foster parents and he is doing well and going to school".

"When last did you check up on him?, I asked her.

"Who are you to ask me this?", she said, her hackles rising.

This was the first time I had met her so I explained that I was the managing director of the Children's Home, and that Jonathan had been to see me.

"Oh, so you are the person who is causing all the trouble in Middelburg", she said.

"No, I am not causing trouble in Middelburg, the children know where to go if they are in trouble", I answered.

"Well, there is nothing wrong with this child", she said, getting up and showing me to the door.

"Miss Grootboom, for your good and the good of this child, I suggest we sit down and talk about him in a calm way to see what can be done in the best interests of Jonathan', I said.

"This child has been living on the street for the last couple of months, and that does not bear well for you, since you are the social worker, the foster parents are claiming grants, he has not gone to school in months, and you are supposed to be supervising the situation. Now can we sit down and discuss these issues", I asked.

She sat down and glared at me. "Jonathan, would like to live at the Children's Home?"

He nodded.

"Can we make some arrangement as he is not happy at home and we cannot let him live on the street", I asked. "At the moment, he is staying with me", I told her.

I gave her my telephone number and she said she would contact me. A week later she phoned me to tell me to bring Jonathan in as there was going to be an evaluation between the Chief Social Worker of the Department of Social Development, herself and the foster parents of Jonathan.

I took Jonathan with me. Jonathan was stand-offish to his foster parents and refused to greet Lucinda Grootboom, although he did greet Mr Pienaar, the Chief Social worker. He was asked in front of the foster parents why he did not want to live with them, and he answered with the exact same things as what he had told me. I thought that this was rather awful, putting him through this, but I was proud of him for standing up for himself. The foster parents were then asked if they wanted him back, and they told the social workers that he was too much trouble and that they did not want him back. Jonathan was then asked if he wanted to be sent to a trade school and he refused. He stated over and over again that he wanted to live with me. Eventually, the social workers agreed and said he could live with me. That was that and Jonathan came to live in the Children's Home.

Within a day, he was back at school in clean and new school clothes and shoes. I had to plead with the headmaster to please give him a chance as he had not attended school for months and was way behind in his studies. I promised the headmaster that he would be helped to catch up. Jonathan never gave us one ounce of trouble. Jonathan was delightful. He settled in well, helped with the other children, was kind to the small ones, entertained them and was a natural leader. He was the most talented artist and actor I have ever seen and was soon the life and soul of the children's home and one of the most popular members of the drama group.

Lucinda Grootboom eventually wrote out the Form 4 on 15 March 2004. In it she states: *During February 2004 Miss Uitlander* (one of my staff) *telephoned me and told me that Jonathan had been living in the care house for a week. I arranged for a home visit to his foster father during which time he told me that they did not see any chance of continuing to care for the child due to his behavioural problems. He gave me a letter to this effect. I made an appointment with them to come to the office. On 19/02/04 the foster father brought the letter to me. I could not convince him to continue to take care of Jonathan. I visited Jonathan at the school and I interviewed his previous and current class teachers. They were both of the same mind that Jonathan would be better off in the Children's Home because he comes to school neat, his school work has improved, his homework is done and he is more enthusiastic about his schoolwork and refuses to return to his foster parents. Contact with Natalie, the person in Johannesburg which whom Jonathan had established a close relationship during his time had been made. She requested a period of 2 weeks in which to make a decision due to the finality of the decision. I have decided to let Jonathan continue to stay at the Care house until a final decision is made by a panel.* It is signed by Lucinda Grootboom and dated 15/03/04. This is as far as the legal side of things went. She never went to Children's Court, never wrote a Welfare report and flagrantly disregarded the Child Care Act.

With the arrival of Lionel, it was back to Lucinda Grootboom, because I found out that this child too, was on the BADISA social worker's books. The history of Lionel was just about the same as the history of Jonathan. He

274

too was an orphan, had been placed in foster care and was unwanted. However, Lionel was not as bright as Jonathan and was lagging behind in school. He also was a bit of a rebel, was a smoker, a glue sniffer and had been on the streets for a longer period of time, thereby making it more difficult to socialize him and get him to settle into the structure, disciplines and confines of the home.

Despite both social workers agreeing to the boys staying with us, they never took the procedure any further to place the boys legally in our care, and it took many months and many phone calls, faxes and letters to get them placed in our care. In the case of Lionel, the social worker did not make out a Form 4, nor did she take him to Children's court or write a report, and she completely ignored the Child Care Act.

Lionel was a smoker. This was a problem as I did not allow smoking at the home. Time and again he would be caught smoking on the premises and time and again he would be sent to the time out room for smoking. Smoking was in his blood and in his nature. I was at my wits end. One day Lionel decided that he and Jonathan would sneak out and go to a tavern. I found out that the boys were missing around ten that night and phoned the police to go out and look for them. As normal, they were too busy and they only had one van available, so I got into my vehicle and combed the townships for them, going into one tavern of drunken people after another, looking for my boys. Drunken men were threatening me, raising knives at me, but I was undaunted: I was looking for my boys.

Eventually at about 1am I found the two little scoundrels walking from one of the taverns, much the worse for the wear. I jumped out my vehicle and in two seconds, I had them by the collars and into my van and I was on the way home, much relieved that my boys were safe. The night staff was relieved, but angry. How dare these children give us such a run around when we were caring for them? But as I told them, boys will be boys and kids will be kids. The next day, while they were still nursing terrible hang-overs, I made them clear the garden of weeds and gave them a good talking to. And Lionel was forbidden to have any money on him, denying him pocket money for a month. No money, no cigarettes. I thought I had this one taped, but little did I know that I still had many heartaches and many nights ahead of me when I would go rushing into the dangerous township to rescue my boys. The township that they would "escape" to for their fun was a township that the police would not enter into unless they had two vans with two police officers. I, in my love for my children, would go in to rescue my children on my own, going from tavern to tavern, pushing my way between drunken men who were usually armed. How I did not get hurt or killed is surely due to my extreme bravery and my fierce confrontational attitude caused by my motivation to find my children.

I would go in there, shouting at the top of my voice in isi-Xhosa, "Where are my children? Who has seen my children?", and for the most part I was left alone. Once or twice a knife was pulled on me, but I always left my door open and the vehicle engine running for a quick get away, and I was always fully aware of what was going on around me. The chances of my vehicle being stolen was virtually nil, as most people were too paralytic drunk to walk a straight line, let alone to think of stealing a car and no one in the township knew how to drive.

Soon after the arrival of Lionel, Jonathan brought Samuel Stement and his father to see me. I told Jonathan that his job was not that of a social worker, and that although I appreciated his need to assist all the boys on the street, our home was already over-burdened with the children we had. I sat and listened to the father of Samuel. Samuel was already 15 years old and was going to soon turn 16.

I was reluctant to take on such an older boy, particularly since he had never been to school. This would mean that we would have to put him in our home schooling program, and I did not know whether he would fit into our programs, or whether he would adjust to the discipline of the home. I was also wary of the possibility that he might disrupt the rest of the children at home as we were a happy and contented family with few problems. I listened to his father who was beside himself. He told me that Samuel was on the street because his new wife refused to allow Samuel in the home. He did not have the guts or balls to stand up to his wife and then if he tried, his wife would beat him up. So poor old Samuel was relegated to the street. The father begged me to take Samuel. He said he would even give me R100 a month to take care of Samuel and to show him the right way.

When I questioned Samuel, he seemed genuine in his desire to turn his life around, if he was just given the chance to learn and a place to live. My heart said yes, my head said no. My heart over-ruled and I took Samuel in. I went to the Department of Social Development social workers and asked them to do the necessary legal arrangements, but it was to no avail. Despite continual requests for Children's Court hearings, the Child Care Act was ignored by the Social Workers.

However, Samuel came to live with us and for a while, all was good. He settled in, was a quiet child and tried his best to learn his school work and catch up with his peers. However, he soon joined forces with Lionel as he too was a glue sniffer and a smoker. The staff had to be on their toes. We started having to frisk the children when they went out and when they came back home to make sure they did not have cigarettes and glue in their pockets.

The way they use glue is to buy the glue that is in a small tin. It costs only R3,50 and is used to glue the soles of shoes. It is beaten up with a stick until it is the consistency of white foam. It is then put into a cardboard milk container. The mouth is placed over the small hole made in the end of the top of the container, and the container pumped to spread the fumes and then the fumes are sucked in, held in the lungs for as long as possible before breathing out. This puts you on a high and takes away the feeling of hunger. It is very addictive. One tin of glue can make ten children completely high for about three hours. The café owners will not stop selling glue to children, despite us having implored them to do so. As they say, it is their right to sell what they want as it is profit to them.

There were some well-orchestrated moves on the part of BADISA, but at that stage we did not know that people could be so vindictive and evil, or that the result of this would end in death, nor could we believe that it was even possible for such things to happen. I was so busy caring for the children that I never imagined that the social workers were up to devious things to discredit our project.

Anton Jali arrived at the Children's Home on 11 January 2004. He was fourteen years-old. We were getting an influx of boys. The story I was given was that he was also a street child that no one wanted. He told me that he felt like hanging himself. I passed this information on to the Department of Social Development to look into. When nothing was done by them, I went to the police station and spoke with Sergeant Engelbrecht who refused to assist us and sign the Form 4. He said that Captain Meiring had instructed that no Form 4s were to be signed and that the Children's Home should not be assisted with such requests.

The day after Anton arrived, an adult male known as Thobela Bisholo arrived at the Children's Home demanding that we pay a sum of money to ensure Anton Jali's safety. This money was owed by Anton because of his involvement in drug dealing in the Old Location, a township alongside of the town. Anton was visibly shaken by this visit and I could now understand why he had wanted to kill himself. He had become embroiled in a drug dealing situation that had got out of control. We reported this to the police but nothing was done about it. We told Thobela Bisholo that we would not be buying Anton's safety and we would be reporting it to the police. He left us alone.

Saving Mandela's Children

By now, we had established that Anton was the nephew of the social worker, Yangisa Makaleni, of BADISA. We informed her that Anton was staying with us, that he was deeply depressed and that he had been living on the streets. We asked her to do something about Anton and to make arrangements for his placement elsewhere. Nothing was done about this either. In the meantime, the child stayed with us, attending school like the rest of the children. He appeared to give us no problems except that he was rather quiet, prone to telling tales on the other children and the staff and often asking to go and see his aunt. This of course, we allowed. Having a house full of children, we should have been more vigilant as to whom he was visiting, but since he was signed out and always returned on time, we felt that this was not a problem that needed to be addressed as urgent. At the time we were caring for over seventy children with a minimum of staff and a minimum of funds.

One afternoon, Jonathan got into a fight with a couple of the boys over the issue of his father. He had said that his father was overseas, that he was a white man and that he had promised to come back for him. The other boys started laughing at him and he started swearing at the boys. The staff got involved and the situation rocketed out of control. I was called to intervene, and once I heard what had happened I confirmed Jonathan's story but said that we did not know where his father was and that it was cruel to laugh at him. I called Jonathan aside and said that he should try not to swear and that I understood his frustration, but swearing at the children and staff would not make things better. He cried and cried in my arms and my heart broke for this child who was waiting for a father who would probably never come. I got a letter from Jonathan later on that day.

Dear Mama D,

The reason why I'm writing this letter to you is I just want to say I am sorry and I'm very sorry and it will never ever happen again mama. I promise you mama and this time I'm very insistent. I promise on ten Bibles on top of my head and cross my heart and hope to die. God can punish me I'm really so sorry. I love you so much and I just know you love me too. Your children love you so much Mama D.

From Jonathan Kaptein.

The poor child was so desperate not to land on the streets again that he took all the blame for what had happened. My heart was broken for him. How I wished that I could make it better for him. How I hated his father at that moment, that he could make a promise to a small child and then forget all about him and his responsibilities. Later that same day, Jonathan wrote a letter to one of our United Kingdom volunteers.

Dear Anna

I'm really sorry about Lionel and me. And I really want to stay by Mama D and I want Mama D to be my foster mother and then will stop my naughty ways. The reason I want to stay here by the Care House is because I've got friends here and all the people that I have is here now and Mama d that loves me. You know why I want you to be my sister is because you look like my little sister that died. I want to stay and live like a child. I don't want to live like a big man who has children. I came here to be loved and to really get a chance in the world. The world is not like a pen because a pen always stays the same. The world is not like that. That is why I want to stay with Mama D because she loves me and I love her also. I really prichiate to live with Mama D and I want to live by her.

From Jonathan.

I don't know what kind of pen Jonathan meant in his letter. He was probably just looking at the pen he had in his hand as he was writing and he thought that the pen remained the same all the time. A pen was just a pen, it never changed its form.

In the meantime I was getting a hard time from the staff, in particular from Niel and Nonqaba. They were not used to dealing with older children who had survived the streets. Nonqaba was wonderful with the smaller children but she had no patience with older children who had a will of their own. Niel was a highly strung and over-the-top homosexual with very creative talents. They were used to dealing with smaller children whom they could tell what to do and when to do it. Here was a group of boys who had a mind of their own, a history of being on a street, and they just could not deal with them. In the minds of Niel and Nonqaba, these were just naughty children who needed a good hiding and if they did not behave, I was to throw them out.

There was one staff meeting after another, while I tried to explain to them the intricacies of the problems that these children had encountered and how important it was for them to be given a chance in life. Unfortunately, my staff were not skilled in child care and as a result, they found this concept hard to understand. I was constantly being bombarded with their insistence that the culture demanded that they get beaten for their insolence, and I had to explain over and over that this was against the Child Care Act.

"Then throw them out because they are giving us a hard time", and I would counter with "This is a children's home and you will abide by the Child Care Act".

And it went round and round. Niel in particular, did not like the children, so I took him off the duty roster so that he had nothing to do with these boys. The boys too, did not like him and therefore disrespected him at every turn. It did not help matters that Neil was a very camp homosexual which the boys found this tremendously funny. With a lack of funds and with no qualified child care workers in the area, I was stuck with the staff that I had. I had to do the best I could with what I had, but the frustrations were often more than I could take. I found myself more often than not playing the middle man between the staff and the boys. The two staff members' dislike of the boys would be one more link in the eventual twist in the tail that led to tragedy.I loved and adored the boys. I found them amusing, courageous, open, spirited, adventurous, compassionate and loving. It was only Anton that was a dark horse. I could not figure him out. He was an enigma. But I thought that with time, I would have him taped as well. But Lionel, for all his stupidity, Samuel for his street wisdom and Jonathan for his intelligence – I adored them. And I would fight to the ends of the earth for those boys – as well as for all the other children.

Lionel was a bad influence on Jonathan. Lionel smoked and got into all kinds of trouble. And Jonathan, because he felt responsible for Lionel, would always be in the wrong place at the wrong time with Lionel. And by his association with Lionel, would end up in trouble himself. The boys went to different schools, but in the same area.

One Friday night, Jonathan's school had a disco dance to raise funds and, after much begging, I eventually allowed Jonathan to take Lionel with him. It was a bad decision. Some of the boys that attended the disco started teasing Lionel about his squint eye and Lionel got into a fight, Jonathan came to his rescue and all hell broke out with the teachers. Because Jonathan already had a bad reputation from his past behaviour at the school, he was immediately blamed for the altercation. I received a telephone call to fetch the two boys immediately from the school. I knew it was pointless to go up to the teaches and try and sort the problem out with the boys and the teachers, so I collected the boys, apologized for their behaviour and took them home.

Once we got home I found out what had happened and, although it was not the boys' fault and I was proud of Jonathan coming to Lionel's defence, the situation had not helped the narrow-mindedness and lack of understanding on the part of the teachers. On the Monday, I did go to the headmaster to try to explain what had happened, but he did not want to hear, continually stating that Jonathan was just a trouble maker. Jonathan was a prolific letter writer and I received another letter from him after the incident, although I had told him that I was proud of him for coming to his friend's defence.

Dear Mama D the reason I am writing this letter to you is that I just want to say that I would still be in the street if it wasn't for you. I love you so much and I won't do such a thing again. That was a mistake Mama D. Please forgive me. I want a final chance to change my manners. Nobody goes to the mother but except through you, you are the new mother. I love you so much Mama D. thank you so much. May God bless you. From Jonathan.

For weeks, the boys were perfectly behaved, although they did not get on with Niel. As long as Niel stayed away from them, or if he was not on duty, things were peaceful. It seemed that Neil rubbed them up the wrong way. I had many talks with Niel, and eventually had to give him a letter of warning for punching the boys on the upper arms with a mandate to stay away from the teenage boys. It was only a written warning as there was no evidence that it was done as a punishment and Niel maintained that it was done in jest. Of course, Nonqaba, who was on duty with him, backed him up to the hilt.

There was to be a school fund-raising function on Friday, 26 March from 7 to 9pm at the boys' school. They had been looking forward to it for weeks. We had to dig around the donation clothes boxes and find the right clothes for the event, and we scraped the money together to buy them trainers. I would not allow them to walk to school alone, as it was dark at that time of the night, so I arranged for Jackson to walk them to school and to fetch them at nine. All the staff had mobile phones and could contact me at any time. When Jackson phoned me in a panic at 9pm and told me that the boys were not at the school and the teachers had told him that they had left the school at eight, I was in a total panic. I told him to wait for me and within a minute I was racing my 4 x 4 down the road to the school.

Jonathan, Lionel, Anton and Samuel had obviously absconded. By now Jackson had let the staff know, and by the time I got to him, they had also phoned me on my mobile and they too were in a terrible state. Losing a child is the second most dreaded thing next to the death of a child.

Jackson jumped into the vehicle and without a second thought we went into Lusaka, the most dangerous area and the area where the children would most likely be. This is the area where most of the taverns were, where the police were seldom seen, where the tavern owners did not mind selling liquor to children, or where adults plied children with liquor and drugs to have their way with them. It was imperative that we find and rescue our children as soon as possible before they were abused.

There are no real roads in Lusaka and without a 4x4, it is impossible to travel around. There are few street lights which stand in the middle of what would be called a street. We negotiated our way around the few street light poles, through ditches and holes, and in my haste, I ploughed through some rather large ones. We screeched to a halt

286

outside the first tavern, our windows open and shouted out to the drunk people standing around outside the tavern, "Have you seen my children?".

Some shouted back, "No", while others started sauntering over to the vehicle.

I put it into gear and drove on. At the next tavern I again shouted out to the group standing outside, "Have you seen my children?".

Everyone in the township knew me and my vehicle and my children. There was no need to announce myself. I had been in and out of the township many times and often in rather dangerous situations, but I never showed my fear, although my heart always beat rather rapidly and my palms sweated. But my desire to find my children outweighed any fear I had. Jackson did not live in that particular township, so he too was fearful. There was a sullen silence from this group. This was the answer I was waiting for. They knew where my kids were. They had seen them and they were protecting them.

I climbed out of the vehicle. Jackson is the most loyal person I know and he would give his life for me, and although he was shaking with fear he too climbed out of the vehicle and followed me. I walked through the crowd, as though I had no fear at all. All the while I was greeting the people, all in Xhosa, talking about the weather, about what a fine night it was for a party, about how difficult it was to bring up children in the old cultural way, that children had no respect for their elders these days, that children thought that they could drink with their elders, that this would not have happened in previous years. I carried on chattering as I moved through this large group of drunk people. Before long they too were agreeing with me that the youngsters of today had no respect for their elders and who did they think they were, coming into taverns and drinking with the older people. I walked brazenly up to the door of the tavern and walked in.

There in a corner were three of the boys with three older men, each child with a beer in his hand. I grabbed Jonathan and Lionel by their collars while Jackson grabbed Samuel and before the astonished eyes of the three older men we frog-marched them out the tavern. The group outside opened a path for us, shouting at the children that they should have respect for their elders, and we put them into the vehicle and drove away. I drove straight home with them, grateful that we were safe and that we had three of them home, safe and sound.

My fear and my relief spilled over into a tirade of tongue lashing when I got them home. I was mad with them. I promptly confined them to school and home for a month, with no visits outside unless under the direct supervision of a staff member and sent them packing off to bed.

Anton was a missing link. I went back into the township and hunted high and low for him. I went from tavern to tavern, from one friend's house to another. Eventually, at midnight, I went to the police station. Jackson and I did not know what to do. The on-duty police officer was Inspector du Plessis. I told him the story about Anton being still missing but he informed me that it was too dangerous to investigate this matter as there were only four policemen on duty at the time.

The staff and I sat up all night, conjuring up all sorts of terrible things that could have happened to him. Of course, in our imaginations we had already buried him by the time he walked in at five in the morning, completely drunk and as high as a kite on dagga (marijuana). He was completely out of it, his eyes were blood red, he could not stand properly, he could not communicate coherently, so I decided to take him to the hospital for the district surgeon to examine him and have a drug test done. The district surgeon said that unless we could narrow down the type of drug he may have taken, it would be useless to take a blood sample to test for drugs as there were umpteen drugs that could have been taken, but that he was under the influence of drugs and alcohol was undeniable.

He then did a rectal examination and confirmed that Anton had had anal sex and that sexual molestation had taken place. Anton was unaware that this had taken place; he did not know where he had been and could give no evidence. We took him home and put him to bed. I asked Jackson to speak to him when he was sober and more responsive. He could still not tell us where he had been or who he had been with. He was morose and unresponsive.

Again, I was pestered by Nonqaba and Niel to get rid of the boys. They were just a problem and I was to tell the welfare to take them away. It took much convincing to try to explain that these children were abused and neglected, that they had lived on the streets for a long time and it would take time for them to settle down. What they needed was love and a structured environment and another chance. Nonqaba was of the opinion that a good hiding was all they needed. I reiterated that no harsh punishments or beatings would take place under any circumstances and that should this take place, that staff member would be fired immediately. I was starting to feel very pressurized by these two staff members as well as by the situation with the boys, particularly with what had happened to Anton.

Anton asked if he could go and visit his aunt and I thought that this would do him good so I gave my permission. He came back from his visit a lot happier and I was feeling more at ease about the situation. Each day, he would ask to visit with his aunt after school and I allowed him to go. He was back at the appointed time each afternoon. The boys were behaving themselves and it looked like we were over the worst.

Wednesday, 7 April 2004, started like any other day. We never knew what the day would bring, what new children would arrive, what children would need us, what new events would lie ahead, what would need to be done next or what problems we would be facing with the social workers. We were constantly on guard for surprise attacks from the Department of Social Development, but never thought that BADISA would also join in the harassment and antagonistic approach to us. The furthest thing from my mind was a problem with the staff or the police.

I wrote another letter to Yangiswa Makaleni, who was the social worker for Lionel Cox, and confirmed the meeting we had had on Monday the April in which she had stated

that I should keep Lionel with me, and I requested that she do the necessary reports so that the matter could be taken to Children's Court. I also sent another letter to Lucinda Grootboom,
Jonathan's social worker and requested her, again, to do the necessary reports so that the matter could be presented to Children's Court. Both letters were faxed through to the BADISA office.

Lucinda Grootboom telephoned me and told me that a Panel Meeting would be arranged for the 25 April before the matter could be settled. I told her that I would be out of the country, and the Panel Meeting needed to be brought forward as a matter of urgency. On the same day, I sent a fax confirming our telephone conversation. I had learned by now to confirm everything that was discussed with social workers in writing, because they would more often than not refute what they had said in the past or they would go back on their word.

There was a loud and insistent knocking on my door, and when I went to open it there were two policemen standing unsmiling at the door.

"Are you Dianne Lang?", they asked.

Immediately, my heart started beating faster. I was afraid and fearful. What had I done wrong? What had happened to one of the children? Were the Department of Social Development making good on their threats to charge me for caring for more children than what I was allowed to care for? Was I going to be arrested? These men knew who I was so why would they be asking me who I was?

"Yes, I am Dianne Lang", I answered, my heart turning over.

"Does Jackson Boboytana work for you?", the tall one asked.

"Yes, he does. What is wrong?", I asked.

"Jackson Boboyana has allegedly sexually molested Anton Jali and we want to take him in for questioning", they said.

I could not believe my ears. This was preposterous. "But Anton is at school", I said.

"No, he is not, he is at the police station with his aunt, Yangiswa Makaleni, the social worker from BADISA, and she has laid a charge of sexual assault against Jackson Bobotyana. We want to take him in for questioning", they said.

I was confused, overwhelmed, completely disorientated, totally shocked and could not even think straight. This could not be happening.

"Can you please call Jackson Bobotyana", they asked.

"Yes, yes, I will", I stammered.

There had to be some logical explanation to all this. This was simply not happening. It was a nightmare. What on earth did they mean... that Yangiswa Makaleni was his aunt? "Just give me a couple of minutes. I will go and get him for you. Please come in and sit down. I won't be long", I said.

I raced down the road to the other Children's Home, my mind in a complete shut down phase. What was happening? Not Jackson. Not my loyal and faithful Jackson. Not the Jackson who sat up all night with dying children. Not the Jackson who loved the children with all his heart. Never, no, never. I could not accept this. It was beyond belief. I got to the Children's Home and called for Jackson. I was out of breath.

"Jackson", I said, "Please don't be frightened. I will do everything I can. But something terrible has happened and I don't understand it. But please be brave. The police have come to take you in for questioning. Anton Jali and his aunt, that Makaleni, says you have sexually assaulted him and now they want to question you. You must come with me", I gushed.

Jackson just stood there, disbelieving. He shook his head. I could see he did not believe what he was hearing. I had to repeat what I had just said.

"I did not do this", he said.

"I know Jackson, I do not understand what is happening, but I will do whatever I have to, to get you out of this mess", I said, hugging him to me.

He was shaking so badly and the sweat was pouring off him. Or was it pouring off me? I don't remember. We returned to the policemen who took Jackson, terrified and shaking, and put him in the back of the police van, like a common criminal and drove off with him. I was devastated and started crying, sobbing, not knowing what to do or who to turn to. I went down to the Children's Home to discuss what had happened with Nonqaba and while I was still telling her, Yangiswa Makaleni, the social worker supporting Anton in this allegation, together with Lucinda Grootboom, arrived to cross-examine us on the alleged sexual molestation of Anton since he was one of their case files. Suddenly, they were now interested in one of their case files, when they had done nothing about this child in all this time. Here was the aunt of the child who had done nothing to assist the child, despite our telephone calls and our letters, cross-examining us on the abuse of the child by our staff.

"We are not going to answer your questions and since you have already laid a charge against our staff member, I suggest you leave the investigation to the police", I said.

"May I ask you where Anton is?", I asked.

"Anton has been placed in care", said Makaleni.

"I think you can leave now", I said, as I made a gesture towards the door. The two of them left, laughing on their way out. I telephoned the local office of the Department of Social Development and informed them of what had taken place. They advised me to immediately suspend Jackson from work until the investigation was completed. Fortunately, Jackson was not arrested. He was released back into my care once I had spoken with the Investigating Officer and told him that Jackson would be suspended from work until the completion of the investigation.

Jackson was completely devastated and shaken up. He told me that while he was at the police station, the two social workers had been there and were talking to Bongani, the Chairperson of the Community Police Forum. Bongani is a civilian and the Community Police Forum is a link between the police and the community. I was the Vice-Chairperson of the Forum. The Community Police Officer for the Forum was Nonqaba's sister. Neil's brother was an Inspector in the police. These relationships would have far-reaching effects for our foundation in the future.

Bongani and I had had our run-ins in the past, particularly in view of the fact that instead of Bongani being pro-community, he was pro-police. Where crime statistics were being purposefully lowered, he would not challenge them as in the case where twenty-three child abuse cases were placed in one docket so that it was recorded as only one child abuse case for the month. The cuddle-up between the social workers and Bongani was not good.

I went to the police station later that day and spoke to two police officers myself about the case. They told me that Anton Jali had told them that he was only joking about being sexually molested by Jackson. I asked them for affidavits which they gave me stating that Anton had told them (on separate occasions) that he was only joking about Jackson molesting him.

The following day, 8 April, 2004, I wrote to the Member of the Executive Council of the Department of Social

Development, the Area Commissioner of the South African Police, the Station Commissioner of Middelburg, BADISA, The Department of Social Development in Cradock (Middelburg's head office), the Independent Complaints Directorate and the Community Police Forum, and gave them the factual situation regarding Anton Jali, how he came to be with us, the lack of service delivery from the social workers, the absconding of the boys, the district surgeon's findings, the affidavits of the on-duty police officers and asked them to assist us to ensure that justice prevailed. I received no response ever from any of these departments.

That night, when the children and I went for our customary walk, we walked past Anton. He was obviously not in care as he was with the bigger street youth, smoking at the corner of the street in town. The following day, Anton assaulted Nonqaba's daughter on her way to school. She reported the incident to the police. Nothing came of it. Obviously, Anton was out of control and the social workers had neither taken him into care nor had dealt with the case appropriately. I did not know what they were up to with this child who obviously was in trouble.

The next total shock was a telephone call from Lucinda Grootboom who informed me that she was removing Jonathan and Lionel from my care due to the fact that my staff molested children. She was making arrangements with Mrs Keeve for the boys to sleep at her home, she was going to get the Department of Social Development to pay her R500 per child, but the boys would be spending the days with me because they were doing well at school.

When I told her that the staff member who had allegedly molested Anton had been suspended, she was still adamant that the interests of Jonathan and Lionel were of her utmost concern and in her opinion this was the best arrangement. She was not going to entertain any arguments.

When I told her that I had been actively trying to find Jonathan's father, she acted surprised. She told me that Jonathan's father was unknown. A year later, I got her records and found that she knew all along who Jonathan's father was. I told Jonathan and Lionel of the new arrangements and they were very unhappy about it. They cried and cried and said that life was unfair. I too thought that it was unfair, but I told them that it would just be for a little while and that as soon as things were sorted out, they could come back.

In the meantime, I was visited by a constable from the police station who brought me some very interesting news. He told me that Bongani and Inspector Vers (Nonqaba's sister) were visited by both the social workers for a couple of hours before the statement about the alleged molestation was made. I also found out that the docket stated that the complainant was Lucinda Grootboom, although Yangiswa Makaleni, the aunt, had made the statement. Thus, the docket was incorrect. How could the complainant be someone other than the person making the statement? This again showed that Bongani was acting in the capacity of a police officer and not that of a civilian.

On 13 April, I wrote to the Chief Social Worker of the Department of Social Development and Lucinda

Grootboom of BADISA and again asked them to reconsider the decision to remove Jonathan and Lionel from my care, specifying all the reasons for them to remain in my care, and stating that the reasons for their removal was insufficient because the Department of Social Development was not removing any of the other fifty children in my care and was, in fact, continuing to place children in our Children's Home. If there was such a threat to the children, why were they so adamant to remove *only* two of them? Again, I received no answer.

In between all the correspondence, the telephone calls, the faxes, the begging and the pleading, I was dealing with Jackson who was in a state of shock and very frightened. At the same time, he was extremely angry with Anton and with the two social workers. I was also dealing with the trauma that was being unnecessarily inflicted upon Jonathan and Lionel and on top of that, the problems of being one staff member short as well as the children who were pining for Jackson. It was a terrible time for all of us. I was overwhelmed with what was going on and I had no one to turn to for help. The authorities were not assisting me in any way, they did not seem to care that the children were being traumatized by the actions of the adults in the scenario, I was not getting any government funding in any case, I was still battling to find funding, and I was just moving from one crisis to another. I was getting very little sleep and was constantly on edge. I was frustrated and I was losing my temper with the authorities and could not get my head around their lack of compassion, their lack of understanding, their lack of knowledge of the constitution, their lack of service delivery, their lack of common decency, their lack of manners and their lack of professionalism.

Jonathan handed me a note just as I was going to bed. I thanked him, kissed him goodnight and got into bed. The next day was the day that the boys were to be handed over to Mrs Keeve. I settled myself into bed and put the pillows behind my head. I picked up Jonathan's note and started to read.

Dear Jesus, Why am I on earth? Why did you bring rules in the world? You must put in real rules and I want you to share your love with me. I just want to know that there is one person that loves me and no one else. I don't know why they don't love me. I want a chance in life Lord. I can't stay living like this with my heart so broken. I wish I could be like you, changing people's lives. Why am I living like this? Why is there AIDS in the world? Why did my mother die? Why does my father not come and take me? Why did you make divorce? Why did you create broken hearts? Like me? From Jonathan.

"Yes, why? God", I asked out aloud. Why? I cried myself to sleep. The next morning Lucinda phoned at four thirty in the afternoon.

"Mrs Lang", she said, "I want you to take Lionel and Jonathan to Mrs Keeve now".

"Miss Grootboom", I retaliated, now sick and tired and frustrated and angry, "collect the children yourself and take them to her. I do not do the work that you are paid to do".

299

"Are they ready?" she asked.

"Yes, they are", I replied, and put the phone down. She was there within five minutes. The boys were with me, with their overnight bags packed. I kissed them, hugged them and told them I would see them in the morning. They walked with her to her car and as they got to the car, they both bolted. They ran down the street, around the corner and were out of sight. I could not help but smile. My boys! They were not going to go without some sign of resistance.

Lucinda Grootboom walked back across the street to me and said, "I am not going to waste any more of my time and money to sort this out. I am going to the gym and I do not want to be late".

With that, she strode across the road to her car, got in and drove away. The boys were obviously watching because they came running back up the street, huge smiles on their faces and almost knocked me over in their bear hugs.

"Oh, you boys", I said, "What are we going to do now? We are going to be in big trouble". "We don't have to go where we don't want to go", they said.

"Well, tomorrow will look after itself ", I thought, as I sent them back inside to get on with the joy of living at home. I went to my computer and wrote a letter to the Chief Social Worker confirming what had just happened and faxed it through to him. Our night had just begun. More was yet to follow and little did I know what an eventful night it would become.

At five-thirty Lucinda Grootboom was back with another member of her team, a person by the name of Marie. She requested the school books of Anton Jali, which I handed over. She told me that she would be returning at six o'clock the next morning to collect the boys to take them from me, and put them in a place of safety in Port Elizabeth for a minimum period of six months. When I argued that the place of safety was a correctional school, and that the children were not juvenile criminals and were not drug addicts and did not fit the criteria for such a place, she responded that it was in the best interests of the children.

When I asked her to justify this, she said, "It is because of the molestation thing".

She then asked to speak to the boys. I called and called the boys but there was no reply. I went to look for them and found them hiding under my bed. I had to pull them out from under the bed, promising them that she would not take them away.

When the children came to the door she told them, "You are going to be sent to Port Elizabeth for six months because you ran away".

Lionel said, "If we apologise nicely, will you allow us to stay?"

"No", she said, "You have already had your chance. And you, Miss Lang, if you do not hand the children over tomorrow morning, I will bring the police to forcibly remove them", she said.

She was still repeating herself when I said, "I have already heard and understood you", and I closed the door on her.

This naturally upset the children and I. I contacted the lawyer who told me that there was nothing more that I could do to keep the children in my care. My mind raced. What to do? How to protect them? They did not belong in a correctional school. It did not make sense for the social workers to remove the two children from me when they were leaving so many with me. This was a personal issue and was not in the best interests of the children. There was no reasonable reason for them to be removed from my care. The children were happy with me, they did not want to go anywhere else and they were well looked after. How could I fight this?

Suddenly I remembered that I could ask for an urgent interdict from the Commissioner of Child Welfare. The Magistrate of Middelburg doubled up as the Commissioner of Child Welfare. There were two magistrates in Middelburg. I tried to phone both of them, but their mobile phones were off. I raced around to their homes, but they were not there. One was in Cradock and the other was on holiday. I then sent an urgent fax to the Public Protector, the highest person in the land to get assistance when a constitutional issue was being violated, and this was certainly a case of a child's rights being violated. I explained the situation in the fax, asked for help and asked for an urgent and independent investigation into the Social Welfare in the area. Still, Lucinda Grootboom was coming to collect the children at 0600 in the morning, and I would not be able to stop her in the time that I had. I would not get a reply from the Public Protector in that time and nor would I get a magistrate in the time I had left. In fact, I only received a reply, despite many letters to the Public Protector, a year later.

The boys were extremely traumatized, as were the rest of the children. I was very upset and did not know what to do to protect the children. The welfare had made some terrible mistakes in the past with children, and I did not want these boys to be subjected to a correctional school where they would be influenced by juvenile criminals and drug addicts and where they would be locked up most of the time. They were in a loving home, and for them to be put into a correctional school for no good reason was beyond my comprehension. I could not let this happen. A plan was growing in my mind, a plan so bizarre and so alien that I would baulk at the idea and chew it over and over as it would entail me asking a favour of someone I had not spoken to for many years and someone whom I had sworn I would never ask for help from. And knowingly, I would be breaking the law. I was in a moral dilemma. There was the law of the land and there was God's law – and which one was I to abide by? Which one did I follow and which one was I prepared to live with? Which one was I prepared to suffer the consequences of? Would I live to regret what I was planning to do?

I had saved so many children from death, from the streets, from rapists. I had stood up to the police and the social workers but this one, Lucinda Grootboom, although I had tried my best to use every moral argument, was abusing her power and not working in the interests of the children. The authorities in power above her were not hearing my pleas, and I was up against a brick wall. To

303

save these boys, I had to buy time. It was a choice between breaking the law of the land and doing what I knew in my heart what was right. I would suffer the consequences. I would do everything in my power to save them. If I went to jail for it, then it would be up to God. I would leave it in His hands.

I phoned my ex-husband. Would he help me? I had not spoken to him for years. We were not friends, and there was too much water under the bridge for a reconciliation on that issue. He came on the line and I told him I needed his help. I explained the problem with the boys and told him I had to buy some time for them so that I could sort something out with the authorities to stop them from being put into a correctional school. Would he hide the children for me for a while? He did not hesitate.

"Phone me when you leave Middelburg", he said, "And I will leave here at the same time and meet you half way".

I was so grateful. After all these years, this man did not hesitate to help me in my hour of need. I called the boys to me. This would have to be a secret that no one else could know about.

"Listen you boys, there is only one way to save you from Grootboom and Erica Place of Safety until I can get something sorted out with the Commissioner. I have to hide you. My friend is willing to hide you for a while, but it is far away. You will be safe with him and his family. No one can know about this. You can never, ever tell anyone what I am doing. Do you promise me that?"

They nodded earnestly.

"Right, what I want you to do is to go and pack your clothes. Don't let anyone see you. Then I want you to go and get a loaf of bread, butter and jam and a cool drink. Bring it into my room and make sandwiches. Close the door so no one sees you. Also, pack a sleeping bag each and a pillow. Put everything under my bed. Then pretend nothing is going on. Do not tell anyone. Later tonight when everyone is asleep we are going to slip away and then we are going to meet my friend half way. OK?"

They grinned at me and nodded. And then they threw their arms about me and hugged me tight.

"Thank you Mama D. We knew you would save us", said Jonathan.

When the home was quiet and the children asleep, I went to Jonathan and Lionel and told them to go and get their things and quietly slip out and into my vehicle while I kept the staff busy. I told the staff that I was going out to visit friends and that I would be back much later. I put on my jacket and slipped out of the house, locking the door behind me. The boys were in the vehicle, hiding under the dashboard. I told them to stay down until we were out of town. It was a very cold night and the windscreen misted up in no time. I used the demister to clear the screen and my heart beat like a wild bird trying to escape a cage. I was afraid.

The boys were excited. The drive out of town was never so long. I told them to stay down until we were at least ten kilometres out of town. I passed two police vehicles on the way out and hoped they would not stop me to find out where I was going at that time of night. I just hooted at them and waved. At last the boys could sit up. I was exhausted. It had been a very stressful day and I still had 200 km to drive to the half way mark.

I called my ex-husband, Rob, on the mobile and told him that we were 10 km outside of Middelburg. The mist on the road that night was very bad. It caused us to have to drive at a very slow speed a lot of the way and my eyes were burning. It felt like it took forever to get to the half-way mark, and there, waiting for us was Rob and his wife, Lesley. It was a very quick goodbye to the boys and they were in his car and they drove off into the night. I turned my vehicle around and drove the lonely trip back home.

When I got home, the night staff were in a terrible flap because they had discovered that Jonathan and Lionel had absconded.

"Just phone the police and tell them that the children have absconded, although I don't blame them, do you?", I told them as I fell into bed, completely exhausted.

It was not without some surprise that Grootboom did not arrive to collect the boys at six the next morning. I wrote to the Chief Social Worker and told him what she had done the previous evening, what she had said to the children, and that she had said that she was going to take them to Erica Place of Safety in Port Elizabeth for a period of six month's because of the molestation problem. I also stated that he had in fact placed all the other children in my care, and that he was satisfied with them continuing to be in my care, and that it made no sense to remove only two children. I stated that because of what she had said to the boys, they had absconded. The police had been notified, and that should the children return to me, I would let them know and, in this event, I trusted that he would intervene and do what was best in the interests of the children. Again, I received no response.

That same day, I received a letter from Grootboom stating that in the best interests of the children they were going to be placed at the Erika Place of Safety due to the fact that molestation was taking place at my children's home. In view of this, I was to deliver the children to her offices as soon as possible and that they would be transferred to Port Elizabeth on Monday. Together with this letter, she attached another letter to the Chief Social Worker's Superior in Cradock, Miranda Botha, explaining that the children would be removed because we had molesters within our children's home. Grootboom had also got Miranda Botha to sign a Section 36(1) order for consent for removal for purpose of observation, examination or treatment of the children for a period of six months at Erica Place of Safety. She was determined to send the boys away to this institution and, by this action, determined to destroy me or these children.

I made an appointment to see the Magistrate, who doubled as Commissioner of Welfare, Mr Mata, and spoke to him about the situation regarding the boys. I showed him all the documents that I had received and sent. He said that he would act as mediator between the social worker and myself. He called Lucinda Grootboom to his office. He requested Miss Grootboom to reconsider her decision to put the children in a place of safety (which is used mostly for children involved in crime), as it did not appear to be in the best interests of the children. He later telephoned me to say that Miss Grootboom was adamant that the children be removed from my care. He said that he was of the opinion that this situation was of a personal nature.

I then wrote and faxed a letter to the Executive Member of the Department of Social Development and explained the Commissioner of Child Welfare's concerns in the matter, and again asked for his help and assistance as well as asking again for an urgent independent investigation into the BADISA social services. Again, I got no response. I also contacted the opposition political parties to see if they could assist me and faxed letters through to them as well. These pleadings also fell on deaf ears.

On the 20 April, I telephoned my ex-husband to put the second part of the plan into operation. I asked him to take the children to the police station to show them where it was. He was then to tell the children to go to the police station the next morning and to tell them that they wanted to go home, that they had run away and wanted to go home to me. They were to give the police my telephone number. With any luck, the police would phone me and then I would go and fetch them from the police station there. This is what they did, and as all good plans fall into place, I got a telephone call from the police station there to come and fetch my boys.

I immediately left Middelburg and collected my boys from a rather amused policeman who could not understand quite what was going on when he saw these two boys jump into the arms of a middle-aged white woman. We then drove around to my ex-husband where I thanked him most profusely for his hospitality and his unhesitating assistance to me. And then we were on our way home. As soon as I got home, I telephoned the local police and reported that I had received a telephone call from the other police station to collect the boys. I also notified the Commissioner of Child Welfare that the boys were back and asked for a Children's Court hearing for the next day. I then telephoned the Chief Social Worker, Mr Pienaar, and told him the boys were back with me and that he should notify Miss Grootboom.

On the 22nd April, Lucinda Grootboom dropped off a copy of a letter that she had given to the magistrate asking for a mandate to order the South African Police to remove the children from me and escort them to the Erika Place of Safety and gave her reasons as being:

The two children are under the supervision of BADISA. There is allegations of sexual molestation of one of the children who is staying at the Care House by one of the staff members (She does not say the child is no longer there and that the staff member is suspended which she knows about) *The chairperson of the Care House told me that I can't go there in the Care House or phone Ms Lang so can you ask the SAPS to go and fetch that children from the Care House.* (this was a lie)

Mr Mata, the magistrate/Commissioner of Child Welfare, whom I had spoken to before about the case, called me to tell me to bring the boys to court at two that afternoon. When we walked into court, Lucinda Grootboom was there, all puffed up in her own self-importance, holding on to her forms, ready to remove the children from my care. Mr Mata called an interpreter in. Lucinda Grootboom started stating her case, that she had the necessary forms to remove the children, that she wanted a police escort to remove the children, and was carrying on so much that eventually Mr Mata told her to behave herself and sit down.

"This is a Children's Court hearing and if you do not contain yourself, you will be excused from my court", he said.

From then on, the Children's Court proceedings proceeded in an orderly fashion, with questions being asked of me, and the boys being questioned extensively on where they wanted to live, how they came to live with me and how they were coping in school. Jonathan was unbelievably quick-witted and intelligent in his responses.

Once he had the idea of how the court worked, he would interject with "Excuse me your honour, but I would like to say something". When Lucinda Grootboom told a blatant lie, Jonathan would say "Excuse me, your honour, but Miss Grootboom is not being truthful...".

And so it went on and on. I was so proud of Jonathan and the interpreter could not help smiling at the discomfort of Miss Grootboom. She had come in so full of herself and, as the proceedings progressed, so she became smaller and smaller in her chair and Jonathan became a bigger and bigger man. I think that even Mr Mata was impressed by Jonathan. Jonathan listened very carefully and would remember what Miss Grootboom said, and if she later said something that was dissimilar to what she had said before, he would jump in with "Excuse me, your honour, but Miss Grootboom said previously that ...". He caught her out on so many lies that unless she was thick-skinned she must have felt like a complete fool. At the end of the court hearing, Mr Mata put both boys in my custody. They whooped with joy and we went out of the door skipping and shouting.

As I walked out the door, Lucinda Grootboom said to me, "You have not heard the last from me".

But my joy over-rode her miserable prediction. We had the celebration of a lifetime that night at home. We sang and danced and ate. Our miracle had happened. I could now go overseas and look for funding with a good heart, knowing my children were safe.

While I was in the UK doing my rounds of presentations to raise funds for the Children's Home, I received a call from Louis Jenner, the House committee chairperson and full time police inspector, to say that they were in Children's Court with Lionel and Jonathan, and that the magistrate had signed the documents for the boys to be sent to Erica Place of Safety in Port Elizabeth.

I went mad. I was screaming and shouting on the telephone, wanting to know what the hell was going on, how could this happen, how could they allow this, could they not stop it and all I was told is that there was nothing that they could do. This was in the middle of May. There was nothing I could do while I was in the UK. I cried and cried. I sobbed and howled and felt completely helpless. I still had to go on and do a presentation, with such a heavy heart, knowing that my boys were on their way to a jail, a correctional school. How had my staff allowed this to happen? Why had they not protected my children? I had a thousand unanswered questions and I felt so helpless. I was so angry as well, but I had to put my heartache to one side while I continued to put another face on while I did my presentations and collected money to take home.

The first thing I did when I landed in Port Elizabeth was go to the Erica Place of Safety to see the boys. They were so sad, so miserable, so unhappy. I promised them that I would get them out of there as soon as possible. I spoke to the Superintendent to find out under what circumstances they had arrived, and was told that they were there because the home that they had come from was unsafe because there was molestation going on. I explained that I was the person in charge of the home, that no molestation had taken place although there was an investigation going on and that the staff member was suspended. She said that she had also had sexual molestation happen at the Erica Place of Safety, and all that happened was that the staff member was suspended until after the investigation and that no children had been removed. She also found the situation rather strange. She felt that the boys did not belong in Erica but there was nothing she could do about it. They could only be removed by the social worker who had placed them there. They were placed there under a six month order. After the six month order they would have to be returned to the original home or to foster parents. I said a very sad goodbye to the boys, promising them again that I would do everything in my power to bring them back home.

I could not wait until I got back to Middelburg to find out how Grootboom had managed to take the children out of my care. As soon as it was possible, I got an appointment with Lucinda Grootboom to discuss the predicament of the boys. She told me that she had a letter from my staff stating that the boys were not behaving, and on the basis of that letter she had them transferred to Port Elizabeth. I asked her for a copy of the letter which she produced. I was sickened to the pit of my stomach.

The letter had been written by Niel and signed by Nonqaba, my own staff members. They had written it on 12 May 2004, and stated that the children had left the Children's Home without their permission and had been brought back by the police on the night of the 8th May. They further stated that they would not listen to the staff, that the staff had no control over them, and that the children were a disgrace and a disappointment.

I told Lucinda that the staff had no authority to write any such letters as they were junior staff members but be that as it may, could she please make arrangements for the boys to return home for the school holidays. I followed the appointment up with a letter requesting the boys to be allowed home for the holidays. My anger at the staff knew no bounds, although I did not show it. I merely asked them who had given them authority to write such a letter, knowing the fight I had had in trying to save them from going to Erica Place of Safety. I was told that Lucinda had told them to write the letter. Whether this was in fact true or not, I will never know. They may even have been in cahoots. I no longer trusted Niel or Nonqaba, considering their attitude to the bigger boys, and I certainly did not trust Lucinda Grootboom. I had no way of knowing who was telling the truth and could therefore do nothing about the staff writing the letter. I did however give them a written warning about writing letters to the authorities without my permission.

I wrote a letter to the social worker, Mr Mendele, of the Erica Place of Safety, requesting that the boys be allowed home for the holidays. Children at the Erica Place of Safety are normally allowed home for holidays unless there is some serious reason why they should not be allowed to do so. Mr Mendele did not see why they could not come home, and said he would discuss it with Miss Grootboom and come back to me. The holidays were fast approaching and I heard nothing from either social worker. I left numerous messages for Miss Grootboom to contact me and eventually telephoned Mr Mendele. He informed me that he had spoken to Miss Grootboom, and that she had said that under no circumstances were the boys to be allowed to come back to Middelburg for the holidays. In between the goings on between the social workers, myself and the various departments of social development, I was telephoning and writing to the boys and driving to Port Elizabeth to visit them.

On my second visit to Port Elizabeth I was most distressed to see them in the condition in which they were. Both boys

314

were covered in scabies and they managed to take me to their dormitory where they slept. The beds were so close together that one had to walk sideways to get between the beds. Our Children's Home was luxury in comparison to what the boys were now subjected to. There was nothing else in the room except beds. The electrical sockets were open with open wires hanging out of them. The windows were broken. The curtains did not cover the windows. There were no cupboards at all in the room. I asked them where their clothes were kept.

"We get given clothes out of the office each morning to wear", Jonathan told me.

"Everyone lines up and clothes get taken out and you get to wear whatever you get given", Lionel said.

I was horrified. This was a government-run institution. Where was the five square metre floor sleeping space? Where was the privacy of the children? Where was their individuality or their individual clothes? This was a jail. What was even more disturbing was that both boys had been tattooed on the back of their shoulders.

"Why did you do this to yourselves?", I asked. "You know that only gangsters and bad boys do this", I said.

"It wasn't us, Mama D", said Jonathan, "they do things to you to make you part of the gang, and then you get a tattoo".

"What things?", I asked.

"You know, things", said Lionel, looking down at his feet.

"No, I don't know. What things?"

"Things, Mama D".

"Jonathan, what things", I asked, now getting agitated and grabbing by the shoulders, and looking him in the eyes. His eyes welled up with tears. Now I was really worried and I felt my stomach tighten. "Tell me Jonathan. You know you can tell me anything", I said gently, taking him into my arms.

"You promise never to tell, Mama D", he asked.

"I promise", I said.

"Tell her Lionel, tell her", he said, prodding Lionel in the chest.

I looked up at Lionel from my kneeling position, still cradling Jonathan in my arms.

Lionel looked away from me and said quietly, "They put their penises in our bums, Mama D".

"Oh, Jesus fucking Christ, not that", I thought. "No, no, no, not that, not to my boys!" I could feel the tears run down my cheeks. The cold wind turned my tears to ice and new tears burned hot as they ran down my face. I had no words to comfort the boys. I reached out my other arm and drew Lionel into my embrace. I held onto them and drew them into me, loving them and trying to convey my love for them through my embrace, trying to heal their hurts and what they had endured, what they had suffered; I tried to take it from them.

My intense irritation and loathing for Lucinda Grootboom and all those who had refused to help these boys was turning to hatred. I wanted to smash their faces in. I wanted to go back to Middelburg and push Niel and Nonqaba's faces into what had happened to my boys. I wanted revenge for these children. I wanted to scream and shout out to the world what the abuse of power of one social worker had done to two lovable and innocent children. The faith I had in the goodness of mankind was now gone. All my many telephone calls, the faxes, the letters had fallen on deaf ears. Who cared about just two children? Who cared what happened to them? The boys pleaded with me not to tell anyone otherwise they would get into big trouble. I had promised not to tell. I would keep my promise but I did go to the Superintendent, Mrs Martin, and complained that the children had scabies and that they had tattoos. She just said that this was normal for children in the institution, but it was her belief that these children of mine did not belong there. The children and I said a very tearful goodbye, again with me promising to do all I could to bring them home.

I again sent all the documents pertaining to the case of the boys to the Erica social worker and asked him to do everything he could to facilitate the return of the boys. I wrote to the Superintendent of Erica and asked her to do the same. She suggested that the Commissioner of Child Welfare in Middelburg write a letter to the Department of Social Development requesting that the boys be returned home. I went to Mr Mata, requesting him to intervene in the case of the boys, as suggested by Mrs Martin, telling him of the condition the boys were living under and showed him photographs of the boys, their tattoos, their scabies and the dormitory in which they stayed. Nothing came of this.

In the meantime, I was still dealing with the issues of all the other children. Jonathan and Lionel were not the only children that were demanding my attention. We had three homes, one for sick children, one for the children who were well and I had a small home in which I lived and where I took in the children who became very ill and from where I ran the office and the entire operation.

Basically, all I had was a bedroom which was not even my own. It was shared with Amore and with whichever child was desperately ill at the time. The rest of the little house was operating as the nerve centre of the entire operation. All three houses were in the same street, in the same block, so it was easy to keep all of us together and under control.

I was learning as I was going along. I had never had a Children's Home so every step was a learning experience for me. I received no guidance from the Department of Social Development so had to muddle along. I learned everything through the Department's policing and harassment of me. It was not long before I realized that the social workers had very little, if any, compassion for the children at all, and that the interests of the children were not their priority.

Saving Mandela's Children

By now I had realized that there was a list of donors on the internet that you could apply to for funding for children, and I sent funding proposals off to 720 donors. Surely something had to come from that. Of the total number of proposals that were sent off in the first year, we received 84 negative replies and three positive ones. The donations were donor-specific, meaning that donations for Home Based Care work, and could not be spent on caring for the children. However, a certain amount of money was set aside for the facilitation and payment of a lecturer for the Home Based Care work, and this money I used for the children as I was doing the work myself. Instead of paying a facilitator and lecturer, I did the work myself and used that money for the children. This teaching and organizing was also taking up a lot of my time. I was sleeping very little as all the administration had to be done in the small hours of the night as there was just no time during the day, and my evenings were taken up by children's needs, such as homework, changing dressings, giving out medication, supper, counselling and dealing with staff issues.

At the same time, Jackson was becoming more and more depressed as the investigation into the allegation of sexual molestation was dragging on. I was also continually phoning the investigating officer of the police to find out when the investigation would be finished or how far they were. After months, I was told that the docket had been submitted to the Public Prosecutor in Grahamstown.

I was still trying to visit the boys at least once a month and making sure that I faxed a letter through to them once a week. I was also phoning them twice a week to let them know that they were still in my thoughts and that I loved them. I was constantly on at the Department of Social Development, writing and phoning all the various managers, social workers, heads of departments, the social worker and superintendent of Erica, Grootboom and her superiors and eventually, the Minister of Social Development. I was harassing the Public Protector and even wrote to the President. Not one of these letters or faxes was acknowledged. The boys, Jonathan in particular, were continually asking me when I was coming to fetch him, and I was continually asking him to be patient, that I was doing everything to bring him home.

In July 2004, Jonathan telephoned me. He was crying and I could not understand what he was trying to tell me. I told him to put the phone down, take some deep breathes and that I would phone him back again. When I phoned him back, he told me that his best friend at Erica had hanged himself because one of the staff had slapped him in the dining room in front of everyone. He was very upset. I promised to visit him the next day, which was a weekend. When I got there, the atmosphere was sombre. I was told by Mrs Martin that Jonathan was particularly affected because Charl and he were best friends and that she would see to it that he got counselling. Jonathan took me to show me where Charl had hung himself. Charl was fourteen years old. Jonathan handed me a letter when I left. It is dated 25 July, 2004.

Dear Mama D, Charl was me and Lionels best friend, but he passed away because one of the staff members slapped him so he hanged himself on Thursday on the steps. He was only 14 years old. He slept in Room 5 and

320

me and Lionel sleep in Room 6. Me and Lionel are full of scabies. The children smoke dagga at this place and they steal our stuff and we don't even go to proper school. I'm getting boils. So please take me home. I'm not happy and I miss my friends. With love, Jonathan.

By the way he wrote his letter and by his unusually bad grammar, I could see that he was a desperately unhappy child, and that he was deteriorating not only physically but mentally as well. I renewed my efforts and again phoned and wrote to everyone who could accommodate me in bringing the children home. Again, I asked if the boys could come home for the next holiday. Again, it was denied.

On 6 August 2004, we received the long awaited news from the police regarding Jackson. *"The Senior Public Prosecutor declined to prosecute anyone in the case Middelburg (EC) CAS 33/04/2004: Indecent Assault: Complainant : AS Jali".* Jackson was at once recalled to work and I immediately set about sending a copy of this document with another request to all the many people I had already requested help from to bring Jonathan and Lionel home. I also sent a letter to the Chief Operations Manager of the Department of Social Development who specifically deals with children who have their rights violated. No response was received from any of them.

On the 25th August, I had the investigation by the team from the Department of Social Development from Bisho. I had given the file on Jonathan and Lionel to Mrs Mathews, and begged her to look into the situation and to try to return the boys to me. Nothing came of this either, despite me phoning her a number of times after their visit.

At the end of August, the social worker from Erica told me that he would be sending someone from their institution to assess the situation so that arrangements could be made to return the boys to me. I was very excited about this and shared it with the boys. By the September, when nothing had happened, I again telephoned him and wrote to him asking him what their arrangements were, because both the boys and I were anxious about their return. He said that he would get back to me. He never did.

Late on the night of the 15th September I got a missed call on my mobile from the Erica telephone. I called back immediately. It was Jonathan on the phone.

"Mama D, if you don't get me out of here, I am going to hang myself exactly like Charl did. Please get me out of here. I can't stand it anymore. I am so unhappy. The other boys are smoking dagga and they are stealing. Please Mama D, I am begging you", he cried.

"Jonathan, please don't do that. Don't do what Charl did. Maybe Charl did that because he did not have someone who loved him as much as I love you. I promise you that I am doing everything in my power to bring you home", I said.

"But Mama D, you have been saying that for a long time".
"I know, my darling, but I am trying, I promise you. I have written to everybody I know who can help us. I even wrote to Thabo Mbeki. I am trying my best and, in any

case, the order from the magistrate said they can only keep you there for six months and the six months is nearly up". "But I want to come home", he cried.

"And I want you home more than anything. I love you Jonathan. You are the most special child in the world and I love you with all my heart. Please don't do anything silly or stupid. If you try to hang yourself and it does not work or you run away, then they will keep you there. You have to be patient and wait. Please, my love". "But I want to come home Mama D, and I can't wait any longer or I will hang myself ", he cried.

I spent at least an hour on the phone to him, calming him down and promising to write to everyone again the next day and promising to fax him a letter as well.

The next day, I wrote to eleven Heads of Departments within the Department of Social Development to get the boys home. Again, I received no response from them, despite having followed this up with telephone calls. I also sent a letter to the Head Office of BADISA for urgent intervention. I received no response. I wrote a letter to Jonathan telling him not to do anything stupid and that I would be sending a letter to the MEC of Social Development by fax every day until they got sick of me and sent him home. This is what I started to do. I started sending faxes to everyone every day, requesting the boys to be returned home.

I wrote again to the social worker of Erica Place of Safety and advised him that the boys had been at their institution for six months on 8 October 2004. I asked him to please

323

do everything in his power to bring the boys home. The placement order was now invalid. On the 11 October he wrote back to me stating that he would be meeting with BADISA to discuss alternative placement for the boys in 2005 and that "*Unfortunately there is nothing more that I can do to assist your cause*". BADISA had refused to allow the boys to come back to me, and Erica was abiding by Lucinda Grootboom's decision.

I wrote a letter to the Commissioner of Child Welfare and took all the documents as well as my latest letter from Erica with me when I went to see him. I showed him the letter from the Erica social worker and asked him to please get the children returned to me as they had now been at Erica for 7 months. He said that he would see what he could do. Obviously nothing was done since there was no hearing and the boys remained at Erica. I again asked for the boys to spend the Christmas holidays with me and I was again refused. I continued asking for intervention on behalf of the children, writing continually to the Public Protector, stating the violation of the children's rights according to the constitution. I got no response.

My visits to the boys were always happy at the start of the visit and traumatic and sad at the end of the visit. Erica never had a problem with my visits and allowed me to take them out for the day. By this stage Mrs Martin, the superintendent, was quite friendly with me. She could not understand what the problem was or the reason why the boys were not allowed to come home to me, or why the boys were being made to stay at her institution.

Jonathan's depression deepened. He said that he could not take it anymore and that he was either going to run away or he would kill himself. I no longer knew what to do. I told his social worker at Erica that I was very worried about him. Lionel seemed to be coping a lot better than Jonathan, but it was perhaps because Lionel had been on the streets longer than Jonathan, or perhaps it was because Lionel was not as sensitive as Jonathan. No matter how busy I was with the other children or with dealing with the numerous other issues concerning the Children's Home, Jonathan was constantly on my mind. I loved him so much. He had crept into my heart and I was very worried about his state of mind.

When I stepped off the plane from Johannesburg after the award ceremony, I switched on my mobile phone. There were dozens of missed calls and messages for me from the children's home. All the messages concerned Jonathan and they were from the Children's Home. "Call Erica about Jonathan", "Phone Erica about Jonathan and Lionel" , "Maybe we can fetch Jonathan and Lionel so call Erica", "Erica wants you to call", "Mrs Martin from Erica called".

I did not even bother to phone. I was so excited that I drove directly from the airport to Erica Place of Safety. I was going to get the boys and drive straight home. What a wonderful ending to an unbelievable time in Johannesburg, notwithstanding the high heeled shoes. I drove to Erica like a woman possessed. The place was deserted. Normally children were milling around the front gate. I went inside and told the porter that I was there for Jonathan and Lionel. He told me to sit down and phoned through. He spoke very quietly into the telephone. A care worker came through and took me into a waiting room. I found this very strange and asked her where Jonathan and Lionel were. She said that someone would be around to see me in a minute and she disappeared very fast.

I started to panic. Something was wrong. I just knew it. This was not the normal course of events when I visited the boys. I got up and went back to reception and demanded to know what was going on from the porter. He said that the stand-by social worker would be along shortly.

"Tell me what is going on", I demanded.

"Someone will tell you in a while", he said.

"No, tell me *now*", I shouted, "Where are Jonathan and Lionel?"

Just then a man I had never met, walked up to me and took me by the shoulder and led me into the room I had just walked out of.

"I am very sorry", he said, "but I have bad news. Jonathan passed away last night".

I went cold. I just looked at him. I could not move. I could not speak. I was numb, paralyzed.

"What did you say?" I asked.

"Jonathan passed away last night", he repeated.

"Bullshit.   You talking crap. I have come to fetch the children to take them home", I said, my mind shutting off the news he had just given me.

"Please bring the children to me", I begged.

"Mrs Lang, listen to me, Jonathan has passed away. He is dead, do you understand", he said, shaking me by the shoulders.

I stared at him uncomprehendingly. "How?" I asked.

"He hung himself ".

"Where? Show me!", I demanded as I stood up.

I followed him as he led me to the place where Jonathan had ended his life. He told me how he had done it. Jonathan had taken some school ties and some string and tied it to the security gate above the stairs. He had then tied the other end around his neck. He had then lain down on the stairs and slid down the stairs until the ligature had tightened around his neck. He must have taken a long time to die and he must have been very determined because his hands were free to loosen the ligature around his neck at any time, and he was able to move himself up the stairs at any time as well. What was in his mind when he did this to himself? Where were the staff when he did this? How long was he missing before anyone looked for him? How desperate was he that he took his own life is such a dreadful, painful and prolonged way? I could still not believe that he had done this, although at some level I understood his pain, his frustration and his need to end it all. I had so many questions but I was getting few answers. I was led back to the waiting room.

"You said I could take Jonathan home. Can I take Lionel too?" I asked.

"We will make the necessary arrangements for Lionel to come back to you, but we have to do the paperwork first" he said.

"Where is Jonathan?" I asked.

"He is at the state mortuary. You will have to identify him and then you can take him home", he answered.

I left Erica and sat in my vehicle, numbed, shocked, unable to think clearly or rationally. I phoned Stuart, our trustee, and told him. I phoned home and told the staff. I phoned the national television program director of Carte Blanche that I had met at the award ceremony. I remembered that he had told me that if I ever needed him, I was to call him. He told me that he had a team in Port Elizabeth and that they would meet me at the state mortuary.

I drove to Stuart and just stood there, completely shocked. All he could say was, "I am sorry. I am so sorry", as he put his arms around me to comfort me. He knew how much the children meant to me. He told me how to get to the state mortuary. He also said he would organize a coffin, a collection from the state mortuary, and a transportation certificate for me to drive home with Jonathan.

He was as good as his word. I was still numb and in shock. I had not shed a tear. I felt that I was walking around in a nightmare from which I would soon wake. When I got to the state mortuary, the film crew from Carte Blanche was already there, as was Mrs Mathews, the team leader from the Department of Social Development who had done the investigation in Middelburg. I greeted them on my way to the mortuary, after asking the directions. I walked in and asked to see Jonathan. I was asked to sit down and wait. After a short while I was called to follow the male receptionist and followed him down a passage. I was surprised at the cleanliness of the place. Along the passage, he pulled a curtain back from a large window and asked me if I knew who the person was behind the window. Covered up to his neck by a white sheet, lay Jonathan, as though he was asleep, his long black hair lying in loose curls around his ears and pushed back from his forehead. I nodded.

"Yes, he is Jonathan", I whispered. I put my hand on the window, trying to reach him, trying to touch him, trying to get to him. From deep inside of me the river of grief broke and cascaded out in ever increasing violent screams of guilt, remorse, anger and frustration as I heard from far away another voice screaming "Jonathan, Jonathan, I am so sorry. Oh! God, I am so sorry! Jonathannnnnn!" And I was running, running, running...

Strange arms surrounded me and held me. Strange voices comforted me. Strange hands pushed tissues into mine. Strange hands wiped tears from my face. I looked around me and noticed I was standing next to a strange vehicle in the car park of the state mortuary. I did not know the people around me. They asked me if I was alright now. I thanked them and said I was fine. I looked over at the other end of the car park and saw the film crew interviewing Mrs Mathews.

With shaking hands, I reached into my bag and took out a cigarette and lit it. I took a deep breath of the nicotine and before it was even out of my lungs, I took another deep breath. I felt it settle in my lungs and I coughed. And the tears flowed down my cheeks but there was no sobbing. There was no noise. I was calm. I went to my vehicle and finished smoking. Then I walked over to the film crew and was just in time to hear Mrs Mathews tell them that the reason Jonathan had hanged himself was because he was involved with drugs and dagga. She did not even look my way as she sauntered off , unaffected by the death of a child that she could have saved. I told the film crew that Jonathan was never involved in any such thing. I remember only this, nothing more. I do not remember what happened between this time and the time I collected Jonathan from the funeral parlour. I have no recollection of what I did, where I went or how I felt. It is strange how some things stick out so vividly in one's mind and yet others are totally obliterated.

Stuart came with me to the funeral parlour. I had to show them my identity document. He had chosen a simple white coffin. We paid for it and then we were asked to reverse my vehicle up to the back of the funeral parlour to load the coffin into the back of my 4 x 4. Stuart had brought one of his employees with him and he reversed my vehicle. When he got out, I noticed that he had tears running down his face. Jonathan's coffin was wheeled out on a trolley and then put into the back of my vehicle. I was numb and did not cry. I remember that. I noticed that there were weeds growing out of the cement in the driveway. I noticed that my dashboard had dust on it. I noticed that Stuart was looking stern. I noticed that my petrol gauge was on full, and wondered who had filled the tank. I noticed insignificant things during the loading of the coffin, but I did not notice my feelings or notice that the coffin had brass handles. That I only noticed much later. The back of the vehicle was closed. I hugged and kissed Stuart goodbye and I drove off, down the road and onto the freeway. I was taking Jonathan home.

Ten months after Jonathan had been taken away from me, I was finally taking him home. I was not allowed to take him home while he was alive, but I was allowed to take him home dead. I had a four hour drive home with a dead child in my vehicle. I dialled the Children's Home and spoke to them via the mobile car phone. I told them I was bringing Jonathan home. I then phoned the funeral parlour in Middelburg and made arrangements for me to bring Jonathan in. Then it was just me, Jonathan, my memories and the road.

If only Patience were with me, this would be more bearable. I cried for Patience. I cried for Jonathan. I cried for the children. I cried for me. After a while, I could no longer see the road, I was sobbing and crying so much that I had to pull over. I sat in the vehicle, looking back at the coffin that held Jonathan and sobbed my heart out. Stuart kept on phoning me to ask me if I was alright and all I could do was sob. He was so concerned about me driving with a dead child. The trip was taking forever. I would pull myself together and then drive on, only to have to pull over again because I was crying too much to see the road.

My grief was mixed with anger towards all the many people who could have helped Jonathan and could have stopped this from happening. Now it was too late. Did they care? Did they even give a damn? My memories of Jonathan were many and those memories filled me with grief. I wondered if there was anything that I could have done that I did not do that could have got him out of Erica. Could I have done any more? Could I have "stolen" him from Erica and hidden him again? Could I not have done more to save him? The torturous trip eventually came to an end. A trip that I will never forget. The ride home with a dead child instead of a chattering happy child in the front seat.

To cut the costs of the funeral, we did the funeral service at home and buried Jonathan next to Luke. I invited all the social workers, but not one turned up. The children were very sad and could not understand why Jonathan had taken his own life. They were only used to children and adults dying from sickness. It took a lot of counselling to help the children over Jonathan's death. I let the children decorate Jonathan's coffin with coloured pencils and paint. Someone painted a large rainbow in the lid of the coffin. I thought that it was symbolic of his life. He was always the sunshine of our lives.

The bigger children all took part in the service, and the words that they said about Jonathan and the part that

Jonathan had played in their lives brought lumps into all our throats. The tears flowed.

It was raining that day, and we all walked behind Jonathan's coffin to the cemetery. When we got to the cemetery, the sun came out. As Jonathan's coffin was lowered into the ground, an incredible rainbow spread across the sky. Somehow I felt that Jonathan was showing us that he knew now that we had loved him.

I asked the Public Protector to investigate the role that Lucinda Grootboom had played in the suicide of Jonathan. I received no reply to my letter.

An ordinary day

I woke to an ordinary day in what I was beginning to think was my ordinary life. It was another blisteringly hot summer's day. As usual, the day lay ahead of me without me having a clue as to what would unfold. I always had a plan for the day, there were always the usual, ordinary things to do, but always, there were the crisis that would spring on me that I would need to deal with.

The first thing on my agenda was to get onto the roof to find the holes that were causing all the leaking. In summer, we have the sudden afternoon thunderstorms with rain lashing down for a half hour or so and then there is nothing, the sun comes out and the steam rises from the hot ground, but we are left with leaks. So, today I was determined to sort out the leaks again. I had had many people go on to the roof, paid them a lot of money and yet, it still leaked. So, I thought, bugger this, I am going to do it myself. There I was, before I had even washed my face, back up on the roof with hammer, roof nails, fibreglass and roof paint.

The roof was so hot that it was burning through my shoes so I shouted for Jackson to throw up the bathmat because when I sat down, I burned my backside. I thought I had done a good assessment and a good job, but the trouble started when I had to come down. My feet just did not reach the ladder and I lost my confidence to come down. There I was, on the roof with no way of coming down. I shouted for Jackson who thought that I was too fat for him to do it alone, so he called Fikile. Between these two brave men, they got me down, both sweating profusely, but proud of the job they had done.

I needed more material for the roof at the office so off I went to the hardware store, covered in roof paint, to buy some more. Over the last couple of weeks, I had been growing seeds in old beer boxes and they needed to be transplanted. All the plants went down to the office, and with some of the children, we got all the plants planted and watered.

It was time to repair the second roof. This time I went up with Jackson and gave him the exact instructions on how I wanted it to be done, and where, and down I came with the help of Fikile.

There was a heap of building sand on the pavement left over from when I re-surfaced the concrete veranda. It needed to be moved before the council gave me a fine. I got two of the bigger boys, two spades and two wheelbarrows, and organized for the sand to be moved to the back of the children's home to a place where it would be needed to replace a fence. The week before I had managed to persuade someone to give me a donation of fifty metres of fencing that was eight feet high. All we needed now was to buy some metal poles and concrete and then we could put the fence up. The fence was desperately needed for the security of our children.

While the roof was being repaired and the sand was being removed, I sat down at my desk to get some things done. The first thing on the agenda was to revise and update the funding proposal, as much had changed since I had worked on it. I sent out three funding proposals that had to go out before February, wrote four thank-you letters for donations we had received, filed a before and after photo of each of the children and answered my emails. Then I called the municipality to come and clear a blocked drain in the street, and sent a deposit to the electricity department for the electricity to be turned on at one of the new houses we had hired.

One of the children who had gone home for the Christmas holidays had not returned, so I sent four of the bigger boys to the township to go and collect him. I discussed the menu for the day and handed out the food, make a list of the shoe sizes for all the children, tabulated it and sent it to Pep Stores, a clothing store in Middelburg, so that they could do the necessary ordering. In between this, there were three phone calls from journalists wanting information, as they were writing various articles on our project.

Three children under the age of nine who had been beaten badly by an adult man came to us for help. I called the police to come and take a statement and to investigate but, when they arrived, they told me that the children had only been beaten once, so it was not a problem. The children said that their fathers did not live in town, that they lived with grandmothers who were constantly drunk, and that most of the time they spent on the streets. After listening to their stories, I got the social worker, Pumza Mobo, to come and assist, but she told me that she was not taking on any more cases because she was too busy. I had no alternative but to take them in, clean them up, dress their wounds, put them into clean clothes, feed them

336

and let them stay until I could figure out what to do about it. These children eventually ended up as part of our family, but it took two years before I managed to get the necessary court orders for them to be legally placed in my care.

Three other children who had gone home for the Christmas holidays to Port Elizabeth had also not returned. The returning of all the children to their extended families for holidays was sanctioned by the social workers when the children were asked for by the relatives. It was a thorn in my side that not one relative would visit or telephone or send anything to the children during the year, or would foster the children, but come Christmas, they would demand that the children be sent to them for the Christmas period. This would be from approximately the 22nd December until the 3rd January. The social workers would then give us a court mandate to send the children to these families, without checking if the situation at these homes was adequate or appropriate for the children.

On a number of occasions, the children themselves would come back to us after just a few days away because they would be left alone while the adults were in the taverns, or they would be abandoned or not be fed. The welfare department would also not give us any finances to get these children to their destinations or to bring them home. They would also not concern themselves with whether the children returned or not, stating that the return of the children was our problem and not theirs. Thus, the return of the three missing children in Port Elizabeth was my problem. I contacted the Port Elizabeth police to get collect of the children and deliver them to Stuart, who put them on the train. I would collect them from the station, 10 km from Middelburg at two the next morning. This meant that I would not get much sleep that night..I had just finished organizing the return of these three children when Marshall, Nkosinathi and Daniel came into the office asking for toiletries. These three boys had come in a couple of days before, without a social worker, a policeman or a parent. They were street children and they had arrived and refused to leave. I had told them that they could not stay, that they had to come in with either a social worker or a police officer. I managed to get them out of the front door but they ran in at the back door. I sat down and spoke to them, explaining to them that we were not allowed to have so many children, and if I took in any more children the social workers would put me in jail.

"But you have enough beds for us", they explained.

No amount of rationalizing with them helped, so I showed them the door, pushed them out after supper and thought that was the end of it. But the next morning, they were in the beds and again refused to leave. They had been with us a while now and were demanding to have what the other children had. I had been delaying giving them anything because I did not want them to think that they could stay. We were well over our quota allowed by the Department of Social Development, and I had already been warned more than once that I would be charged with contravening the Child Care Act if I took in any more children. I did not want to give these boys any false hopes. I sent them to the social worker and told them that if she agreed to them staying, they could have the toiletries. Off they went, but in a short while they were

338

back, saying that she did not have time for them, and they wanted what the other children had.

They were not leaving even if I chased them away, and said, "We will just come back in again, so you can't do anything about it, Mama D. You are our mother and we are your children. You have known us since we were small on the street and now we are living with you".

Subject closed. I issued them with the standard toiletries and got Jackson to sort out clothes for them. I would deal with the consequences but first I would teach the children that if anyone asked how many children lived at the home, they were to say "twenty-six", even if they counted more than that. It was obviously not good to teach children to lie, but it was a case of necessity. That night, Jackson and I had a teaching lesson with the children in lying.

"How many children live in this house?" we asked.

"Seventy-two", they shouted.

"You are right and you are wrong. Remember that if anyone asks you how many children live in this house you have to say twenty-six", we would repeated over and over.

"How many children live in this house?" we would ask again.

There would be some who shouted "twenty-six" and some would shout "seventy-two" and then they would start fighting with one another.

"OK, OK", Jackson said, "We don't have to fight about this. We know there are seventy-two of you, but if anyone asks then you have to say twenty-six. Do you understand?"

"Now, how many children live in this house?" I would ask again.

"Twenty-six", they would all shout.

Over the next couple of weeks, we would do this over and over, but still there would be those who would say "seventy-two". I hoped that the day when they were asked by a social worker they would get it right. And they did. They were asked and they got it right. They said "twenty-six". How proud I was of them that day.

The soup kitchen that was run by the Catholic Church for the street children had closed. Father John who ran the soup kitchen had had a heart attack, so I had to do something about feeding the street children. I made twenty large posters on the photocopy machine saying that we would feed all street children at the home between 1 and 2 o' clock each day, gave out some coloured pencil crayons to the middle-sized children and got them to decorate them. Once this was done, we went and put up the posters around the town.

The children had broken a window earlier in the morning when they were playing with a ball so I went and measured it, bought the glass and putty and taught one of the bigger boys how to replace it. In the meantime, the "qualified" carpenter that I had got to scrape down the door frames, doors and shutters had given my very expensive sander to one of the children to use. The child broke the top part of it and the part would cost R400 to repair.

My blood pressure was rising. Tools were lying all over the place. The little ones were playing with them, the staff were cleaning the house instead of supervising the children, so I had to sort that out first and then I took all the tools up to the office, made a stock book for the tools and locked them up in one of the cupboards in the office. Better care needed to be taken of the tools. Now they would have to come to the office to collect tools, sign them out and in. This way, tools would not go missing, broken or be played with. And the day was only half way through.

I had an appointment with the social worker at two o'clock so I dashed off to the office. She was late, as usual, working on African time. It annoyed me that they would keep me waiting but I always had to be on time for them. She came forty-five minutes late. While I waited for her, I made some photocopies for the children for school and then the photocopier ran out of toner. There was none available in Middelburg or Waltons, our stationers in Port Elizabeth, and the other place that sold it in Port Elizabeth was closed until the following week. I knew I had an extra toner somewhere, but the head sometimes did not work so well, not with so many things going on at one time. I got the whole team, which consisted of Jackson and four of the bigger children, to turn the office upside-down looking for the toner and they found it. I jumped for joy. What little things made me happy in those days. The copying was completed.

Still waiting for the social worker, I started on tracing a container of Xmas gifts that had been sent to us from Beresfords Solicitors, a donor from Doncaster in the UK. The container had been sent with DHL long before Christmas, had been paid for by the donor, and had never turned up. Eventually, I found where the container but was told that it was being held by the government until I paid thirteen thousand rand import tax. I tried to explain that these were Xmas gifts for a Children's Home and that everything had been paid for and declared on the waybill by DHL, but they would hear nothing of it. I decided to take the DHL donation situation higher up the ladder. I faxed a letter through to the Minister of Inland Revenue and in no time I received a telephone call to say that I would not have to pay the import tax and that the container would be shipped to me in Middelburg. I could not believe what they were saying.

"How are you going to ship the container to me?", I asked.

"By sea", I was told.

"Excuse me, Sir", I said, "But we are inland, are you going to use the ships of the desert? Camels?".

"Ooh, is zeh no sea zeh zen?", he replied.

"No".

"Zen you must pay for it to be zent to you zen", he said.

"No, I am not paying. The payment was already made by the sender to DHL. You must see that it gets here".

"Listen to me lady, you no pay, you no get container. OK?".

"No, you listen to me. The sender already paid DHL to deliver the container to my door. I am not paying you again. You will see that the container is delivered to my door".

"You no pay, we burn container".

"You mean you will steal the things in the container".

"You try get clever wiz me?"

"What is your name because I am going to speak to the Minister again and I want to tell him about you".

"No need for zat. I work it out".

"What is your name?", I repeated.

"No name, I sort it out".

"I want a confirmation letter faxed to me within 20 minutes that the container will be delivered to me within a certain amount of time... *to my door* ... otherwise I am going to report this to the Minister. Am I clear?".

"Yes Lady", he answered.

Before the social worker arrived, I had a fax on my desk confirming that the container would be delivered to my door within the week. Needless to say, the container only arrived in January. It was a mad scramble to purchase gifts from our already over-strained budget the day before Christmas when we finally came to the realization that the container would not be arriving on time.

The social worker, Pumza Mobo, arrived with a mother who wanted her child back. I could not believe that the social worker had arrived with the mother and that she had condoned this action. How could the social worker arrive with the mother and assist the mother in requesting that I return the child? The child had been placed legally in my care by the Commissioner of Child Welfare pending an investigation by the police into alleged child abuse by the mother. I had to explain the Child Care Act to the social worker and to the mother, that no child was allowed to go back to the mother while the mother was under investigation for child abuse, and nor was I allowed to hand a child over to anyone unless I was authorized to do so with a court order by the Commissioner of Child Welfare. In any event, if the Commissioner of Child Welfare authorized such a move while the mother was under investigation, this would be contravening the Criminal Procedures Act. The social worker pressurized me to make an exception in this case.

I refused, explaining the Child Care Act and the Criminal Procedures Act to her again. When they left, I could only shake my head in disbelief. This was a social worker, employed by the Department of Social Development and she did not even know the Child Care Act. Everything in this hell-hole called Middelburg was beyond belief.

I put together five children's files, ready for the next day to start getting birth certificates for them. This would be a slow and laborious task. I would have to first find the mothers and, if they were alive, their identity documents if they had them. If not, the mothers would have to apply for an identity document, which could take up to six months. If the mother did not have a birth certificate, then she could not apply for an identity document. She would have to get her mother's identity document or her mother's birth certificate, and then apply. If the mother was dead, I would have to get her death certificate from a relative. I would also have to get a clinic card for the child. This would mean that I would have to find out the correct surname of the child, find out the approximate age of the child, and go to the hospital and search the records to see if the child had been born there. If so, I would have to ask for a copy of the clinic card. If the mother, under investigation for child abuse, I was unlikely to get co-operation from her.

If the child did not have any family at all, then I would be unable to get a birth certificate at all because a child over the age of ten days cannot be registered as a foundling. The child would then be a non-entity and be entitled to nothing. This is where our law and our constitution is not in sync. The constitution states that a child has a right to a name, and nationality but if a child is an orphan and there is no way of getting an identity document, then the child has no right to a name and a nationality. I got a phone call from one of the Home Based Care workers. She told me her son in Johannesburg had just died from AIDS. She wanted to know how to bring his body home for burial. I was feeling so pressurized by then. I still had to order the food and we had run out of washing powder. I told her that I would help her in the morning. As I put the phone down I heard running feet and sobbing and crying and looked up to find a young boy I knew, Julian, standing at the desk. He told me that he had been told to "fuck off " out his home because he was using the foster parents' money to eat and he was eating too much. The children know where to come when they are in trouble.

I sat him down, wiped his tears, gave him a cold drink and told him that we would sort it out. After all, his parents are given a foster care grant to take care of him. How could they do this to the child? What kind of adults do we have in this world? When he had calmed down, I got him to call his mother. They spoke on the phone. Things were better. He would go home. I told him that if things got really bad or if they beat him, he was to come back to me and I would do the necessary to see that he got put in my care. He was happy about that and left. I ordered the food, did a number of other necessary things and then closed the office to see that the children were fed.

As I was walking to the house where I sleep, something extraordinary happened. One of the seventeen year-old boys who has just moved in shouted "Mom, mom, mom" to me and came running towards me.

That in itself was strange because all the children call me Mama D. I thought something was wrong. All the houses are in the same street so it is easy to see what is happening at each one. When he got to me, out of breath, he took my hand in his and put his other hand on my back.

He looked into my eyes and said, "Mom, I think I love you".

"I love you too", I replied, amused.

"I want to be someone one day, so I have decided that if that is going to happen, then I am going to make you my mother".

And off he ran back to the house where he was sleeping. These were the little things that made my ordinary days worth while.

I had just got into the house, closed the door, kicked off my shoes and was going to sit down when there was a loud banging on the door. It was after eight o' clock. The only people who banged on the door like that were the police. Before I could get there, they banged again.
"OK, OK, I'm coming", I shouted.

My head throbbed. I was exhausted. I just wanted to rest for a while because I had to be up and driving to Rosmead to collect the children from the train at two in the morning. I was right. The police were at the door. With them were two small children, a boy and a girl. The boy was five year-old Jerome and the girl was three year-old Jessica. Also with them was a sixteen year-old girl by the name of Nancy who was holding a two year old female child on her hip. The two smaller children were from one household and Nancy and her baby were from another.

Jerome and Jessica both had swollen and bleeding faces. The police told me that the grandmother had beaten them up and that they had arrested her and that she was locked up in jail. Nancy had also been beaten by her grandfather and was afraid for her life and the life of her baby. However, they had not arrested the grandfather because Nancy would not press charges against him.

Having had to learn the hard way, learn from being harassed and policed and having had to learn the Child Care Act in the dark hours of the night, there was not much more I needed to learn, but the authorities did not know much about it. This made it very difficult to work with them in the area of children's rights. I asked the police to sign a Form 4 for me before I could take the children in. They said that they did not know how to sign such forms and had never heard of them. I had to explain to them the legalities of taking children in as a Place of Safety. I also had to explain that since the children had been abused, they would need the District Surgeon to complete a J88 immediately, confirming the children's injuries, and that the J88 had to go into the docket so that the public prosecutor could prosecute the off ender. I asked them to take the two little ones to the hospital and get the District Surgeon to complete the J88 form which was available at the hospital. I also told them that the District Surgeon had to by law be available. They took the children with them. In the case of Nancy, this was not necessary because she refused to make a statement, so we could not open a docket of abuse against her

348

grandfather. I could only offer her a place to stay for the night.

Nancy was left with me while the police officers went to the hospital with Jerome and Jessica. Nancy then told me her story. The baby was actually the product of incest between herself and her grandfather. She was very afraid of her grandfather who would often get drunk and either beat her or her grandmother up. She was very protective towards her grandmother, and wanted to go home because she was afraid her grandfather would kill her grandmother. Her grandmother did no know about the incestuous relationship between herself and her grandfather. She had been living with them since her mother had died of AIDS, and her grandfather had been having sex with her for as long as she remembered.

She refused point blank to make any statement about it as she was too afraid of her grandfather. When the police came back she asked them to take her home. Because she refused to make a statement, there was nothing we could do about her situation.

What shocked me terribly was that the District Surgeon had refused to come out to see the children. He had told the police that he would see the children the next day. I then took my camera and took photographs of the children's injuries myself. The police left the children with me. The next day I took the children to the hospital for the J88, but the District Surgeon again refused to come out because it was a weekend. He only saw the children at his office on the Monday, at which time the injuries were not so severe and the only obvious signs were the cuts in their mouths which were made by their teeth when they were assaulted across their mouths. The J88 stated that there was no evidence of abuse.

I contacted the investigating officer and told him that although the J88 stated that there was no evidence of abuse, the examination had been done three days late, and that I had taken photographs of the injuries and that he could use them as evidence. There was also the evidence of the two policemen who had picked them up. I took copies of the photographs and the Form 4 to the social workers at the Department of Social Development for them to process the placement of the children. Nothing was done about it for months. Eventually, after a long battle, the children were put on to a Form 5 which meant that they were legally placed for a period of 60 days, pending a more permanent placement. The Department of Social Development never revisited the case to place them permanently with us or with anyone else. The Child Care Act was contravened by keeping them on a Form 5, despite us continually asking them to process their documentation.

Time moved on and the children were put in school. A year went by and Jerome passed his first year of school. Another year went by and Jerome passed his second year of school and Jessica went to school. I followed up the investigation which had come to a standstill. There had been rumblings from the Department of Social Development that the children were going to be placed with their grandmother, but I was determined that until the investigation was completed, this would not happen. How they could even think of placing the children with the grandmother, when the grandmother was a victim of domestic violence and the grandfather already had a child through incest with his grandchild.

Eventually, I was notified that the investigation was complete and that the Public Prosecutor had refused to prosecute due to lack of evidence. When I asked why there was no evidence, I was told that the J88 stated that there was no evidence of abuse. Again, when I said that there were photographs and two policemen who could vouch for the abuse, I was told that unless it was police photographs, the evidence was inadmissible. When questioning whether the police had a camera, I was told that the only camera they had was in Cradock and that if one was needed, it had to come from Cradock, which was 100km away.

After more than two years, Jessica and Jerome were taken away from us and returned to the grandmother, without the grandmother ever having visited the children once or the children having seen their grandmother once during this time. The social worker came with a removal order, collected the children and that was that. We made a follow up visit to the children to check on them and it broke our hearts to see them. They were dirty, had lost weight, their eyes were dull and they were listless. The grandmother was drunk.

At a quarter to two, I drove to the train station and collected my children from Port Elizabeth. I was asleep before my head touched the pillow.

Maggots, barking children and circuses

The circus was coming to town. The posters were up all around and the children had seen them.

"Can we go to the circus Mama D?" "Please Mama D, can we go to the circus?", they would ask. And it went on and on. I wanted to take them to the circus. If only I had the money. How could I deny the children the circus, but how could I get them to the circus without money? The ticket prices were over the top and when you added up all the children, it was totally out of the question. I wrestled with this problem. How to get the children to the circus? Somehow I had to try. I went to look at the poster and found a telephone number. I would ask for 80 free tickets. I would need that many because I would have to take the staff as well. If I was going to ask for one, I may as well ask for 80. What could they say? They could only say no. What a cheek, I thought, as I picked up the phone to dial the number. But what the hell, I also thought. "Please God, let the person who answers this call say "yes"", I sent up a silent prayer as the number was dialling.

"Good morning", I said brightly. "I wonder if you would be so good as to give me 80 free tickets for your show in Middelburg for my Children's Home?" I asked.

"No problem, come and see me when we get there. My name is Keith", he said.

I nearly dropped the phone. Just like that; as simple as that. I had the tickets and we were going to the circus. The children were so excited they were whooping with joy.

352

The day of the circus eventually arrived and we walked in our usual 2 x 2 way, all dressed up warmly as it was a cold evening. We were lucky to be able to all sit together and I had my camera with me to take photos, although I only took photos of the children's faces. The children loved the animals and the juggling acts and the high wire acts. But the clowns were another thing altogether. They did not think they were funny. They did not laugh. They were horrified and some of them were crying. It was then that I realized how very damaged these children were. The clowns acted as though they were drunk. My children had lived with drunkenness all their lives and the result of drunkenness was violence. Drunkenness was not funny. It was horrible and degrading and disgusting. And the clowns represented everything that they no longer wanted to have anything to do with.

The drawings the children did after the circus were of everything but the clowns. When the children first come into the home, they draw coffins, cemeteries and crosses. Within three months, they start drawing flowers, houses, birds and butterflies, using more colours in the drawings. It is an amazing thing to see how they change in the way they express themselves.

One day, a community member brought in a small boy of about four years old. She said that she was just a concerned person and thought she would bring the child in. All she knew about the child was that his name was Slow and that he had been living with dogs and that he could not talk. Slow was an animal child, which we soon realized. He was dressed only in a pair of raggedy short pants and a shirt that was equally raggedy and very small

353

for him. He did not say a word. When she left, we tried to get him into the bath as he was covered in scabies and lice. It was only then that we realized that he must have been living with dogs for a long time and had had no communication with humans. He bared his teeth at us and growled. He put up such a fight that it took three of us to get his clothes off and into the bath. The fight was on.

We could not have him in the home with lice and scabies, as it is very contagious and it would have spread like wildfire through the house. What life had this child had? Where had he been? What was his background? He fought us and bit us but we managed to get him cleaned up and into some clothes. Then it was time to get him fed. He ate from the plate just like a dog. I was afraid he would run away, back to where he came from, so it was lock down. All the children knew what lock down meant. This means that all doors are locked until the new child has settled down. The other children know where the keys are to get in and out but the new child does not.

The first thing I did was to change his name. Slow was not a good name for a child. I gave him the name of Ntlantla. We called an emergency meeting of the staff to plan a program for Ntlantla. We had never had a child like this before and a program was needed so that we could work with this child. It was a slow process that took a long time and much patience from all of us, including the other children, but within six months Ntlantla was indistinguishable from the others. Ntlantla now goes to school, and if there is any residue left from his past, we have yet to see it.

On Christmas eve, 2003, an aunt dumped her dying sixteen year-old niece with us saying, "I don't want her. She is spoiling our Christmas", and with that she was gone in her car.

Yolanda was barely conscious and smelling terrible. We got her into my bedroom and lay her down. We needed to see why she smelled and between Niel, Fikile and myself, we stripped her to give her a bed bath. When we turned her over, we discovered the source of the smell. She had a huge big hole in the lower part of her back over her coccyx. There were maggots in the wound and it was suppurating. This could only have been caused from a bedsore, and then not dressed or cared for. She was pathetically thin and her bones were sticking out. She looked like a skeleton covered by skin. She was by this stage unconscious and I decided to call the doctor to her. I also called the social worker, Johan Pienaar, to come urgently to my home and would not take no as an answer. I told him that if he did not come and a child died in my care, that not only I but he too would be in serious trouble for not coming.

The doctor arrived and told us that Yolanda would not be alive the next morning, Christmas day. Johan arrived huffing and puffing. He took one look at Yolanda and wrote out a Form 4 immediately. This was the only time that the social workers ever wrote out a Form 4 immediately for me. I then phoned Father John and told him that another one of our children was at death's door. This time he was aggravated. I don't really blame him, because I was always calling the poor man out to come and bless the children in the middle of the night because they were touching heaven's door.

"Dianne, you keep calling me out for your children who are dying and then they don't die. Now you have seen me bless them, baptize them and give them the last unction so many times that I think you can do it yourself ", he said.

"But I don't have the stuff, the oils", I protested.

"Use what you've got", he replied.

"Right, thank you Father", I said, putting down the phone. Yolanda was blessed, baptized and given the last rites with olive oil. Strange how small things start mattering in a crisis. My mind became overloaded and clogged up with the thought that if I did not get Yolanda a Christmas present then she would be dead by the next day, Christmas day. All the children had their Christmas presents ready and waiting, but here was a child with nothing waiting for her for Christmas day. I had to get her something. I could think of nothing else but that present. It became an obsession in my mind.

I left Niel watching her and went to buy her something. There was a beautiful porcelain doll at the chemist, and it cost more than I could really afford, but I thought that it would be a beautiful sight for her if she opened her eyes on Christmas day. I bought it, wrapped it up and put it at the bottom of the bed. Yolanda did open her eyes on Christmas morning and she did see that doll. And we did get her up and into a wheelchair three weeks later. By

April, she was back in school. So Yolanda became another one of our children, still weak and sickly, but she was a participant in our home. She was really good with the little children and everyone got on well with her. We got her mother's death certificate from her aunt, and began the long process of getting her an identity document because she was sixteen years old. She would be entitled to a disability grant if we could get her the identity document.

In September Yolanda fell ill with meningitis. Meningitis is an opportunistic disease in HIV positive patients. It is also contagious. There were a number of cases of meningitis in the township as well. Whether Yolanda got infected by one of the children in the township, or whether it was lying dormant in her anyway, we will never know. Within days, one after another child came down with meningitis. Meningitis is a notifiable, which in South Africa means that the Health Department has to be notified. It was not long before the Department of Health put us under quarantine. The hospital was full with children who were ill, many of them with meningitis, and the doctor said that he just did not have the space to take our sick children. All the children and staff had to move into the biggest house and we were quarantined for three weeks. No one was allowed to leave the premises and the Department of Health came and gave us all injections. Our food had to be delivered, left on the veranda, and when the delivery people had left, we could go outside and collect the food and bring it inside. We managed to keep ourselves busy and occupied, and stayed in our own backyard and indoors. Some of the children became really ill, but with good nursing, a lot of love, paracetamol and bactrim, they all pulled through. However, a number of children in the township died.

A letter was sent to us by the Department of Health stating that the reason we had an outbreak of meningitis was because we were over-crowded. The Health Department sent a copy of the letter to the Department of Social Development as well as to the local Environmental Health Department.

This caused a huge problem for me as the Health Department had stated that the number of people staying in the house were all the staff and all the children. They did not break down the number of children staying in the three homes, nor did they subtract the staff from the children, the staff not living in the children's home, but staying in their own homes in the township. The Department of Social Development and the Environmental Health Officer would not take my word for it that these numbers of people were not the number that usually stayed in the house.

Numerous letters were written to the various departments stating that the cause of the outbreak of meningitis was not due to over-crowding but was a result of an opportunistic disease in an HIV positive child. I also pointed out that no child had died in the Children's Home, and that meningitis was rife in the township where numerous children had died. All this fell on deaf ears and this situation was brought up by the investigation team from the Department of Social Development that came from Bisho. They too did not understand that three houses of people were put into one for the quarantine, nor did they understand the opportunistic diseases of HIV. All they were interested in was the fact that I was over-crowded. This was the word they focused on.

Yolanda was well for another five months before she got ill again. This time, when she came down with her second bout of meningitis, I had her hospitalized. She became increasingly worse, so I asked for her to be transferred to Livingston Hospital in Port Elizabeth. Again, she rallied and came home. Her identity book arrived and we applied for a disability grant for her.

The social worker, Pumza Mobo, let the aunt know when the disability grant was approved. We were unaware of the grant being approved. Suddenly, the aunt arrived and wanted Yolanda back. Yolanda had been with us for eighteen months and the aunt had not come to visit her once. I sent the aunt to Pumza and within a day, Pumza arrived with the aunt, brandishing a court order for the release of Yolanda back into the care of the aunt. It was then that I found out that Yolanda's disability grant had been approved and was being paid into the aunt's bank account. How often this had happened. Children became a financial commodity. How it sickened me. How I wanted to fly into that aunt and give her a piece of my mind. Where had she been the last eighteen months? How had she cared for this child that she could let maggots eat the child while she was still alive? What kind of neglect was that? What kind of a social worker was Pumza Mobo? Again the Department of Social Development had disregarded the Child Care Act.

We had not been notified that a Children's Court hearing was going to be held. We were not notified that Yolanda was going to be returned to her aunt. Yolanda was not at court, which is a requirement when a Children's Court hearing is held. Yolanda was given no warning of her impending removal from our care. There was no re-unification process put in place. We had not received any grant or safety fee for caring for Yolanda, but the social worker could treat us with contempt and make decisions about Yolanda without any regard to the child's interests. I bit back my words. It would make no difference to either of these people. They were without compassion or reason and I had not a leg to stand on. They were standing there brandishing the court order. I said goodbye to Yolanda, knowing that she would not be cared for properly and knowing, too, that she would soon be dead.

Yolanda was not our first child to be snatched from us like this. There had been others, and they did not survive long outside of our sheltered home with the love and care we gave to our sick children. I saw Yolanda only once more, standing in the township in a thin cotton dress, her arms and legs sticking out like a scarecrow with an obviously pregnant bump in place of her tummy. She hid her face in her hands when she saw me drive past. Six months after she left, Yolanda was five months pregnant and dead.

The home schooled children had been working hard for two years and it was time for them to leave the nest to attend regular government school. At the beginning of the year, we bought them the school uniforms and enrolled them at school. It was a terrible blow for them to be told that they would have to start with the first year children, and that they would be monitored to see whether they could be promoted up the grades. There was no system in place to assess their abilities prior to them going into a grade. The children baulked at this. What would everyone say if they were to go into a baby class? After all, some of them were teenagers! It took a lot of encouragement to get them to agree to go to school and start in the baby class. The fact that they were a group assisted in their agreement to go, but it was not easy for them, nor was I happy about it.

There should have been some system in place to assess the children, and the school could have done something to help us to alleviate the embarrassment of these children who were so disadvantaged. However, they were unwilling to do anything out of the norm to assist us. This lack of compassion and unwillingness to provide anything extra for us contributed to further problems with Mark and John a couple of months later.

Most of the children progressed rapidly through their grades and soon were on a par with their peers, and two of the children surpassed the grades of their peers. We were very proud of them. However, Mark and John dug their heels in. They were good friends and they decided that they would not cooperate in a baby class, so that is where they stayed. They were thirteen years old, going to school with children who were six years old. This was obviously a bad situation and they were disruptive in class and the teacher was resentful.

I had numerous meetings with the teacher and the headmaster, chats to the boys, meetings with the social worker assigned to their case, but it all proved unsuccessful in getting them promoted to a higher grade. During this period, John and Mark became more and more determined not to go to school, until they started playing truant. They would walk to school with everyone else and then disappear when the bell rang. They would then re-appear when it was time to walk home. This I only found out by accident after weeks of them playing truant. There was no more moaning coming from the boys, and when I asked them about school they told me that it was good. There were no more complaints from school and I was breathing a sigh of relief. I happened to go to the school on another unrelated matter and met up with John and Mark's teacher.

"I am so glad that John and Mark are settling down in class now", I said.

"They have not been in class for weeks", she said.

"But why have you not notified me?", I asked.

She just shrugged her shoulders and walked on. I immediately made an appointment with the headmaster to ask him to notify me if any of my children were absent from school without permission. I always notified the school when a child was ill and was not going to be at school, so I found it completely irresponsible of the school not to notify me that children were not attending class.

I had some very strong words to say to Mark and John when they got home. They apologized profusely for not telling me the truth, but they were adamant that they would not return to school. By this stage, the home schooling had been abandoned since we no longer needed it, and also because we had been told by the Department of Education that if we wanted to continue to school the children ourselves, we would have to register as a school and employ a certain number of qualified teachers. This was beyond our financial capabilities. After much investigation, the only possible solution for the boys would be a boarding school that offered special education. This was discussed with the social worker. Eventually, she came around to talk to the boys. She wanted to have a private meeting with them, which I thought was quite in order.

After her meeting, she told me that she had decided that since the boys did not want to go to school and nor did they want to go to boarding school, that they did not have to go to school at all. They could just stay at home. I was flabbergasted and completely lost for words. Here were two thirteen year-old children who had just dictated what they wanted and the social worker had agreed to their demands. They would no longer have to go to school and I was to just allow them to stay at home. It was simply unacceptable to me.

"Pumza, this is totally unacceptable. Children need an education. These children are not old enough to make such a decision. It is not in their interests to stay at home. More than 30% of the youth here are illiterate. We cannot just simply allow them to stay at home. They either go to school, or you find a place for them where they are forced to go to school", I said.

"If they don't want to go to school, then they don't want to go to school. There is nothing I can do about it", she replied.

"Yes, there is. You can transfer them to an industrial school where they can be trained in some trade. They are minor children. You have the power to make a difference here" I fumed.

"There is nothing I can do", she said as she walked out.

There is nothing you are prepared to do, I thought. I went outside and spoke to the boys, where they were still sitting after their meeting with Pumza.

"Well, boys, how was your meeting?", I asked.

"We don't have to go to school", they said gleefully, smiling from ear to ear.

"Well, in my home you go to school. I don't have children who don't go to school. Children who don't go to school end up as stupid adults who can't read and write. Now, do you want to end up as someone who will not be able to get a job, who will be on the streets and will not be able to look after himself or his wife and children?", I asked.

"We don't care. We don't have to go to school. The social worker said so", said John in a cheeky manner.

"I don't need your cheek, John. If you want to use that kind of attitude, go use it on the social worker, but not on me".

He dropped his face sullenly. I had a problem, a big problem. What had this social worker done here? I appealed to Mark.

"Mark, will you please go to school so that you will make something of your life, so you will one day be able to be someone you can be proud of? Will you make me proud?"

He shifted uncomfortably in his seat and looked at John for direction or some sort of assurance. John would not look up. His lips were pursed and puffed out like a bullfrog. Mark was actually brighter than John and he had a much better chance of success than John. I was getting angry. I wanted to smack his face, but it was the last and worst thing I could do. My frustration levels with these boys was over the top. I had done everything possible for them, had cared for them for almost three years, and I was getting nothing but grief back from them. I had used every method in the book and then some to win them over with the school issue, but had not won on any of them. I had run out of ideas. The soft touch had not worked. I could not allow them to dictate terms to me as they would then influence all the other children.

I made up my mind, as difficult a decision as it was. They would either have to go to school, or I would have to get the welfare to remove them from my care. There was no other way out. I would appeal to the welfare again to place them in an appropriate place which would ensure that they attended school, but if that was not done, then there was no more that I could do. This was it. If I said it to the boys, there was no turning back. I would ask them one more time; give them one more soft touch chance.

"Mark and John, please listen to me. Look at me while I speak to you. John, lift your head please. Look at me while I speak to you. Thank you. I have cared for you for a long time and I love you both very much. I want you to go to school because I love you and I want the best for you. If you go to school, you will be educated and you will go on to university and you can become anything you want to be. You will also make me very proud. Will you please, please go to school, even if it is just for me. I will speak to the teacher and the headmaster to put you in another class. Will you go to school please?"

"The social worker said we don't have to go to school", said John, again sullenly.

"And you Mark?" I asked.

He hesitated before he answered, "No, I won't go to school".

"Then you make me very sad", I said, "but I have also made a decision. If you won't go to school, then you cannot live with me anymore. Will you go to school?" I asked again.

They both shook their heads. "OK then, boys. I will speak to the social worker again and she can make the arrangements for you to leave our home. She will let you know". I contacted the social worker and told her of my decision, again begging her to make the arrangements with the industrial school. She said that she would do what she could. She did what she could, which was very little indeed. She got the release papers for the boys and the boys left our home. I was sad, very sad.

The boys went back to the streets. The social worker surely had done what she could. It was not even a year later that the boys were in juvenile court for robbery. Mark started asking to come back home, but I had to refuse, as by then he was addicted to marijuana. All I could do for him was to continue to feed him as we were doing for all the street children.

The schooling system proved to be another challenge. It did not run smoothly. One of the issues we had was obtaining the correct uniform. Apart from the expense of the uniform, it was not easy to obtain. The uniform for the junior school, to which thirty of the children were attending, had a yellow shirt, maroon dress, maroon socks with a gold stripe, sash and black shoes for the girls, with a maroon jersey with a gold stripe around the neck, sleeves and bottom for the boys and girls. The boys had the usual grey trousers, socks, white shirts and black shoes. The problem with the uniform for the girls was that the yellow shirt was only obtainable from one particular shop in Cradock, 100 km away. The dress was not obtainable from any shop and had to be made to order. The money had to be paid up front. The reason for this was because the school governing body had decided to create jobs for people in the area, and only those who had been given permission to make the dresses were allowed to make the school uniforms. The price of the dresses was exorbitant and could have been made for a sixth of the price. The material for the dresses was only obtainable from one outlet in Queenstown, 220 km away.

The socks and sashes could only be purchased from the people who had permission from the school to sell them.

These were people in the township and again, the price was excessive. To further exacerbate the situation, the children were not allowed to go to school unless they had the correct uniform on. The school jerseys had to be made to order in the same manner as well. The school tracksuits for winter had to also be obtained in the same manner. The tracksuits were five times more expensive than what could be purchased in a shop. None of this has changed. We still have the same problem, but we pass the uniforms down as the children grow out of them.

Another problem was the school fees and the purchase of the school materials. I applied to the School Governing Body for a reduction in the school fees as we had so many children, but they refused to reduce the school fees. Our Constitution entitles children to basic education, but the Department of Education makes it mandatory to pay school fees or children may not attend school. The Constitution and the legislation of various state departments are not in line. In 2007, the Department of Education placed a large advertisement in all newspapers claiming that parents and guardians could make application to the school governing bodies to waive school fees. This we did, and our reply from them was that they had no knowledge of such a mandate and that, unless we paid the mandatory school fees, the children would not be allowed to attend school. This mandatory school fee is responsible for the large numbers of children who do not attend school, and for the more than 30% of illiterate youth in our area.

At the beginning of the first year we learned a lot about how to deal with the long lists of school materials that the teachers sent home with the children. The children needed all kinds of things, from flip files and crayons to calculators. Although money was tight, I wanted my children to have what they needed and did not want them to feel that they were different to the other children in school. We provided everything on their lists. After their first day, they came home without anything in their school bags. When I asked them where their things were, they told me that their teachers had taken them. However, when it came to doing their homework a week later, they did not have the pencils, calculators or files to do the work. I again asked the children where their things were, and again they told me that the teacher had taken them.

On enquiry, I found that the teachers had taken the files and calculators and these were now the property of the school. The children did not need the calculators as they had to do their work without calculators. I again issued pencils to the children and wrote each child's name on the pencils, threatening the children with dire consequences should they go missing.

"Money does not grow on trees. Bring your crayons and crayon bags home with you tomorrow. Tell your teacher I want you to bring them back every day so you can do your homework", I said.

It was only a week after the start of school so imagine my shock to see the crayons that were only half and a quarter of the original size.

"What happened to your crayons?", I asked.

No one answered me.

"You can't possibly have used so much of your pencil crayons. What has happened to your crayons?", I asked again.

"We broke them in half and gave them to the other children", Sylvia replied.

My mouth fell open in disbelief. "What?", I exclaimed. "Why did you do that?".

"Because you told us that we must always share", Sylvia replied.

What could I say to that? I had taught them to share. But I did not have the money to supply the whole school with pencil crayons and I did not have the money to replace the pencil crayons for more than forty school going children.

"You are right, I did teach you to share, but you must first share with your family. And we are family. All of us here! And after us, then we share with others. We don't have a lot of money and I can't afford to buy you new crayons so we have to look after what we have. I don't want you to share your crayons with anyone else now. Do you understand? Your crayons are now too small to share, so no more sharing. These crayons must last until June".

There was no more to be said. I tried to write their names on each individual crayon, although it was pointless on some of them as they were less than 1 cm in length.

Then there were the inevitable fund raising events at school. The children had to have money for this fundraising event or that fundraising event. Although the average fundraising event cost was only ten rand when you had to multiply it by the number of children in our care, it was becoming completely out of control. I went to the school to explain to them that we were a non-profit organization and we ourselves were struggling for funds and could not assist them with their fund raising. They were adamant that the fundraising amounts were to be paid, or the children could not attend school. We would just have to find the money. The fund raising money was to put a playground into the school and for the seven years of fundraising that we have been contributing towards, the playground is nowhere to be seen. School is an expensive exercise in South Africa.

The children are walked to school in the morning, and collected and walked home from school in the afternoons by a staff member or by myself. This is to ensure the children's safety, as the crime rate in the area is exceedingly high and child abuse and rape are common. However, despite the numerous meetings concerning the safety of the children with the school principal and teachers, teachers would still send children home alone for various reasons, to collect money for raffle tickets or to collect some item needed by the school. No amount of complaints made any difference.

One day, Nkosinathi came home in the middle of the morning, sobbing his heart out. Nkosinathi was only eleven years-old at the time. He flew into my arms, his little skinny body shaking with sobs.

"What is wrong my darling? Tell me, what is wrong?", I asked, cuddling him in my arms.

"Mama D, they chased me out of school because my school fees are not paid", he managed to get out in between his crying and sobbing.

I was livid. I was so angry. How dare they do this? How dare they send a child out of a class, make him feel embarrassed, tell him this in front of everyone and send him home? What kind of compassionate people are we dealing with? I thought. My heart filled with contempt for the teachers and principal and ached with the pain of rejection and embarrassment that Nkosinathi was feeling.

"I have paid your school fees, Nkosinathi. Honestly. I have. We will sort this out. Come with me to the office and I will phone the school now".

I phoned the school and asked them why they had sent Nkosinathi home for not paying his school fees. The school secretary informed me that I had thirty-one children at the school and I had only paid for thirty children.

"If that is the case, could you not have just phoned me to come in and pay? Why send a child home like this?", I asked.

"We do it to all the children", she responded.

"But it is damaging to the children", I said.

There was a sullen silence on the phone.

"Are you there?", I asked.

"Nkosinathi cannot come back to school until you have paid for the extra school fees", she said and she put the phone down on me.

I told Nkosinathi he could stay home for the rest of the day, took some money out of petty cash and drove to the school.

"Right", I said as I got to the secretary, "show me which child has not paid school fees because I know that Nkosinathi has paid school fees".

With deliberate slowness and only slightly veiled annoyance, she walked to the desk behind her and looked at her books and files.

After about ten minutes she came back to me and said, "I don't know which are all your children because they are all in different classes, but I do know you have thirty-one children and you have only paid for thirty".

I quickly thought about the situation. My financial documents went to the auditors in Port Elizabeth at the end of every month. To get proof of the paid school fees would take at least a week. This would exacerbate the situation with Nkosinathi. There was no point in further aggravating the situation. The most simple solution to this problem would be to simply pay for an extra child's school fees.

"I will pay the extra school fees", I said.

The secretary smiled, took the money and put it in her drawer. "Thank you", she said, dismissing me.

"May I have a receipt for the school fees?" I asked.

Immediately her face took on a disgruntled look again as she reluctantly took out the receipt book and issued me the receipt.

"Thank you so much", I said as I flounced out of the school, calling out that Nkosinathi would be at school the next day.

Nkosinathi was not the last child to be sent home alone on a ridiculous errand, but the one that really made me angry was when Donovan was sent home. Donovan was six years old and sent home by his teacher to get a new pencil because he had lost his. He had to walk alone, through a very dangerous township. Despite our continual requests to the school not to send the children home unattended due to the dangers of the township, the school teachers continued to do it. I can only believe that the angels were protecting our little ones that they came to no harm during these irresponsible errands the teachers sent them on.

More sinister dealings with the schools had to be endured. Nombasa's high school class teacher constantly came to school so drunk that he could not teach a class, or he would just not come to school at all. I wrote to the principal, and the Head of the Department of Education for the area, but nothing was done about it. At the end of the year, when Nombasa was to collect her school report, after writing the examinations, the teacher was too drunk to give the class their reports. We had to wait until the opening of the school the following year to get the reports.

Class teachers at both the schools would often not come to school when they had been paid. They would simply take the day off to do their shopping. The children would then stay at school playing until we collected them, or the children would decide to come home on their own. We were often surprised by the children all walking home together early in the morning, and on enquiry being told that the teachers had gone shopping.

The most shocking incident that I had to deal with concerning the school was with Aya. She was an eleven year-old child who was introverted and stubborn. The best way one could get something out of her was to ask her nicely and never to order her to do something. In fact, she is still like this. Her older sister is an extrovert and is liked by everyone, and Aya lives in the shadow of her sister.

Aya is more beautiful than her sister, Kholiwe, and is an incredible dancer with a lithesome body, but does not have the confidence of Kholiwe. She is still battling with the demons of her past. Aya came home from school with a swollen eye and cheek. When I asked her what happened, the other children who are also in her class told me that the teacher had hit her. I was fuming about it. Here was an abused and neglected child who had been assaulted by a teacher. It was against the law! I tried to pacify Aya, but she was having none of it. She had retreated into her own world. She just went to her bed and lay there, not communicating with anyone, just staring up at the ceiling.

Not even Kholiwe could get her to talk about what had happened.

The following day I went to the principal, letter in hand, complaining about the assault on Aya, and I sent a copy to the Head of the Department of Education again. The principal said he would look into it. I heard nothing from either the principal or the Department of Education, despite many follow up letters. Aya simply got up that morning and went to school as though nothing important had happened. She still refused to discuss what had happened as though this kind of treatment is all she deserved. Life continued.

As I sit here, writing about this incident, I recall my emotions about what happened. I think of what more I could have done. I could have gone to the police station and charged the teacher with assault. Aya would have had to make a statement. But she was not talking. Somehow, maybe I could have got her to talk, or at least got the other children to make the statements. But every case that I took to the police on child abuse was never investigated properly, and every single case was thrown out by the prosecutor. If I had laid a charge against the teacher, the result of that would have been victimization of not only Aya, but all the children.

I have become wise to the reactions of state officials and persons working for the state after the years of working in this field. If you cross them or question them, they become vindictive. Vindictiveness together with the power they wield and the contacts they have will make a life almost impossible to live. Did I sacrifice Aya unconsciously because I knew that it was pointless to charge the teacher, or because I was afraid of the consequences of rocking the boat? I don't know.

When the cat's away...the mice will play

Summers in Middelburg are always scorchers. The temperatures can easily go up to over 45° Celsius. The children run around near naked in the afternoons after school. During the first two summers, I had managed to hire a private swimming pool in town where we taught all the children to swim, but the lady had left town and now we no longer had this possibility of cooling down.

The council had sold the town swimming pool to a private person for a song, and it had been left to go to wrack and ruin. I think that the person wanted the ground and not the pool. Without a swimming pool, I had to devise some method of cooling them down that would also be fun. With so many children playing in the back yard, there was no grass left, just a few bits growing along the sides of the property. Planting grass had been a dismal failure as the soccer games put paid to any growth that might have been possible. Mud! The fun would have to do with mud.

Eventually I got my idea and went to the hardware store where I bought metres and metres of weatherproof plastic sheeting that is used under the tiles of a roof. I laid this on the ground, poured dishwashing liquid on it and then ran the hosepipe on it until it was soaking wet. I put the hosepipe down flat on one end, balancing it there with a brick and I demonstrated the first run on the "slipslide" as we started calling it.

With all the children standing around in their underwear, I took off at a run, fully clothed but barefoot, took a leap and intending to slide along on my feet fell immediately onto my backside with a jolt and slid off the other end scraping my heels on the dirt. The children were doubled over in laughter and then they all wanted to do it together. I had to get them to line up and do it one at a time, all the while rubbing my backside and trying not to limp where the skin had come off my ankles. I would have to remember that I was half a century and not a kid anymore.

This was when I was having the best time of my life. There was no other place in the world that I would rather be, than with the children in that moment. All the frustrations with the authorities, all the worries about the finances, just disappeared and I was living in the moment, like a child with the children. I was happy, so happy with them. I loved them with a passion, with a fiercely protective passion. They were mine and no one would harm them. I would fight for them with my last breath. Oh, God, I said silently, thank you for these children. Help me to keep them safe from harm. In these moments I knew that I was doing the right thing because I was happy. I was truly happy and contented. I could feel the children's love for me and I could laugh with them and play with them. I loved them and they loved me. We were a family in every sense of the word.

Children are colour-blind when it comes to love, and this was demonstrated numerous times. One day there was a knock at the door and Jane called me, "Mama D, there is an umlungu (white person) at the door".

"Jane, I am an umlungu", I said.

"No, you're not", she said as she skipped away.

I had to chuckle at that. Another time, one of the older children who had been listening to the news said to me, "Mama D, did you hear that there was a bus accident and all the people were killed?"

"No, I did not hear that", I replied.

"Well, thank goodness they were all white people", he said.

"But I am a white person", I replied.

"No, you are black", he said adamantly.

The children honestly saw me as being the same colour as they were but everyone else was definitely of a different colour. It is only love that makes people colour-blind as another child demonstrated. I was sitting in my vehicle one very hot summer's day, waiting at the school to collect the smaller children, when a small child climbed up on the running board and leaned into the window of the cab. I started talking to her in isi-Xhosa, making conversation.

She looked at me quizzically with her head to the side and eventually asked me, "Why are you white if you speak isi-Xhosa?" In her mind, there was something wrong with the colour of my skin, not with me.Pure love, innocent and naïve love, compassionate and protective love; it is only this love that is the antidote for racism, oppression and for the abuse of children.

Not all our encounters with the schools were negative. The positive experiences were entirely due to the perseverance and aptitude and once due to the beauty of our children. There was a Miss Nonyaniso Junior School Competition at school, which of course was part of their fundraising efforts. We entered all the girls. There was so much enthusiasm and excitement as we preened them and dressed them and braided their hair. They left very excited with Jackson in charge of them. I did so hope that one of them would come home as the Miss Nonyaniso for the year but I did not hold out much hope. My children were all beautiful to me, but then beauty is in the eyes of the beholder. There were celebrations for a week when Evelyn came home as Miss Nonyaniso 2004. I was so happy for her since she deserved something good in her life after the traumas she had suffered.

The end of every year also brought a lot of celebration with the end of the year examination results. Year after year, every child would pass with good marks, except the one or two children who would have been placed in our care in the last term of the school year. This was an incredible percentage pass rate for such a large family, and was in my opinion a result of children who were becoming well adjusted and balanced. Traumatized children did not do well at school. Even our little Xolani, who had been tested and found to be only trainable, was passing every year in a normal school environment. We had a lot to be proud about.

A major triumph for us was winning the competition that was organized by the Department of Arts and Culture for the region. We had been doing drama and cultural dancing and gumboot dancing as part of the children's home activities. We put a dancing and gumboot dance program together and entered the competition. This was open to everyone, but most of the entrants were adults. The children won the first round, which was for Middelburg. They then went into the semi-finals which were held in Cradock. They won that round as well and went into the finals held in Queenstown. The children won the competition and were awarded with a certificate and R500,00. After the prestige of winning the award, the children were often asked to perform for various government dignitaries or, to entertain at various public memorial days for the community. The first state department to always ask us to perform for government dignitaries is always the Department of Social Development. It is a pity that this has never been acknowledged or that the children have never been praised for this. They have only been used by the local government officials for self promotion to impress the dignitaries, but the organization itself has never been acknowledged.

Once a week the children and I would take a walk to what we called our building society. Whenever we walked anywhere we would go in our usual 2 x 2 manner, all of us singing at the top of our voices. We knew a lot of songs. And our singing would bring all the people out of their houses to look at us. And I would lift my head higher with pride in my children. I knew that they thought me strange and crazy. What on earth would a woman want to do with all those children? Any normal person would be at home with a husband, minding her own business and not be out collecting unwanted street children. I could just see it in their faces.

Our walk went right through town on to the road that led to the Army base. We would then climb through a fence and walk into the fields until we got to a great flat rock that had many small stones lying around. This area may have been a result of some earth movement millions of years ago, because the area around looked as though it were a giant pot of boiling porridge that suddenly solidified. In this area there are many of these bits of erupted rock with lots of stones around. It was at one of these places that we had our building society.

The whole point of the building society was to build a wall of remembrance, and to leave our worries at the wall with those that we had loved and lost. Every stone in that wall was for a mother, a father, a sister, a brother, an aunt, an uncle or someone else we had loved who had died. Every stone in the wall was a hurt and a worry. Every week the wall got higher and higher. At the same time, I was teaching them how to build a dry stone wall, one that would stand for years. We loved going to our building society. We went in all kinds of weather; nothing stopped us from going there.

We also walked and sang every evening in summer. We walked around the town, skipping, singing, walking and playing games. We would do this while the staff prepared the dinner. The little ones would be in the prams, and often there would be seven or eight prams being pushed by the older teenage girls. It was a joyous time. From late

November we would start singing Christmas carols. The favourite of all time was "Oh! Come all ye Faithful".

We would deliberately go into the police station and give them a rendering of the latest song we had learned. Of course, the constables on duty would love it. We never did have a problem with the constables; it was only the police at the top, the ones who made decisions, that made life difficult for us. We would also make a point of walking to the hospital at least once a month and visiting the patients and giving them a couple of our songs. They too would love the singing, as did the nurses. The nurses loved it when we visited, and they would take the babies up in their arms and walk them around the wards.

It was during these times that I would take the opportunity of getting medication out of the hospital for my sick children. Either I would get the help of some compassionate and friendly nurse to help me fill up a bottom of a pram with medication and cover it with a baby blanket, or I would help myself when no one was looking. I did not have the money to buy the medication and mothers will do anything to keep their children alive. Bactrim was what I needed most, and that is what I got. The antibiotic would keep my HIV babies alive for longer, and I did not have the anti-retrovirals, the government was not giving them and I could not afford them. I assuaged my conscience by donating to the hospital, when I got donations, anything they needed that I had more than enough of.

Money was a constant concern. We were always in dire need of money. Something had to be done fast. I decided that I would try to raise funds by going to the UK and working there. The staff could look after the children while I was away. I could then bring the money home that I earned. I made contact with a friend in Edinburgh, and asked her to book me onto a number of healing fairs where I could give inspirational talks. Anyone could book a place at these fairs, pay for a space and a hall, and the organizers would advertise that you would be giving a talk. I would charge £5 per person. I thought that, at the end of each talk, I would also tell people what I did back home and the reason I was doing the talks and ask for any donations. These fairs are on every weekend at different towns and cities all over Scotland in the summer. I decided to go over and work every Saturday and Sunday for six weeks. During the week, I would try to make contacts and raise awareness and get donations. I booked my air ticket, Claudia, my friend in Scotland, booked the fairs, I left instructions for the staff , enough money for six weeks and off I went.

My determination and motivation were at fever pitch. I was so desperate to keep the children and so worried about our financial situation that I asked everyone for donations. From these fairs I built up a contact base of people who gave me donations of anything from £5 - £10 per month. This money was either sent to me via cheque or bank transfer. We soon realized that the transfer costs were so high that most of the donation was taken up by bank charges. Stuart negotiated with the bank to reduce the cost of foreign cheque deposits and slowly our income improved in this way. However, our donation base never grew to the point where I could breath easily. Our expenses always exceeded our income.

I managed to come home with enough money to pay my overdraft and to pay for everything for the next two months. And this is how we started to live. I would go over to Scotland and do the same thing, come home and pay the overdraft and have enough for one or two month's expenses. However, the more children we got, the more staff I needed, the more money we needed. It was a never-ending problem.

And in the winter months there were no fairs. But by now I had managed to get a number of contacts in Scotland, and I started going to schools and giving talks about the Children's Home. The school would then do a fund raising activity for us and we would then receive those funds. I was getting very tired, trying to run the Children's Home, deal with the harassment from the social development, and cope with the staff, the children, the police, the finances, the funding, the administration, the correspondence, the maintenance and the racism.

More often than not, I would have to dip into my private overdraft to pay the wages and for the food, the electricity or for whatever was needed for the home. If we got money in, I would then have to pay it back into my overdraft because by then my bank manager was breathing down my neck. I made a wish list for myself that I wrote out and stuck up above my computer. It read: "I want enough money to look after the children. I want a country that cares for its children. I want a little place to call my own". That list I put up five years ago. While I write this I look again at that list. How sad that it is still just a wish list.

One of the problems that I encountered was that, when I was away from the Children's Home, the staff did not economize, and the savings that should have been in place went out of the window, so when I came back the expenses were over the top. The phone bill was doubled, the electricity was doubled, the food bill was doubled and the theft of goods from the children's home was unbelievable. This would make me despair completely, as there was no one who could understand that money was a problem. The staff just thought that I was a never-ending supply of money and no amount of explaining could change that fact. They believed that white people had money and that was that. This was a result of the indoctrination from the lead up to the elections which gave us the new government, and there was no changing their mind set.

I could not just fire people for theft. I would have to prove it, and with the new labour laws, dismissal of staff is very difficult. I would have to work with these people and try to work around the problem. The children were safe and I felt that was the most important thing, so the problem with the theft of goods and food and the misuse of the telephone was secondary.

I put codes on to the telephone to stop the misuse. I placed a standing order for food from the supplier and gave instructions that no other orders could be delivered unless ordered by myself, and I thought that this would at least put some measure of prevention of theft into place.

However, after my next trip I found that the food had been "used" in the first week and the children had been fed on bread for the rest of the time. No washing had been done because the washing powder had "finished" in the first week. I issued final written warnings to all the staff for neglect of duty. I also notified the Department of Labour because I had not followed their prescribed laws but told them that the staff had contravened the Child Care Act. The final written warning is the last warning before dismissal before a disciplinary hearing. The staff got a fright, particularly since there are virtually no jobs available in Middelburg.

Before my next UK trip, I put a standing order for food and consumables in to be delivered once a week. This arrangement worked a lot better than the once a month delivery.

I had to continually watch for theft from the home. Since no one other than the children and staff had access to the homes, it was obvious that the only way goods were disappearing was via the adults who were leaving the Homes. This was a particularly unpleasant situation for me. I spoke to all the staff, telling them that they were not stealing from me, but stealing from the children, but they did not comprehend this. They still felt that I was white and therefore had a lot of money. The staff were very quick to blame the children for the missing food, clothing and linen.

I then told the staff that I was going to do an experiment. I also let them all observe me when I placed R50,00 in loose notes and change on the top of the television set. I told them that I would leave the money on the television set for twenty-four hours. If the money was still there after twenty-four hours, then the children were not thieves. Twenty-four hours later, the R50,00 was still on the top of the television. Not one of my children has ever taken anything that did not belong to them. I have only three rules in my Children's Home. Everyone was forbidden to tell a lie, use violence or steal. All other problems are easily sorted out.

While the children never stole a thing from the Home or from school and seldom told lies, this was a different matter with the staff. However, this would change over time, as staff were weeded out through their contracts coming to an end and other staff being employed. Whatever could go wrong would go wrong when I was away, and if the Department of Social Development wanted to do something mean, they would do it when I was away.

Eventually, I too got wise to that, and went to see the Commissioner of Child Welfare and asked that no Children's Court hearings be held if I was not available. Nevertheless, this too was a waste of time, as the social workers continued to get hearings without us being notified. Those first years were very hard and I learned a lot about the nature of human beings.

For the umpteenth time I decided to approach Johan Pienaar, the Chief Social Worker for the state, for safety fees. The children in my care were placed with me through the Children's Court on a Form 5 and at that time, the court order stipulated that the Department of Social Development was to pay us R8,00 per day for each child on the Form 5. Some children were siblings, so the family would be on one Form 5. Again Pienaar told me that Mrs Ferreira, his superior in Cradock was the only one who could authorize safety fees. I asked him to ask her. Again I phoned him and he told me that she had refused to authorize payment. I then wrote to Mrs Ferreira, asking her to please claim the safety fees that were due to us. She wrote back to me stating that the department did not have the funds to pay safety fees. Every so often I would ask for the safety fees and there was always a different slant on the reason for the non payment of safety fees.

I eventually found out that we were entitled, as a registered Children's Home to apply for funding from the Department of Social Development. I obtained the correct procedure and form from the department and submitted it to Mrs Ferreira. Again, I received a negative response. The department did not have the funds to fund our children's home. Every year we have applied for funding from the Department of Social Development, and every year we get a different reason for their refusal to fund us, from not being written in the correct format (which was not true) to not having made a budget for funding. The first year we were told that we were not going to be funded because we did not have a committee.

I quickly established a house committee, with the stipulated seven members. I decided to ask members of the community to join the committee, so that the Children's Home would be open and transparent to the community, and could act as a liaison between the community and the Children's Home. I managed to get a nursing sister from the hospital, Diana Jagers, a police officer, Louis Jenner, a social worker, Johan Pienaar and, a number of community members. We held regular monthly meetings and all activities within the home were discussed as well as our financial position. The only person who never attended a meeting was Johan Pienaar. However, the following year, there was another excuse as to why the department would not fund us.

One of the most disappointing refusals has been from the Nelson Mandela Children's Fund. We have requested funding from this fund every year, and each year we have been refused funding. The one year we were refused because "we do not believe in institutionalizing children". Another year we were refused because "your foundation does not meet the requirements of a children's project" and yet another year we were refused because "your project is not in line with youth and child care". If our project is not caring for children and fighting for their rights, then who is? Who is the voice of the children of South Africa?

Another disappointing refusal was from Save the Children's Fund. This refusal came back as "We regret to inform you that we do not fund children's projects. We are an advocacy group only". How many people are supporting this fund on a regular basis, thinking that their money is supporting children around the world?

It was back to sending out hundreds and hundreds of funding proposals and receiving sixty percent of them back with "we commend your efforts but...". From all these rejects, I have learned thousand ways to say no. If it were not for my funding trips to the United Kingdom, we would not have been able to survive. The donors from the United

Kingdom were mostly private donors. I found them to be very compassionate people as opposed to the South Africans who had become compassion fatigued.

Themba and Patricia

Themba was brought to us on after midnight on a Friday night by the police. He was eight months old. His mother had thrown him out of the window in a drunken fit and the police had locked her up on a charge of attempted murder. The little one had a cut on his head and was cold, wet, hungry and crying. We nursed him and cared for him over the weekend.

On Monday morning were told by the social worker to take him to Children's Court. Naturally, we assumed that this was to place him in our care or to have him placed in a relative' care. I took the little one to court and to my surprise I found the mother, the social worker, a man who claimed he was the father and the Magistrate/Commissioner of Child Welfare waiting for me. I sat and listened to the proceedings. The social worker was speaking on behalf of the father. The father stated that he lived in George. He wanted his son to go home with him. He said that he had a job, and that he had his mother living with him who could take care of the baby. The social worker confirmed that this was true.

The Commissioner then asked the father if there was any chance that the mother would have any contact with the child, because she was out on bail on a very serious charge. The father said there was no chance of the mother having contact with the child. The social worker said that the mother would have to stay in Middelburg because of her bail restrictions, and that the father was going to George with the baby.

This satisfied the Commissioner and he asked me to hand over the baby to the father. I duly did this, but I did not feel good about this decision. Something did not feel right about it, but I could not put my finger on it. It seemed too smooth, too straightforward. My gut feeling was that something was fishy about what was happening. From my experience with this social worker, Pumza, I did not believe that this was a straightforward case. However, I had nothing to go on but my gut feeling, and the Commissioner would definitely not listen to me talking about intuition.

In any event, I now had confirmation that the Commissioner was more than just Pumza's friend. I had heard rumours about it and I had made it my business to check whether this was true or not. The more information I had about what was going down in Middelburg with regard to government officials the better. This was the only way I was going to be one slippery step ahead of them when it came to saving the children. I found out that it was true by checking up myself late one night. It was indeed true that they were lover's so unless I had absolute proof of something when it came to Pumza, I would not offer just an opinion to the Commissioner.

We all walked out the Commissioner's office together, the father carrying the child. When we got to the street, the father handed the child to the mother. I looked at Pumza with a questioning look. She looked away. I called to her.

"Pumza, wait a moment please". I walked with her to her car. "Pumza, do you think this is alright for that child? I have a feeling that the mother is going to take that child.

Already she will be able has access to the child when the Commissioner does not want that to happen".

She shrugged her shoulders. "It is not your business anymore", she said.

Later that day when I was driving through the township I saw the mother with the baby. The father was nowhere to be seen. The mother was as drunk as a lord. "God, protect that baby and keep him safe", I prayed. My life was so busy and so full with the children in my care that all I did for that one was to send a prayer for his safety.

While for some children I wonder if I did enough, with others I feel I did everything I could. Patricia was one of those I did all I could for, but it was not enough to save her.

Welile Falake, the man who would one day leave three children on my doorstep, is a man who has great compassion for street children. He no longer lives in Middelburg as he has moved to Cape Town. The community saw him as a laughing stock. He was always walking around with a group of dirty, barefoot male street children, himself a scruffy, smelly man with a bald and shiny head the shape of an egg. He had started a street children shelter with the help of the Catholic Priest, but it was poorly organized. However, it was done with compassion and passion, and I tried to assist him as much as I could during the time that I was doing my HIV awareness work in Middelburg.

In June 2001, I noticed a child amongst his group of boys who looked very much like a girl. I spoke to Welile and asked him whether he realized that he had a girl in the group of boys. He was completely nonplussed about it and asked me to take the child and check on his/her sex. I was right. She was a girl.

"Welile, this child is a girl. I think you should take her to the welfare and sort something out for her. It is not right that she is with all these boys. She is dressing like a boy because she is afraid of being raped", I told him.

"I will do something about it", he said.

Almost two years later, this same child was one of the children that I took on a cold May night when they arrived at my door. I recognized the child, but could not place her. While looking through my photograph albums, that I recognized her as being the girl who walked around with Welile.

I called him in a few days later to ask him why he had not done anything about the child with the Department of Social Welfare. He looked offended.

"Have you worked with the Department of Social Development?", he asked.

"Not really, I only know they do not care very much and they have no facilities for street children", I replied.

As usual, he was carrying a dirty and battered briefcase with him. "Look here", he said as he sat down and opened his briefcase. He ruffled through his papers, some of them dog-eared and old, some folded in half, others just scraps of paper. Eventually he pulled out a brown manila folder marked "Field Worker – Peter Stephens". He pushed the folder towards me.

"You don't know what it is like to work with these social workers", he said, clearly agitated and still offended. "They do nothing for the children. They don't care about the children and they are jealous of me. I don't get money for the children. I look after them because I do it with my love. They get paid for their work and they do nothing, nothing, nothing. I do reports and nothing gets done. Look at this", he continued, again pushing the folder towards me.

I took it and opened it. The date on the report was 31 August 2001. The report stated that Ntombixolo (who we called Patricia at her insistence) was found to be a child in need of care. It was recommended that she be placed in a place of safety pending placement in foster care. In two years, the Department of Social Development had done nothing for Patricia and she was still on the streets. At the time of the report, she was ten years-old, wearing boys clothes so that she would not be "rachered". She was now twelve years-old, and raped so many times she could not remember, and, she had been gang-raped the night she came to live with me.

My blood boiled with anger at the lack of compassion and the lack of service delivery by the social workers of the Department of Social Development. In the Field Workers report, there was the name and address of Patricia's mother. I took the details down, determined to make someone responsible for the neglect and abuse of this child.

At this point, I was still unaware of the intricacies and the procedures of the Child Care Act, and was still dependent on the information fed to me by the social workers. I was very new at what I was doing. Naïve and innocent! All I really knew was that what was happening to the children was wrong. Mrs Ferreira had told me that I may not keep the children because I was not registered as a Children's Home, and I was doing everything I could to speed up the process of registering it. However, she was delaying the process as much as she could. Eventually, Mrs Ferreira put the first three children in my name as a place of safety, and told me that it was only temporary until a foster parent could be found. When I suggested that I become a foster parent, I was told that it was not possible because of the cultural difference. This too boggled my mind.

What did culture have to do with it? Was the culture difference between myself and the children a good enough reason to leave them to die on the streets, to continue to be abused and neglected rather than to live with me? I found this totally absurd. There was no questioning of my background to see whether I was culturally similar to the children. I had been brought up under a tribal system, was accustomed to the culture of the ama-Xhosa, and therefore I was more suited to the children than any number of black people brought up in towns or cities. The problem they had was to do with me being white and the children black, and not anything to do with culture. Culture was the new politically-correct word for racism.

I did two things that I was inexperienced enough to believe would solve the problem of Patricia. The police would protect the children's rights and the Commissioner of Child Welfare would act in the best interests of the child. Off I went to see both of these people, my heart filled with hope. How little I knew, and how much I still had to learn in those early days. I went to the Commissioner of Child Welfare, who was at the time a Mr Vermeulen. He was less than friendly to me. I told him the story of Patricia and asked him to help me with putting Patricia into my care permanently as she was in need of psychological care.

"Mrs Ferreira has the last say and I cannot be of any assistance to you", he said as he ushered me out of the door.

I began to think that Mrs Ferreira was the law, the beginning and end of all rights of the child, and what she said even superseded what a commissioner said. This was beyond what I had imagined, although I was too raw at this stage to know about the Child Care Act. I was only going on the information supplied to me as I was moving from one official to another.

My next stop was the police station, where I was assisted in opening a case of neglect against the mother of Patricia. I was even told to come back the next day to get a docket number, which I did. I very proudly put the docket number, (K) MAS 6/6/2003 in a file, thinking that at least someone would be held responsible for what had happened to Patricia. Needless to say, no investigations were done and the prosecutor refused to prosecute due to lack of evidence. It took two years to get this information.

A little while after her arrival, Patricia's mother arrived to see me. She had a message for me from Johan Pienaar.

"Johan Pienaar said that I must come and fetch Patricia from you because you have too many children and you are not allowed to have them".

I could not believe what she was saying. "Are you telling me the truth?", I asked.

"Yes", she answered.

"Then I will write down what you have said and you will sign it and we will witness what you have said".

I wrote down what she had said and she duly signed it. I don't know why I did this, but something inside me was starting to let me know that I had better start collecting evidence about what was going on with the children. Something did not sound and feel right. There was something more to the whole manner in which the way children were being dealt with that did not make sense. Somehow, I would get to the bottom of this. Looking back down the years, I realize now that by doing this, I was able to save
a number of children from being put back on the street, although in cases such as Jonathan, nothing helped.

I told the mother that I would not let her take Patricia until she proved that she was a caring mother, and that she could start by cleaning up her act, by coming to visit Patricia, and by showing that she cared. If she wanted Patricia then she could go to the police and the Commissioner of Welfare and Mrs Ferreira, and come back with the police to fetch Patricia. Over my dead body was I going to let Patricia go with her.

Patricia's behaviour was very disturbing. She was constantly fidgeting and biting her nails down to the quick. She could not sit or stand still. She jumped and startled at every sudden movement. If I moved too quickly towards her she would put up her hands to protect herself from being beaten. She scratched her arms until they were raw and bleeding. Her concentration span was extremely poor. She had never been to school and her ability to read a letter on a page was almost impossible. She could not draw except for making small black crosses in the corner of a page.

With good food and care, Patricia was putting on weight and developing, but her mental, emotional and psychological scars were getting no better. She was also beginning to get aggressive with the other children. On numerous occasions I asked Pumza Mobo to come in to assess the situation, but each time she would either not arrive for the appointment, or would cancel it at the last minute.

I was getting desperate. We did not have much money, and private consultations with psychiatrists were extremely expensive, and Middelburg did not have specialists. However, I was so worried about Patricia that I took the financial leap and made an appointment with a psychiatrist in Graaff-Reinett for her. He put her on medication, and thus began our expensive monthly trips back and forth to Graaff-Reinett. The medication stopped Patricia from pacing up and down and from scratching her arms, but did little for her other symptoms. In most cases, if there was going to be an upset in the house about something between the children, it was invariably Patricia who would start it. Patricia was hard work.

A number of children who were HIV+ were on Bactrim and they would line up in the kitchen for their medication twice a day. Because we do not have anti-retrovirals, we use Bactrim to keep the opportunistic diseases at bay. Patricia got it into her head to start teasing them about being HIV+. This caused so much trouble in the home with a lot of tears and unhappiness. My head spun. How to deal with this? The only thing I could think of was to make everyone positive. The whole house!

I called a meeting of all the children. I often had to do this when something happened that needed an explanation, or a problem solved with the children. Meetings are held in the dining room and the whole family, including the little children and staff, take part. We always begin a meeting with a prayer and then end it with a song.

I started the meeting, "Right, there seems to be a problem in this home with the taking of medicine. I want you all to know that there are some people in this home who are negative and some people who are positive. We are all positive. Negative people are sad and miserable people. Positive people are happy people. Now can you tell me if we are negative people or positive people?", I asked.

"Positive people" shouted most of the children.

"Right, as positive people I have decided that to become more positive we are all going to take medicine and pills. This medicine and pills is going to give us more energy. Everyone in this home, including the staff, from today, will line up in the kitchen for their medicine. Are we all positive people?", I asked.

A resounding "Yes" was shouted.

"And, what is more", I continued, "I don't want to hear another word about anyone being negative in this home. We are all positive people. Am I understood?"

Another resounding "Yes, Mama D" filled the room. From that day on, everyone was given Vitamin B complex and Multivitamins. I made sure that no one was ever treated in any way differently to any other child. I had learned another lesson from the children.

In July 2004, Patricia's father, who had been released from prison, arrived at the home, smelling badly of alcohol, his eyes yellow and bloodshot, leaning on the doorjamb to stabilize himself in his drunken state, and demanded we release Patricia into his care. He caused quite a scene in front of the children, pulling at the security gate, shouting obscenities and accusing us of stealing his child.

Patricia asked if she could go with him. I refused to allow him to enter the premises and I refused to allow Patricia to go with him. She started screaming at me, he was screaming all kinds of bad language at me, and eventually

I closed the door on him, calling the police to have him removed. Patricia went berserk. She kicked out at anyone within her reach. She threw the chairs around. She screamed at all of us for keeping her prisoner. We tried to calm her down but it was becoming mayhem. I fetched a tranquilizer and tried to get it into her mouth. She bit my hands and tried to bite my arms. She was flailing her arms and kicking and screaming.

The other children were standing around open-mouthed. We had to get the situation under control quickly. I asked Monea to take the children outside and asked Jackson to help me grab Patricia and get her into one of the rooms. Once we got her forcibly into a room, I held her down on the bed, her arms at her sides and Jackson had her legs in a vice grip. Now what? What to do next? I had never been in a situation like this. I tried again to get the tranquilizer into her mouth but it was impossible. I could think of no other alternative but to get her to hospital. With a lot of effort, with Jackson and Fikile holding her, we got her to hospital where, thankfully, my friend Diana was on duty. She immediately reacted by injecting Patricia with something or other that calmed her down, and we put her into a bed in a private ward. I was exhausted. Diana phoned the doctor. At least Patricia was calm and in a safe place, but I had no idea of what to make of the situation or of what to do. I waited for the doctor. The doctor was the district surgeon and he did not come out unless it was an emergency and this was obviously not an emergency. I would have to wait until he came on his usual rounds. I waited and waited and eventually Diana told me to go home. She said that she would phone me when the doctor had been around. Patricia was by then sound asleep.

Just before Diana went off duty she called me to say that the doctor had decided not to do rounds that day, but that she would be on duty early the next morning and would let me know what he said. When she called, she told me that the doctor could find nothing wrong with Patricia and that she had been discharged. I went to collect Patricia and she was her normal self.

Patricia was fine for three days, and then she absconded. She had now been in our care for fourteen months and she was part and parcel of our lives. She was loved, despite the problems. Even though she was the first child to runaway, the pain and worry of a run-away child never got any less for me. I immediately phoned the police to look for her, but they were not very helpful. They told me that they would look for her after the change of shift and if they had enough vehicles to do so. They also wanted to know where she might be. If I knew where she was, I told them, I would not be phoning them. I then got into my vehicle and without any thought to my safety, drove into Lusaka, the township where I knew her father lived. I did not know exactly where he lived, so I just drove up and down the streets, stopping to ask the children if they had seen Patricia. Most of the children told me that they had seen her but they did not know where she had gone. I continued my search.

I had been driving around for about an hour when I thought I saw a glimpse of her between two houses a street away. I knew that by the time I drove around to where I had seen her, I would have lost her, so I jumped out my vehicle and ran through the little lanes between the houses in the direction that I had seen her. As I came around the corner I saw her go into one of the houses. When I got to the door it was closed and I banged on the door, shouting for her. The door remained closed. By now, I was out of breath, angry and desperate to get her home. I shouted in isi-Xhosa for the door to be opened, or I would call the police all the while banging both my fists against the door. The door opened and I was faced by a very drunk father and behind him a couple of his equally drunk friends.

"I have come to fetch Patricia", I said.

"She is my child and you can't take her", he replied aggressively. My heart was beating rapidly, not from running, but from fear.

"Give me Patricia immediately", I said taking a step inside.

He pushed me away and tried to close the door. Suddenly I found myself pushing him back with strength I did not know I was capable of. I pushed him so hard and violently that he fell back against his friends and they too stumbled.

I shouted "Patricia, where are you?", as I ran towards and through the only other open door.

Patricia was sitting on a bed. I didn't know at the time why she did not fight me. I grabbed her by the arm and pulled her along with me. I was heading out towards the door by the time the father recovered. He tried to stop me by barring my way at the door, but I had the strength of a lioness protecting her cub. Still holding on to Patricia for dear life, I kicked him as hard as I could between the legs.

He just folded and we were out, running down the lanes towards my vehicle. I don't remember driving back home.

As I walked into the house, my legs started shaking. I was in shock but Patricia was safe. She was safe, but she was drunk and under the influence of dagga. Now I knew why she did not fight me. And so began our round of absconding and rescue. The scenario was always the same; Patricia, the father, the alcohol and the dagga. In the meantime, I was desperately trying to get the social workers to assist me in getting help for Patricia. Numerous letters were being written, appointments made and cancelled by them, and our trips to the psychiatrist were not helping. The psychiatrist said that Patricia needed to go into a mental hospital for treatment, but private treatment was out of the question for us. We could not afford R750.00 a day for her and, on top of that, the cost of her medication.

Patricia was exhibiting periods of extreme aggression and violence in between her times of absconding. There is a procedure within the Criminal Procedures Act and the Child Care Act that prohibits anyone from luring a child away from a Children's Home. This is a criminal act punishable by law. I had asked the social workers again to place her in my permanent care so that I could lay a charge against the father for enticing her away from the home. I could not do this if she were not permanently in my care. The social worker, Johan Pienaar, again told me that Mrs Ferreira was the only person who could allow this, and she would not sign the necessary forms. I eventually found a way of getting Patricia into a government facility for care. Although I was now equipped with the letter for her admission to the Komani Psychiatric Hospital, I could not admit her because she was a minor and I was not legally her guardian nor was she legally placed in my care.

I wrote a letter to the Commissioner of Child Welfare explaining my predicament with Patricia and requesting urgent intervention so that she could get the necessary medical care. However, this was also ignored.

When one is faced with a situation where every legal alternative and avenue is thwarted, one then has to become creative. I could no longer allow the situation to continue as it was. Patricia needed professional help. On the 24 August 2004, I phoned the hospital in Queenstown and made the arrangements to bring Patricia in the next day for admittance. We all made a big fuss about the trip so that Patricia could look forward to it. We bought new pyjamas, slippers and packed magazines, cold drinks and biscuits. A big party was held that night for her.

The trip to Queenstown was uneventful, with Patricia gazing out the window and asking various questions about the hospital. The real test for me was when I got there. I would somehow have to get her admitted without the necessary documentation proving that I was her legal guardian. I sent a prayer up to all the archangels I could think of for protection. I asked God to put the right words in my mouth. I asked that He put the right people on duty. And all the time I kept on thinking that I was after all the only person who gave a damn anyway, so what the hell... a couple of lies between saving this child from herself and no life at all.

Whether it was the minions of heaven, the right people at the right time or my smooth talking, I was accepted as Patricia's foster mother. She was introduced to the others on her ward, we were introduced to all the nursing staff and she was left in their capable hands. I drove home feeling that I had at least accomplished something good.

Patricia was released three weeks later. She had been diagnosed with dagga related psychosis and delirium. When I collected her, she was prescribed a low dose of tranquilizer. She was cheerful and relaxed on our way home, and very happy to be going home.

We had a blissful week with no upsets and then the round of absconding, drunk father, dagga and alcohol began again. The aggression and violence returned. By now, she was inciting Betty to abscond with her. I could not allow this to go on. Returning her to the psychiatric hospital was out of the question because the maximum stay was three weeks. She would then just return to the same environment, and without the authority to lay a charge against the father for enticing her to leave the home there was little I could do to keep her from alcohol and dagga.

On 4 October 2004 I hand-delivered a letter to the Commission of Child Welfare asking for assistance in transferring Patricia to a place of safety as she was a danger to herself and others.

The next day, I hand-delivered a letter and spoke to Johan Pienaar, requesting an immediate transfer for Patricia to another facility, again explaining the circumstances. I also gave him copies of all the medical reports on Patricia. To make sure that something was done, I sent a copy of this letter to Mr Makasi, District Manager of Social Development, Mrs Ferreira's boss.

On 6 October, I hand-delivered a letter to the Clerk of the Court, requesting him to follow up on a Children's Court hearing for the transfer of Patricia. All hand-delivered letters were now being signed for by the recipients, all telephone calls were being followed up with a letter confirming the telephone conversation. All letters sent were being registered and all faxes were being attached to the fax print out. The various recipients could not say that they had not received the relevant documentation or information on the children. I did this for every child in our care.

On 14 October a Children's Court enquiry was held by the new Commissioner of Child Welfare, Mr Mata. I gave him all the evidence I had and requested him to have Patricia transferred to a facility that was better equipped to deal with her problem. I explained that we were a Children's Home and that we were not equipped to deal with aggressive and violent children that were a danger to themselves and others. The commissioner issued a Court Order for immediate transfer of Patricia to the Erica Place of Safety in Port Elizabeth for a period of six months. Thereafter, the situation could be reassessed and she could come back to Middelburg. Erica also had a school and she would be attending school. Mr Mata informed Johan Pienaar to escort Patricia to Erica in Port Elizabeth. After all the times I had collected her from the township, Patricia thought I was her enemy.

Patricia went off with Johan Pienaar, evidently very pleased with herself that she would now no longer have to live with my rules. I told Johan that I would deliver her suitcase to his office which I did straight away. I was very distraught about Patricia leaving but at the same time, I knew that this was her only chance of getting better. She needed to be away from the influence of her father, and, away for long enough to get over her dagga addiction. It never occurred to me to check whether Patricia had actually been taken to Erica. I assumed that a court order was a court order, and that since Patricia had gone off with Johan that she was safely at Erica. I continued with life at home, dealing with a thousand and one issues, from trying to get a registered Children's Home to coping with sick children.

It was by chance that it came to my attention that Patricia had, in fact, never been taken to Erica, and that she was living in the township. My friend Diana at the hospital had been on leave, and when she got back she mentioned to me that Patricia had been hospitalized sometime between 14 October and 3 November following an assault by persons unknown. This meant that within a week of the court order she had been assaulted and had been hospitalized. It was on the 17 November that I received this information, and I immediately wrote a letter and hand-delivered it to the Commissioner of Child Welfare, informing him that the court order had not been carried out and that the child was in Lusaka. I requested that the court look into the matter and take the appropriate action. Again, I assumed that this would be dealt with speedily and appropriately. However, I was again, as I would continually be throughout the years, astonished at the lack

411

of concern when it came to children from any of the state departments.

On the 27 December of that year, Patricia arrived back home. She had had enough of the township. She had never been to Erica. She was hungry, dirty and in a terrible state of neglect. She had a great deal of bruising on her face and her right eye was bloodshot. She was sober and looked pitiful and helpless. My heart went out to her and my love for this child poured out. I took her into my arms and rocked her, telling her over and over how much I loved her. Then I took her inside, fed her, bathed her and put her into clean clothes.

The next day, I requested to see Mr Mata, the Commissioner of Child Welfare. I refused to leave until he saw me, much to the annoyance of the Clerk of the Court. When I told him the story of how Patricia had never been taken to Erica, despite his court order, that she had been living in the township with her father, that she had been assaulted, hospitalized and made vulnerable to dagga and alcohol, he phoned Pumza Mobo, the social worker.

"Why has Patricia Ngesi not been taken to Erica?" he asked.

When he put the telephone down, he told me that Johan Pienaar was the social worker on the case, not Pumza, and that Johan was on leave. The reason Johan had not taken Patricia to Erica was because the child had been involved in a case of theft. I told Mr Mata, that I could find out about the theft case, because this had not happened while she was in my care and that I would come back to him immediately. I went to the police station. I found out from the police that Patricia had been caught stealing from Pep Stores on the 3rd November 2004 at 15h35 and that she had been arrested and fingerprinted. The case number was 10/11/2004 and the case would be heard on the 30 December 2005.

The court order to place Patricia in the Erica Place of Safety was dated 14 October 2004, more than two weeks before the case of theft. I took this information back to Mr Mata, who immediately called Pumza Mobo to court. He issued another order. Pumza Mobo was to transfer Patricia to Erica within 24 hours and I was to take care of her until that time.

On the 30th December, Pumza had still not come to collect Patricia, so I accompanied her to her theft case at court. This case was postponed until 21st January 2005. When I got back from the court, I telephoned Pumza and asked her why she had not collected Patricia yet. She informed me that Erica was closed for the holidays and would only open again on the 20th January 2005.

She said that she had spoken to her supervisor, Mrs Ferreira, and Mrs Ferreira had asked why I, Mrs Lang, could not keep Patricia until that date. I again explained that we were a Children's Home and not a secure unit, and it was not in the best interests of Patricia or the other children for her to remain at the home for any period of time.

Something about the conversation with Pumza did not ring true. I could not understand how a secure unit for children

413

would close during the Christmas holidays. I phoned the Erica Place of Safety myself and spoke with Mr Andre du Plessis, the manager. He told me that they never closed, and that they were open for admissions at any time.

I was starting to get frustrated and exasperated with the continual lying by the social workers. They got away with murder because their word was law. The Commissioner of Child Welfare made his or her decision based on the reports by the social workers. The supervisors of social workers believed every word they said. How was I to deal with such lying, manipulating, lazy people?

When I phoned Pumza with the information that Erica Place of Safety never closed and were open for admissions at any time and that I had got this information from the manager, her reply was "I will phone Erica myself and phone you back". There was no embarrassment, no shame and no apology for her lies.

When I had not received a call from Pumza by the next day, 31st December, I called her myself.

"I have not been able to reach Erica yet and I am going off at 11h00", she said.

"Pumza, can you try and carry out the Court Order to transfer Patricia because she is being aggressive and I cannot keep such an aggressive child", I pleaded.

"I will try", she replied.

By the 3 January, the situation with Patricia at home was deteriorating at such a rate that I had to make a decision about her transfer to Erica. There were no social workers available as they were all on holiday and not answering their telephones. I decided to drive Patricia to Port Elizabeth and put her in Erica myself. At last she was safe. Nothing was done about Johan ignoring a court order or about his lies or about Pumza's lies. This was just a way of getting out of doing what they were paid to do, never mind that a child's life was at stake or that a child's best interests are supposed to be a priority. I knew that Patricia's best chance of getting well and educated would be at Erica Place of Safety.

On 24th March 2005, one of my staff members saw the Erica Place of Safety vehicles drop Patricia off at her father's home in the township. He was so upset he came running to the home, even though he was not on duty, to come and report it to me.

I immediately telephoned Erica and spoke to Mr Mendele, the social worker there, that it was inappropriate to leave Patricia with her father for the holidays because he had already assaulted her in the past, and explained what went on at that house. He said that he would contact the driver to bring Patricia to me. This did not happen.

On the 26th March, I sent a letter to Erica, again voicing my concern as Patricia had been seen very inebriated in the township. This time, I received a letter back stating that Patricia's case worker had made the decision that it would be to her benefit to return home to her father for the holidays. There was nothing more that I could do. At the time, I thought that the case manager was someone at Erica. I did not know that the case manager they were referring to was Johan Pienaar.

The school term started and Patricia was still in the township. I contacted Mrs Martin, the supervisor for Erica. I informed her that Patricia was roaming the township and that she was supposed to be in the care of Erica, and asked her to kindly look into the matter. She said that she would contact Johan Pienaar.

Again, life in the home took over and I was busy with numbers of other children, various other things and again, stupidly, thought that Mrs Martin would have sorted everything out with Patricia. This again was not to be. Patricia arrived back on my doorstep, again dirty, hungry and assaulted. She wanted me to phone Erica and tell them to come and fetch her. It was now the 10 May. She had been roaming the township since 24 March. By now, I was extremely angry. I could not believe how unprofessional, how uncaring and how indifferent everyone in the system of child care was. I was ranting and raving.

Patricia was not the only one I was fighting for. There were dozens of them, and every child had a story, every child had a right, and every right was being violated, over and over by the very systems and people that were being employed to safeguard their rights. I was not being paid. I was doing it for the love of these children, but I was being treated with total disrespect. I was being treated like dirt. I was being policed and harassed by these people. I was sick of it. Patricia was indoors, being taken care of by my loving and dedicated staff, and I was walking up and down, fuming. My thoughts were flying from one direction to another. How dare these people treat these children and me like this? Who the hell did they think they were? They were taking home fat salaries at the end of the month. They were going home to their lovely houses at the end of the day, forgetting all these children and living in luxury, while I was constantly working, sleeping little, with no luxuries to speak of. I had not had a day off in 4 years.

I was angry, bitter and frustrated at the audacity of these people and the state Department of Social Development that was constantly giving me such a hard time while they said nice things about how much they did for the children, when in fact they did nothing. Nothing at all! The hypocrites! The dirty, dirty hypocrites! I lit one cigarette after another. I had hardly put one out when I lit another. Was there no one out there that cared the same as I did? Was there no one out there that wanted to make a difference to the children, that cared where the hell this fucking country of ours was going? Damn that Ferreira! Had she ever put a black baby on her lap and watched the child die of AIDS? The fucking bitch! What was an Afrikaans woman doing anyway with the ANC? Why could she not allow any one of the social workers to make a decision without her say so? Because she was still of the old school and a person of colour could not make a decision. Could these fucking people not see that? Had they not heard me? When it suits her I must look after Patricia, but it does not suit her for me to get even an R8.00 grant for a child? It did not even suit her to put Patricia in my name to protect Patricia from her father's

417

influence. The children and I must struggle for every cent. But the corruption and fraud and the no care attitude to the children can go on and on! And I smoked and I fumed and I ranted and I raved and I wanted to scream in frustration. So often I had gone to bed in despair, but now I was angry. Damn the Department of Social Development! Damn the MEC! Damn the Minister of Social Development! And Damn the President!

Between the 10th and 19th May, Patricia was in and out of our home constantly, and I was in constant contact with Margie Martin, the supervisor of Erica. We had long discussions about Patricia and eventually, Margie understood my love for Patricia and Patricia's background. She was astonished that Johan Pienaar had given them nothing to go on. I emphasized that since the court order had placed Patricia in her care, she was ultimately responsible for Patricia and, that should anything happen to Patricia, she would be held responsible. What a joke! No one is held responsible for what happens to the children in South Africa. Complaints to everyone, right up to the Public Protector are ignored.

However, what I said must have made an impression because she got Patricia collected by the police and delivered back to Erica. Whatever happened between her and Johan Pienaar, I do not know. When I contacted Margie to find out how Patricia was doing on the 26th May, she informed me that Patricia had an Sexually Transmitted Disease and was in an advanced stage of HIV, and that all the staff were very upset as they had not had an HIV positive child admitted to their institution yet.

I was not surprised by this news as it was indicative of the township situation that she had been left in by her case worker, Johan Pienaar. However, I was shocked when Margie suggested that in the circumstances, it would be best if she returned to her family. Again, I said that this would not be in her best interests, so she suggested that she should return to me until suitable foster parents could be found. She said that she would make these arrangements with Johan Pienaar.

Later that same day, I telephoned Margie Martin again to tell her that Patricia was in the township. She was shocked as she had made arrangements with Johan Pienaar to drop her off with me. She said she would contact him immediately to collect her and to bring her to me. On the 31st May, we again told Margie Martin that Patricia was still not with us. She again contacted Johan Pienaar. On 8th June, Margie contacted me and told me that on numerous occasions she had spoken to Johan Pienaar. She was now going to put it into writing and if the child was not put into the Children's Home immediately, she was to be returned to Erica. Margie sent me a copy of the letter she sent to Pienaar. There was little room for him to manoeuvre out of his clear duty in this letter. However, he still continued to ignore his duties. The following day, Johan Pienaar did not answer his telephone, so at eight o' clock that night, I went into the township and found Patricia staying in a child-headed home.

Child-headed homes are rife in the Eastern Cape, where many parents have died from AIDS, and where there are no adults to take care of the children and where social services are unavailable. Children then take to living together and wandering the streets begging for food and, not going to school. Many of the smaller children in the townships were by now living in the Children's Home, but due to financial restrictions and restrictions put on me by the Department of Social Development, I could not take in any more children.

I took Patricia home, hoping that Margie would be able to do something so that either Patricia could be put into my care legally or she could be sent back to Erica. I found out who was having sex with Patricia. Her "boyfriend" was an adult male by the name of Thanduxolo Matshisi who lived at 6 Silvertown, Lusaka. As a minor child, her boyfriend could be charged with statutory rape. I went to the police and charged him. Nothing came of this matter either.

It was not long before Patricia absconded again. I continued to harass both Johan Pienaar and Margie Martin to do something about Patricia. Patricia was coming into and out of my life. She would spend three to four days a week at home, clean up, eat, sleep and then she would be off again for a couple of days, only to be back again, dirty and hungry.

On the 19th July, Patricia arrived with her friend Maria. Maria had lived with us for a couple of months a year previously, when she was pregnant. She was only 13 at the time. She had had her baby, a girl, and the social workers had sent the baby to foster parents in George. Maria had received no counselling, and she had been told that she could go back to the township and live in the child-headed home that she had come from. She was a child prostitute and very street-wise. Maria had brought

Patricia to me so that I could bandage her up. She had received a severe beating from her father. Her right forearm was swollen and lacerated, as was her wrist. I did what I could, fed the two girls and they left.

I telephoned Pienaar again and told him that if he did not do something about Patricia, she would either die from AIDS or she would be murdered sooner or later. The following day I received a phone call from Pienaar.

"Can you go and fetch Patricia and bring her to my office?", he requested.

"It is easy to find Patricia. You can easily go to 6 Silvertown and go and fetch her yourself ", I said.

"Then can you call the police the next time she comes and tell the police to take her to Port Elizabeth?", he asked.

This was the first contact Pienaar had made with me about the transfer of Patricia to Port Elizabeth; two months after Margie Martin's request. On the same day, Captain Meiring of the police telephoned me and asked me to telephone him the next time Patricia visited me. I told him that I would do so. Obviously, Margie Martin was starting to make waves because both Pienaar and the police had contacted me about Patricia.

The next day, 21st July, Patricia and Maria came to visit, again for food. I telephoned Captain Meiring. He sent two police officers who collected the children. Later that day, Pienaar telephoned me to say that the police were not going to Port Elizabeth and that he could not take the

421

children himself. He asked me if I would take Patricia to Port Elizabeth. By now, I was more than fed up.

"Johan, I took Patricia to Port Elizabeth the first time. I do not get paid for it and I do not get any money for petrol. You get a state vehicle and petrol and get paid to do a job. I do not even get a subsidy to take care of the children. I am not going to take Patricia to Port Elizabeth again", I told him. "This is your job and your problem".

Three days later, both Patricia and Maria arrived back at the Children's Home. They were breathless and frightened, and it was obvious that they had been running. They wanted to move back home permanently because they said that if they stayed any longer in the township, they would be killed. Patricia also said that her boyfriend was starting to beat her up. They told me that Mr Pienaar had told them to wait in the township until Mrs Martin came to pick them up but they were too scared to stay there. I notified Pienaar and Mrs Martin.

On 29th July 2005, I telephoned the Clerk of the Court to get an appointment with the Commissioner of Child Welfare to discuss the problem. I wanted to take both the girls with me so that they could tell the Commissioner the story themselves. Maria had gone to the township to fetch something so I sent Patricia to fetch her, never dreaming that Patricia would be in danger. The Clerk of the Court never called back with a time for the appointment, but Patricia arrived back at half past two. She had been severely assaulted by a group of boys who had attempted to rape her. I called the police, who said I was to take her to the hospital so that the district surgeon could complete a J88 form for the docket. I took Monea, one of the staff members, and Patricia up to the hospital and left them there to wait for the doctor. At six o' clock that night, Monea and Patricia walked home as the doctor had still not arrived and the sister on duty had told them that he was not coming to the hospital. I drove them back to the hospital and asked the sister to please call the district surgeon as this was an assault and the police wanted a completed J88. Of course, it was the duty of the police to do this, and not me.

She phoned and the doctor said he would see her in the morning. I did not want Patricia to bath and change or to tamper with anything that may change the evidence so asked the sister if Patricia could stay the night in the hospital for the doctor to see her the next morning. She agreed to this.

Early the next morning I was at the hospital. The doctor did not arrive. We waited and waited. I had to get back to the home and the office as the work was piling up. I left some money with Patricia to phone me as soon as the doctor arrived and told her that I would only take three to four minutes to be with her after she called. When she had not called by twelve-thirty, I got a lunch together for her and took it to her. The doctor had still not arrived. I left her there and went back to work. At five o'clock, I took up some more food to her, telling her I would return at six o'clock, which I did. We waited together for the doctor. Again and again, I asked the sister in charge to phone the doctor. She said that she had phoned several times, and that he had said that he would be in later. We could do nothing, but wait. I had the J88 form with me. I was taking no chances. Eventually, at seven o'clock he arrived, as drunk as a lord. This was not the first time, nor would it be the last time, that I would have to deal with an inebriated doctor. However, an inebriated doctor is better than no doctor at all. This is what we get to accept in rural Africa.

Eventually, I got Patricia home to a bath, clean clothes, good food and a bed. Whenever Patricia came home, no matter how long she had been away, no matter how aggressive she had been in one of her moods, the other children were always happy to see her. For all the problems she gave us, there was a lovely side to her and we all loved her. I took the J88 to the police the next day and went with Patricia and Maria to give the police their statements, as they had been asked. Inspector Fredericks was the Investigating Officer on the case. He was patient and kind in his questioning, but when Captain Meiring saw me in the passage and asked me why I was there, he had little time and patience for me.

"Agh, that Maria and Patricia... wasting our time again", he commented as he walked away laughing. This same man would tell me that I was wasting his time and paper when I went to him with a witness to a murder plot two years later.

The best that Pienaar could do was to tell me that I should allow Patricia to sleep at the Children's Home, but to give her free reign in the township during the day. I was not prepared to do this. It was detrimental to the children and to Patricia. The children would then also want to have free run of the township during the day. If I allowed this freedom to Patricia then they would want it too. I was not a shelter for nights only, and I was not about to be dictated to by this man.

I told him that Patricia needed to be in a secure environment, that I would only take her in if it was a legal arrangement, or he must find alternative care for her where she would be given the treatment for her HIV and would be in a safe environment. I could not guarantee safety for her if I was only providing a sleeping space. I also told him that I was not a hotel but a registered Children's Home and that acting as a hotel did not comply with the Child Care Act. I could no longer be a hotel for Patricia to come and go as she pleased. She had to choose either to live with me permanently, or she would have to go her own way, and hopefully, Johan
Pienaar would find her a safe place.

I told Patricia my conditions. She could come and live with me permanently, but she would have to abide by all our rules. She would no longer be allowed to come and go as she pleased. The pull of the township, with its alcohol, its dagga, its excitement was stronger than the safety of our home. She chose to leave.

I wrote my final letters to Erica Place of Safety and Johan Pienaar, with a copy to Makasi, the Area Manager of Social Development, pleading with them to intervene in the life of Patricia.

Patricia did not live long enough to see Christmas that year. She was murdered by someone in Lusaka, beaten to death. I am glad the Investigating Officer is Fredericks, the one who so patiently and kindly questioned Patricia the day that she had been assaulted by that gang of men. Officer Fredricks arrested Thanduxolo Matshisi, the same man that I asked the police to arrest for statutory rape, which they did nothing about. Does anyone else give a damn?

This is only the beginning ......

"The reward of the ending of apartheid will and must be measured by the happiness and welfare of the children. The children who sleep in the streets, reduced to begging to make a living, are testimony to an unfinished business. There can be no keener revelation of a society's soul than the way in which it treats its children."

What inspiring words spoken by such a great man! What ideals to strive for! What fights to fight! What burdens to carry! What disappointments to endure! What discrimination to suffer! What losses to bear!

Writing the stories of just some of my children has been exceedingly painful, reliving the trauma and hurt of the moment, the frustration and anger.

Emotions live in our very tissues, they are not something that are in the past, like remembering a sunset or how I painted the bedrooms for the children, or when we put in the carpets or the feeling of the cold nights, or remembering how the washing on the line freezes solid in winter. The emotions return in our bodies instantly, as though it is happening in the moment; so as I was recalling the stories of these few children, I hurt, I ached, I angered, I cried and I screamed.

And I grieved all over again for my losses. As I grieve today for the many losses I feel. My story and my journey have not ended. Both are still just somewhere there, developing, moving onward, continuing the struggle as the journey reaches ever higher mountains, the story gets more twists and turns. Does one's story ever end or one's journey ever finish? I fear my mission to make a difference in the lives of the children has become my biggest enemy and my greatest friend. It is what wakes me in the morning and what fills me with despair. The children in my care were happy and healthy, doing well at school, but we were constantly under threat of the social workers. We were also constantly at risk because of lack of funding. The joy of the children always made me feel that the work I was doing was right and good, and since there was nothing I would rather do, I continued to do it. I was still fighting for their rights and still fighting to keep them safe. I would save most of the children in my care through tenacity and stubbornness, through long hours of studying the Child Care Act, of going out and finding what the situation was like, that the social workers were going to put the children back into the street and fighting for them in the Children's Courts, but I did not always win.

Where do you go for help for the children when you have gone to every person in the land; when you have appealed to the Minister, the President and even Nelson Mandela? Archbishop Tutu replied to my letter that his words were falling on deaf ears and that he was resorting to prayer. I have tried the Public Protector, the highest authority in the land when it comes to the Constitution. And while this all took years to work its way through the avenues of state departments and red tape, our children continued to be abused, neglected, orphaned and abandoned.

The winds of change were in the air and the tide was turning. Unfortunately, the tide turned not for my good, nor for the good of the children. I would end up spending more time defending myself in an attempt to keep the children safe as life spiralled out of control. My forthrightness and my truth had bred numerous enemies in various state departments. Life would become a nightmare, an unbearable, unending horror. I would learn to live with death threats, with the brunt of insults and being ignored, with being treated with contempt. I would learn to keep my mouth shut as long as a child was not in danger. I would learn to take every insult and more. I would learn the game of politics and lies. I would learn the game of silence.

I would learn that truth gets vindictive responses. I would learn that the Constitution, of which I was so proud, meant absolutely nothing to the children or to me. I would learn about the abuse of power. I would learn about the effects of affirmative action gone wrong. I would learn that what people said is not what people meant, and not what they would do. I would learn that trust was something you could not afford to give to anyone.

I would be investigated and followed. I would be videotaped and my phone calls recorded. I would be charged with so many alleged crimes that the police could not tell me how many as they had lost track. I would be searched and raided. I would have every document and computer removed. I would be burgled over and over. I would have my tyres slashed, home trashed, stones thrown at me and my life made impossible to live. Any adult I had daily contact with became a target as well.

I would have to hire a bodyguard to watch me while I slept. I would be sworn at and assaulted.

Eventually, I would have to pack and leave in the middle of the night.

When I took in those three children that cold winter's night, I never knew that I would lose my home or that I would lose my identity as a white South African. I never knew that I would lose everything, my home, my family, my children, my community, my land and worst of all, that I would be filled with revulsion for the very country that gave me birth.

This is not the end of my story. It is only the beginning. I no longer see the microcosm of the little town of Middelburg with its lack of service delivery to the children, but the macrocosm of neglect of the children of South Africa and further still, of the children of Africa. Life, with its cruel twists and turns has taught me much. It has prepared me for my journey that has only just begun. It has prepared me to fight the bigger fight, the fight for the freedom of all the children in South Africa.

If the individual state officials and organs think that what they have done to shut me up about the atrocities that are committed daily against the rights of children has been effective, they are mistaken! I have tenacity and resolve. They cannot destroy my spirit. And the pen is mightier than the sword.

I love those children in South Africa passionately, protectively, with my heart and soul. I will fight for them with every last breath or until I cannot do it anymore, until that day... Mandela's children, my children...are dying, starving, begging in the streets, neglected, abandoned. They are not free.

What reward is this for the ending of apartheid?

APPENDICES

The Scorpions (National Prosecuting Agency) carried out a search and seizure operation on the author's home, the children's home, the auditors and other people connected with the author on 6th December 2006.   They confiscated all documentation, financial records and computer hard-drives. The only documentation that was not seized was files pertaining to the children.

The documents that are evidence that what I have stated herein is the truth, is available in the first edition of the book, published by AuthorHouse. Those documents had been sent to the United Kingdome for safe keeping just months prior to the search and seizure.

To date, no case has been opened against the author and all documentation seized was returned on 17 December 2008.

Dianne Lang © 2007

Printed in Great Britain
by Amazon

42242253R00258